Gender, Conflict and Peace in Kashmir

Invisible Stakeholders

Seema Shekhawat

CAMBRIDGE
UNIVERSITY PRESS

CAMBRIDGE
UNIVERSITY PRESS

Cambridge House, 4381/4 Ansari Road, Daryaganj, Delhi 110002, India

Published in the United States of America by Cambridge University Press, New York

Cambridge University Press is part of the University of Cambridge.

It furthers the University's mission by disseminating knowledge in the pursuit of education, learning and research at the highest international levels of excellence.

www.cambridge.org
Information on this title: www.cambridge.org/9781107041875

First published 2014

Printed in India at Sanat Printers, Kundli, Haryana

A catalogue record for this publication is available from the British Library

Library of Congress Cataloging-in-Publication Data
Shekhawat, Seema.
Gender, conflict and peace in Kashmir : invisible stakeholders / Seema Shekhawat.
    pages cm
Includes bibliographical references and index.
Summary: "Discusses the role of women in militancy in Kashmir from a historical perspective"--Provided by publisher.
ISBN 978-1-107-04187-5 (hardback)
1. Women--India--Jammu and Kashmir--Social conditions. 2. Feminism--India--Jammu and Kashmir. 3. Social conflict--India--Jammu and Kashmir. I. Title.
HQ1744.J35S443 2013
305.40954'6--dc23
2013010249

ISBN 978-1-107-04187-5 Hardback

*I dedicate this book to
my mummy and papa*

Contents

Preface

Traditional international relations (IR) has ascribed gender a low priority in the discourse on conflict and peace. Despite increasing feminist scholarship in reshaping international politics, gender appears a minor candidate, if not a pariah, in the domains of war and peace making. This book endeavours to interrogate such a deep-rooted notion by locating women at the centre of the discourse while focusing on one of the protracted conflicts in South Asia – Kashmir. Gender being an inseparable part of the social frame and a crucial component of every aspect of collective human endeavours including conflict and peace, it cannot be detached from them and their flow. The discourse on conflict and peace must be gendered, viewed from a gender prism, scrutinized, interrogated and explained through gender, not sans gender. Women are competent in conflict as well as peace building and their role in both needs to be acknowledged. The book throughout the analysis runs in salience with two crucial and inter-related assumptions. First, literature on conflict has mostly been inclined, with few exceptions, towards a gender-blind masculinized discourse. Second, this gender-blindness gets extended to the theory and practice of peace making in post-conflict scenario. It is crucial to recognize the role of women in conflict to make the case for their rightful role in peace.

The book is a modest effort in centrally engaging gender in the conflict and peace discourse in Kashmir, the idea of which came to my mind while pursuing doctoral study on militancy-led victimization of women. Though not a native of the Indian state of Jammu and Kashmir, I grew up, studied and worked there for 23 years with my parents settling in the state in 1985. This was the time when a fertile ground was laid for a protracted internal armed conflict in the region. At an impressionable age I witnessed the rise of militancy and consequent socio-political changes. I moved out of Jammu and Kashmir in 2007 when violence in the region had substantially declined. I, hence, had the opportunity to observe the onset, growth and decline of the violent separatist movement from close. Several visits to the militancy-prone areas of the state prepared the background for this study. During my doctoral and post-doctoral studies I came across narratives of unremitting agonies of Kashmiri women, with occasional references to their crucial roles in the sustenance of the separatist movement. My interactions with Kashmiri women helped comprehend their told and untold experiences of encounters with conflict. At one end of the spectrum women were the victimized lot: the rape victims underwent physical, mental and social trauma; the widows lost sole breadwinners of the family; and bereaved mothers lost their only sons, and at the other end of the spectrum they were the perpetrators – propagandists, caretakers and facilitators. Conflict impacting women in Kashmir has been the focus of many works, including some of mine. However, women impacting conflict has remained under-researched. In this study I locate Kashmiri women in militancy beyond victimization, as agents, not in an exercise to either commend or criticize their involvement but to make a case for their due place in the peace process.

Militancy could not have sustained in Kashmir for such a long time without the participation of women. The women not only shouldered the burden of being a mother, wife, sister or daughter of a male militant but considered the struggle for freedom 'a family matter' that needed support of one and all. Though Kashmiri women did not take up guns, they aided militant operations in significant ways. The violent movement could not have been as widespread and effective in challenging the Indian state without the gender component as women could execute tasks such as hiding weapons behind their veils, or acting as couriers and messengers, which were difficult for male militants. Women displayed unparalleled courage in confronting gun totting Indian security forces, numbering thousands, during mass protests. As I witnessed scenes of violence during my surveys, and personally escaped some, the women in the initial days of heightened militancy appeared liberated, even though in a limited way from the traditionally framed concept of being a female. This limited liberation vanished with decline in militancy and dawn of a peace process, pedalled irreversible and sustainable. Women appeared in conflict and disappeared in peace, at the behest of the patriarchal separatist leadership. At the end, it was the male leadership that decided, and the female followers abided. The leaders strategized the inclusion of women in conflict and exclusion in peace. Interestingly, Kashmiri female separatist leaders who shared the credit for mobilizing women to support the violent struggle were in fact followers of a chauvinistic orthodoxy that facilitated instrumental use of women during conflict and marginalization afterwards. The all-women separatist groups could successfully organize women for abetting violence but failed to negotiate a place in efforts towards peace. Male-dominated decision-makers at both sides of the spectrum – militants as well as state authorities – did not feel it necessary to include women or their concerns in peace efforts. The simple arithmetic that none of the committees and groups constituted to facilitate conflict transformation in Kashmir duly represented women or paid due attention to their concerns provides ample testimony to the gender insensitive conflict and peace discourse in Kashmir, which finds resonance in many other conflict situations across the globe.

This work could not have been possible without the support and encouragement from family, friends, respondents and uncounted others. I am grateful to all of them. I am thankful to my respondents from Kashmir, Punjab, Odisha, Manipur, Nepal and Sri Lanka for sharing their experiences. I am indebted to my dear friend Janette Davies for her invaluable support during the course of the work. I am grateful to Veronica Fynn and Jenny Francis for their timely help during the preparation of the manuscript. Special thanks are due to Evelin Lindner, Linda Hartling and Immanuel Ness for their encouragement and thoughtful insights. I am thankful to Rekha Chowdhary, P. L. Dash and Renu Modi for their crucial support over the years.

This study has been completed with financial support from the Berghof Foundation. I am particularly grateful to Johannes Zundel who believed in the work and extended support throughout.

I owe sincere thanks to Suvadip Bhattacharjee at Cambridge University Press, for his enthusiastic support throughout the publication process. His motivation and optimism made the entire process less painful than it could have been.

I am fortunate to have a caring family, for which I thank the almighty. The constant personal and professional support of my husband Aurobinda is beyond the confines of words. He shares credit for every goal I achieve. He read and re-read the manuscript and offered constructive criticism. Without him the work would definitely have taken much longer to complete. I express my gratitude to my 2-year-old son, Asim for making my life beautiful. The fatigue of long hours of writing disappeared when he prodded me to play his favourite song on my computer so that he could dance. I hope one day he will read this book and understand and appreciate why I spent days away from him. I owe thanks to my nephews, Aditya, Ayush, Amar and Naman and niece, Shreya for always making me smile. I am forever beholden to my dear sisters, Laxmi, Amrit and Susheel, and brother, Shailendra for their unstinting support. They selflessly extended all help though I often failed to reciprocate and took them for granted. I sincerely appreciate the encouragement from my brothers-in-law, Dilip, Sunil and Vishal, and sister-in-law, Renu. Finally I thank my parents for always encouraging me to pursue my ambitions and supporting me at every step without fail. They always had faith in me and stood beside me in trying times. For me, they are god and it is to them that I dedicate this book.

Chapter 1

Feminism, International Relations and War

'As a scholar and teacher of International Relations, I have frequently asked myself the following questions: why are there so few women in my discipline? If I teach the field as it is conventionally defined, why are there so few readings by women to assign to my students? Why is the subject matter of my discipline so distant from women's lived experiences? Why have women been conspicuous only by their absence in the worlds of diplomacy and military and foreign policy-making?,' noted feminist and international relations (IR) scholar Ann J. Tickner aptly posited these questions in her study *Gender in International Relations: Feminist Perspectives on Achieving Global Security* (1992). Many feminist scholars, by challenging the masculinized theoretical and practical structure, have emphasized on broadening IR to include a gender perspective. However, even after two decades the issue of gender invisibility remains relevant and IR has still a long way to go to make both the discipline and the scholarship gender inclusive, especially in the context of war and conflict. A number of questions remain unanswered including where women stand in war and conflict situations, how war impacts women, and more importantly, from the point of this book, how women impact war and what kind of roles they play in violent situations. Though literature on these issues is increasing, much needs to be added, for instance, by focusing on regional specificities.

The role of gender in shaping our global political perceptions has become one of the concerns of contemporary international relations. Many scholars question why gender has remained at the periphery of traditional IR with most concluding that conventional areas that are of importance to states such as power and security have dominated the discipline. R. B. J. Walker argues that the obsession surrounding the concept of sovereignty has relegated all other issues as marginal.[1] IR, traditionally defined as the study of states and their security, has been an overwhelmingly male-dominated discipline as not only the actors (leaders) but also the analysts have been men. Women have played a crucial role in IR but the masculinized nature of both players (leaders) and commentators (analysts) has ensured that their roles as well as viewpoints remain insignificant. The international relations system is constituted by gender hierarchies, which in turn contribute to the subordination of women. Gendered IR is crucial to respond to this suppression and to correct the inadequacies in both theory and practice. In fact, it is not just about gender but also about the way in which international relations operates and is analysed. Only through a gendered analysis of IR can the differential impact of international developments on women and men be appropriately understood and appreciated. V. Spike Peterson contends that feminist scholarship commonly agrees that gender is socially constructed and that it produces subjective identities that shape the global realities for us.[2] Similarly, Christine Sylvester argues that introduction of feminism in the discipline of IR has to do with 'disordering and space-opening – for women, theory and alternative practice.'[3] Cynthia Enloe asserts that a study of IR will remain incomplete without taking gender as a unit of analysis.

> Feminist-informed investigations by academic and activist researchers have revealed that many forms of public and private power are dependent for their operations, legitimation and perpetuation on controlling popular notions of femininity and masculinity. It therefore follows that if we do not become seriously interested in the conditions and lives of women, we are likely to craft analyses of international power dynamics that are at best incomplete and at worst faulty and unreliable.[4]

Enloe makes a lucid argument for according due place to gender in IR in her book *Bananas, Beaches and Bases*. She elaborates how heavily everyday manoeuvring of global power depends on gender constructions. Through an interesting analysis of various under researched roles that women play ranging from being wives of diplomats to being part of sex tourism she argues that international relations cannot survive even a day without the structures of gender.[5] All these women who play crucial roles across the globe to sustain masculinized international relations share invisibility. Jonathon D. Wadley points out that ignoring gender means making the masculine knowledge universal and thereby leading to the building of partial theories. Gender neutrality makes an analyst 'blind to processes through which these gendered identities are produced – processes that are in many ways central to the operation of world politics.'[6]

Feminist IR has emerged as a crucial approach for understanding global security.[7] Broadly the term is attributed to works that bring gender concerns into the understanding of international relations. It does not solely emphasize on issues related to women. It involves looking at how international politics impacts both the genders and vice versa. The origin of feminist IR can be traced back to the late 1980s and the early 1990s. The end of the cold war and the broadening of the traditional discipline of IR to take account of non-traditional concepts provided a fertile ground for the growth of the approach. The IR discourse was reshaped in the sense that an array of traditionally neglected issues such as human rights and civil society were accorded place, although on a limited basis, due to increasing voices for looking at alternative perspectives. It is now globally accepted that the concept of security should not be merely studied from a state centric perspective. A humane perspective, wherein the concept of security can have different connotations for different people, needs to be an integral part of the overall discourse. For instance, for women the concept should address issues such as rape and violence not only from the 'enemy' but also from those belonging to their 'own group'.[8] Traditionally these issues have never been a part of analysis; as a result policymaking too has remained gender exclusive and even demeaning to women. Hence, the advocacy for a humane feminist security, a new kind of security factoring gender.

What is Feminist Perspective?

Virginia Sapiro argues that, 'feminism is both a way of thinking about the world, and a way of acting in it.... [It] is a perspective that views gender as one of the most important bases of the structure and organization of the social world.'[9] A feminist approach focuses on the historical oppression of women and stresses on the intersection of theory and practice to eliminate it.[10] Susan Okin categorizes feminists as those who believe that sex-based discrimination is unacceptable and women should have the same rights and opportunities that men benefit from.[11] All feminists agree that gender inequalities exist and need to be addressed. Challenging the centrality of men in both the theory and practice of local, national as well as international relations is the predominant issue in the feminist approach across disciplines, including in IR. Feminist perspectives create a standpoint to observe, analyse and criticize the traditional perspectives on IR.[12] The emphasis is, thus, on engendering IR. For Sarah Brown, a feminist theory of IR is an act of political commitment to understanding the world from the perspective of the socially subjugated. She argues, 'there is the need to identify as yet unspecified relation between the construction of power and the construction of gender in international relations.'[13] Cockburn contends that feminist gender analysis is unified on the issue that 'the differentiation and relative positioning of women and men is seen as an important ordering principle that pervades the system of power and is sometimes its very embodiment.'[14]

Different perspectives exist in feminist scholarship on the whys and hows of discrimination and subjugation and also on ways to overcome them. For instance, many feminists contend that patriarchy, simply understood as a male dominated structure, is the primary reason for the oppression of women.[15] Others argue that gender is only one among many reasons of subjugation. There are many other factors such as race, class, caste and ethnicity that lead to oppression.[16] Diversity exists within the scholarship though the focus remains same, that is, making IR gender inclusive. Sylvester elaborates on this unity in diversity:

> Feminist theories are diverse, but generally concur that the invisibility of gender issues within mainstream social theories, and of women in 'important' public domains of human existence, cannot be remedied simply by adding a pinch of women – to the state, to capitalist processes and to theories – and stirring. Visibility requires considerable analysis of the points in the international system, and in the theories which depict it, where women's behaviors and contributions are choked off and men's are taken as the norm.[17]

A crucial term for the feminist perspective is gender that 'refers to the complex social construction of men's and women's identities...[and] behaviors... in relation to each other.'[18] It is, argues Laura Sjoberg, 'a system of symbolic meaning that creates social hierarchies based on perceived associations with masculine and feminine characteristics.'[19] Judith Lorber interprets gender as,

> A social structure that has its origins in the development of human culture, not in biology or procreation...[and] exhibits both universal features and chronological and cross-cultural variations that affect individual lives and social interaction in major ways. As is true of other institutions, gender's history can be traced, its structure examined, and its changing effects researched.[20]

To put it simply, gender is a social invention that apparently has nothing to do with the biological differences between males and females. It is a social categorization that puts human beings in a relationship of power. Joan W. Scott defines gender as 'a constitutive element of social relationships based on perceived differences between the sexes, and...a primary way of signifying relationships of power.'[21] In this relationship of power, women are at the receiving end. Gender is a set of socially and culturally constructed characteristics in which attributes such as power, autonomy, rationality, activity and public are associated with men and their opposites such as weakness, dependence, emotionality, passivity and private are linked with women.[22] Thus, generally the qualities associated with gender are structured as dichotomous pairs such as 'rationality/irrationality, civilized/barbaric, autonomous/dependent, active/passive, and powerful/weak – all of which map onto the dominant signifier pair of masculine/feminine.'[23] A cursory glance at these gendered dichotomies provides ample guidance to comprehend how discriminatory the social construction has been.

What is War?

Wars have traditionally been a crucial subject of IR. Fought between two or more states in the form of pitched battles, wars dominated the global scenario until the Second World War. The concept underwent a noticeable change thereafter and is, many times, used synonymously with conflict, as I am doing in this book. Though the post-cold war world witnessed decline in inter-state warfare it also inversely witnessed the rise of conflicts confined within states, which were hence termed internal conflicts. The term conflict, owing to its fluid nature, is applied generically to various kinds of situations. When conflict becomes violent and includes weapons of destruction, the term used is armed conflict. Armed conflict can be defined as when actual and perceived incompatibilities result in destructive violence.[24] The data set of conflicts compiled by Uppsala Conflict Data Program and International Peace Research Institute, Oslo defines armed conflict as a 'a contested incompatibility that concerns government and/or territory where the use of armed force between two parties, of which at least one is the government of a state, [and] results in…deaths.'[25] This data set categorizes conflict keeping in view the number of deaths in a single year. 'War' involves at least 1,000 battle-related deaths per year, 'intermediate conflict' has between 25 and 1,000 deaths per year, and 'minor armed conflict' has at least 25 deaths per year.[26] Internal conflicts are defined as

> Protracted armed confrontations occurring between governmental armed forces and the forces of one or more armed groups, or between such groups arising on the territory of a State [party to the Geneva Conventions]. The armed confrontation must reach a minimum level of intensity and the parties involved in the conflict must show a minimum of organisation.[27]

Modern day conflicts are complex in nature. Though many of them are intra-state, there are instances of their linkages across the formal boundaries of the state. From the beginning of 1990 the world has witnessed more than 100 armed conflicts, most of which were civil wars, often confined to one region of a country but internationalized through the involvement of outside powers.[28] Warfare, as an open conventional clash between two or more state armies in battlefields have been replaced by irregular and guerrilla style conflicts where no battle lines are drawn and the confrontation is not direct.[29] This results in heavy men and material losses for civilians. Joshua S. Goldstein details:

> Guerilla war, which includes certain kinds of civil wars, is warfare without front lines. Irregular forces operate in the midst of, and often hidden or protected by, civilian populations. The purpose is not to directly confront an enemy army but rather to harass and punish it so as to gradually limit its operation and effectively liberate territory from its control....In guerilla war, without a fixed front line, there is much territory that neither side controls; both sides exert military leverage over the same place at the same time. Thus guerilla wars are extremely painful for civilians. This situation is doubly painful because conventional armies fighting guerillas often cannot distinguish them from civilians and punish both together.[30]

'New Wars'[31] are increasing and correspondingly increasing the scholarship on them from various perspectives including gender.

Women and War

War and security are two core issues of IR with which feminist scholars have engaged on various fronts. Traditionally the equation between women, war and security has not been a major subject of study. Wadley argues, 'nowhere is the silence toward gender more deafening than in the field of International Security. The study of war, anarchy, alliances – all observably gendered processes – stand to benefit the most from the recognition that the key actors do not act without, or outside gender.'[32] Since the leaders of states as well as fighters are generally men, they form the focal group in the history of war. Elaine Showalter contends:

> Women have been left out of history not because of the evil conspiracies of men in general or male historians in particular, but because we have considered history only in *male-centred* terms. We have missed women and their activities, because we have asked questions of history which are inappropriate to women. To rectify this, and to light up areas of historical darkness we must, for a time, focus on a *woman-centred* inquiry, considering the possibility of the existence of a female culture within the general culture shared by men and women.[33]

Absence of women-centric war narratives has prompted a few scholars to conclude that war is gender-free.[34] Feminist scholars contend that gender is crucial to understanding the issues related to wars and conflicts since gender impacts war and vice versa. They share the concern that women are a disadvantaged and discriminated class in both theory and practice of IR. They intend to change this male dominated scenario in both the spheres. Beyond this agreement there seem to be differences within the feminist scholarship on why and how gender intersects with war. There is no commonly agreed feminist approach to war and peace since 'feminists are not only at war with war but with one another'.[35]

Though feminists have broadened the scope of research to study gendered aspects of IR and themes such as foreign policy and decision-making and social institutions such as family, they have largely shied away from analysing the concept of war. As Sylvester argues, 'feminists understudy war relative to other trans-historical and transnational institutions, such as the family and religion.'[36] Even when wars are studied from a gender perspective, either women's role as peace makers or more commonly their experiences of victimization are highlighted. Women perpetrators of violence are on the margins of war related discourses.[37] Feminism may lose its relevance if 'it does not speak "of" and "within" the margins.'[38] From this perspective, the discourse on women making war has assumed increasing significance.

Theories of war generally revolve around the assumption that men fight wars and hence women are irrelevant to the study of war. War is described as 'a masculine endeavour for which women may serve as victim, spectator, or prize.'[39] Ralph Pettman points out, 'statemaking and warmaking are cognate activities and warmaking has long been a way of defining and demonstrating a range of stereotypically masculinist traits.'[40] Even a cursory glance at the traditional literature on war would suffice to reinforce the postulation that men make war and women make peace.[41] The iconic image of war is men armed with weapons and, in continuation of that, woman mourning the dead, fleeing, searching for food, struggling to care for children, or as victims of sexual abuse.[42] In this context, comes to picture the 'protection discourse' that plays a crucial role in legitimizing war; making violent actions by men commendable and justified. Lauren Wilcox opines that without this discourse a number of wars would become futile and unnecessary.[43] Under this framework, wars are fought by men to defend the vulnerable section of society including women from potential or actual threats. Men are protectors and women are protected and the protector and the protected cannot be equal.[44] Iris Marion Young argues, 'the male protector confronts evil aggressors in the name of the right and the good, while those under his protection submit to his order and serve as handmaids to his efforts.'[45] Jean Bethke Elshtain in her classic work *Women and War* (1987) introduced the notion of the 'Beautiful Soul' and the 'Just Warrior' as gender identities that legitimize war since the 'Just Warrior' wages war to protect the 'Beautiful Souls' who are 'too good for this world yet absolutely necessary to it.'[46]

Feminists often have to confront the accusations that through a gendered debate they imply that women are more peaceful than men.[47] Tickner argues that most IR feminists reject this labelling on various grounds including:

> The association of women with peace and moral superiority has a long history of keeping women out of power…. The association of women with peace can play into unfortunate gender stereotypes that characterize men as active, women as passive; men as agents, women as victims; men as rational, women as emotional…. Moreover, it detracts from what feminists consider to be more pressing agendas, such as striving to uncover and understand the disadvantaged socioeconomic position of many of the world's women and why women are so poorly represented among the world's policymakers.[48]

Are women more peaceful than men? Can war and men be synonymous and women and peace be linked without any exception? These questions have been debated and discussed cutting across boundaries of disciplines not only in social sciences but also in science disciplines. There can be no easy answers though across the globe it is commonly assumed that women are more peaceful. If we accept this argument we have to delve further to understand as to why this is so. Women's peaceful character is sometimes attributed to biology and at other times to sociology (socially constructed). The most convenient way to analyse this issue is to look into the nature versus nurture or as Sherry Ortner puts it 'nature versus culture'[49] dichotomy; women are more peaceful because nature has made them so versus because they have been socially constructed to be more peaceful.

All is Natural

Plato believed in the concept of 'idea', an abstract entity of which all objects in this material world are imperfect manifestations. It is not difficult for students of political thought to recall endless list of examples cited by professors such as the particular chair and the particular horse as imperfect manifestations of the ideal chair and the ideal horse. Essentialism draws some of its basics from this Platonic concept. Diana Fuss in her book *Essentially Speaking* (1989) writes, 'essentialism is most commonly understood as a belief in the real, true essence of things, the invariable and fixed properties which define the "whatness" of a given entity.'[50] Essentialism holds that for an entity, there is a set of 'incidental attributes' necessary to its identity and function.[51] The approach is based on the notion that things and beings have specific inherent and enduring qualities. These innate traits are crucial for distinguishing all non-living and living beings from each other, including men and women.

Essentialist feminism considers that all women are in essence similar. Women, irrespective of class, caste, race, religion and culture across time and space, share common characteristics. Elizabeth Grosz explains this approach as 'the attribution of a fixed essence to women....Essentialism entails the belief that those characteristics defined as women's essence are shared in common by all women at all times....Essentialism thus refers to the existence of fixed characteristics, given attributes, and ahistorical functions.'[52] Notwithstanding disagreements as to what defines the essence that all women share, many scholars hold that gender identities are unchangeable due to permanent underlying, primarily biological, factors. In simple terms, you must be born a woman to be a woman. Nature and not nurture define gender differentiation, as elaborated by Inger Skjelsbaek:

> For men in power, the essentialist position can be taken to mean that there is something about men's power status which originates in their gender identity – that is, the 'true' nature of men. The fact that women have stayed at home and taken care of the house and children is also explained in terms of women's 'true' nature. This interpretation suggests that throughout history men and women have tended to do what they are naturally good at. Gender difference thus becomes a matter of nature rather than nurture.[53]

Essentialist feminism resonates with the difference feminism approach that contends that there are deep-rooted real gender differences. This strand of feminist theory is based on the assumption that women are dissimilar to men in that they have an alternative way of looking at the world.[54] They are ontologically different from men due to the possession of distinct natural qualities, which include being peaceful and cooperative.[55] Many difference feminists, including essentialist ones, advance a major theoretical claim relevant to this book – women are inherently peaceful and less aggressive and men are relatively violent and more aggressive. This strand of feminism believes that women should not fight wars to preserve their 'feminine' qualities. Virginia Wolf, though not an essentialist, in her work *Three Guineas* (1977) comments,

> Scarcely a human being in the course of history has fallen to a woman's rifle; the vast majority of birds and beasts have been killed by you [men], not by us [women].... Obviously there is for you some glory, some necessity, some satisfaction in fighting which we [women] have never felt or enjoyed.[56]

Goldstein summarizes various arguments that primarily relate men to violence and women to peace into five categories: (1) men's genes make them violent; (2) testosterone makes men comparatively more aggressive than women; (3) men are bigger and stronger than women; (4) men's brains are programmed for aggression; and (5) women are biologically tailored for nurturing roles that preclude participation in violence.[57] A boy attains manhood by, among several things, participating in war.[58] A girl attains womanhood by becoming a mother and this role is considered central to the assumption of women being innately peaceful. Due to their nurturing roles, primarily as mothers, women are more inclined to give life and not take it.[59] Skjelsbaek points out,

> We regard motherhood as the central marker of the transition from girl-hood to adult womanhood, and war-related activities as markers of the transition from boy to man.... When femininity is conceptualized as inherently peaceful, it is the concept of motherhood which is emphasized and cited to legitimize the claim.[60]

Elshtain criticizes the viewpoint that all women are peaceful and all men are violent contending that it 'dangerously overshadows other voices, other stories: of pacific males; of bellicose women; of cruelty incompatible with just-war fighting; of martial fervor at odds – or so we choose to believe – with maternalism in women.'[61] Sex is immutable while gender is a social and historical construction. All women may not necessarily possess 'feminine' qualities and similarly all men may not possess 'masculine' qualities. Also, a feminist view based on the essentialist construction cannot be a true representative of all women since 'we have yet to be able to specify some essence that is genuinely common to all women.'[62] There are possessions that have essence and some, such as gender, do not, argues Andrew Sayer.[63] 'All women are women, no woman is only a woman,'[64] and, hence, differences exist within gender emerging from several other socially constructed identities that women possess. Judith Butler points out:

> If one *is* a woman, that is surely not all one is; the term fails to be exhaustive... because gender is not always constituted coherently or consistently in different historical contexts, and because gender intersects with racial, class, ethnic, sexual, and regional modalities of discursively constituted identities. As a result, it becomes impossible to separate out *gender* from the political and cultural intersection in which it is invariably produced and maintained.[65]

A major critique of essentialism is that it undermines the role of nurture in societal processes, attitudes and behaviours associated with constructing femininity and masculinity. There is no scope for change in behaviours or attitudes since they are considered innate. Growing evidence of women's participation in violence both directly and indirectly challenges the assumption that women are inherently peaceful.

All is Artificial

Since the late 1980s and early 1990s, constructivism emerged as a major school of thought within IR. The term brought theories that emphasize the socially constructed character of international relations into a single fold.[66] Constructivism views IR through the prism of broader social relations.[67] Its proponents believe that cultures and societies shape all aspects of a state's behaviour including international security. They argue that identities and interests are socially constructed. Every construct is human invention and there is nothing natural about it. Nothing is fixed or predetermined. Human beings are not born with a specific set of behavioural and attitudinal patterns. A complex set of social processes imposes specificities on human beings to behave in a particular manner. Alexander Wendt by contending that power politics, a core realist concept, is socially constructed – that is, concepts are shaped by social practices and interactions and not by nature and hence, they can be reshaped by human practice – paved the way for scholars to pursue research on a wide range of issues, including gender, from a constructivist perspective.[68] This strand of feminist thinking believes that gender differences are socially constructed and, therefore, no characteristics generally associated with either of the gender are natural or universal.[69] 'Doing gender means creating differences between girls and boys and women and men, differences that are not natural, essential or biological,' argue Candace West and Don H. Zimmerman.[70] Gender differences are history and culture specific.[71] Gender identity is not determined from within but from without of the individual. It is shaped by the 'transaction' between individuals.[72] Identities are not natural; they are forced on individuals through the process of socialization. Skjelsbaek argues:

> When we enter the social world as male or female there are patterns of behaviour and thinking which are 'available' to us. Parents may choose to dress their baby daughters in pink and baby boys in blue; boys may be given cars to play with while girls are given dolls, sons may be encouraged to study natural science and daughters to study languages. All these choices parents make emphasize differences between the genders. When the young girl or boy grows up, the opportunities and experiences he/she has had will be part of the background which determines future experiences and choices.[73]

Gender is not a readymade natural category; it is a tailor-made artificial one. 'One is not born, but rather becomes, a woman,' asserts Simone de Beauvoir while arguing that women across the globe are considered homemakers because they are socialized to become one and there is nothing inherent or natural about it.[74] Enloe argues, 'conventionally both masculinity and femininity have been treated as "natural", not created. Today, however, there is mounting evidence that they are packages of expectations that have been created through specific decisions by specific people.'[75] Hence, gender differences may be conceptualized as 'the construction of masculinity and femininity in their distinction from each other.'[76] Some scholars argue that men do not make war; in fact it is the opposite, war makes men. A man may not be naturally inclined to be violent or aggressive; he can be trained to become so. Men become violent through military training and by sports, stories and movies.[77] Enloe analyses a number of encouragements that are used to enlist men in the military including 'first-class citizenship' and 'cultural superiority'.[78] Men in military are taught to become 'real' men and 'much of [their] basic training involves overcoming men's reluctance to kill.'[79] Exploiting 'fears, vulnerabilities, prides and prejudices' masculine military programme train men to kill and

> There may be high costs to transgressing the culturally imposed [gendered] boundaries....Men who refuse to fight risk being ridiculed, imprisoned or even killed for their lack of "courage" or masculinity. Equally, women who contradict female stereotypes by [for instance becoming a warrior and] killing [others], are often regarded as much more deviant or unnatural than men.[80]

Both men and women can be violent as well as peaceful. Women can behave exactly like men in both peace and war and vice versa. Taking a cue from this argument, a strand of feminist approach, liberal feminism, stands for gender equality in all spheres, including combat. Many scholars argue in favour of women's right to fight, discarding the nature versus nurture debate regarding intersection of gender and peace.

Right to Fight

Drawing from classical liberalism, liberal feminists emphasize equality between women and men in both political and social spheres. They contend that 'female subordination is rooted in a set of customary and legal constraints that block women's entrance to and success in the so-called public world,'[81] and seek gender equality by overcoming these constraints. The adherents emphasize on inclusion of women in all aspects of war ranging from fighting to negotiating peace.[82] Put simply, men and women are equal in terms of capabilities to make peace or war. Women can be equally capable warriors and men can be equally capable of making peace. Liberal feminists criticize gender exclusion in IR but are not convinced that a greater or equal participation of women will bring change, positive or negative, in global affairs. They demand an equal role for women in IR, not to make it gender sensitive but to make it gender inclusive, so that women have a fair chance to participate in international affairs. Based on the gender of the leader at the helm of affairs, there is no difference in a state's decision to go for war or peace in a particular situation.[83] Margaret Thatcher, former British Prime Minister, is often referred to as a classic example in this context since she used military force in a dispute with Argentina in 1982. Golda Meir is considered a war heroine for winning a nearly week long war against the Arabs. In India, former Prime Minister Indira Gandhi led a war against Pakistan in 1971. Under her leadership, India won the war and there emerged a new state in South Asia – Bangladesh. From being dubbed as *goongi gudiya* (dumb doll) in her early days in politics to being called 'the only man in the cabinet' due to her stronghold on Indian politics in later years, liberal feminism does find an apt example in Indira Gandhi, as to how, if provided an opportunity, women can play dominant roles in political spheres.

Based on such exemplars scattered across the globe many scholars argue in favour of greater gender integration in all areas, including military. This inclusion, among other things, will ensure tapping of additional available human resources and thereby improve the quality of military forces.[84] The argument in favour of insertion of women in combat operations has led to a fiery debate in both scholarship and political circles. The discussion continues with focus on the pros and cons of inclusion of women in militaries. Those who seem to be less bothered with this debate are mushrooming non-state armed actors who are challenging the sovereignty and integrity of states in many parts of the world on accounts ranging from ethnicity to self-determination. Many women play a crucial role in sustaining these armed movements.

Contextualizing Kashmir

In the context of the Kashmir conflict, a crucial but less analysed aspect is that the women played a crucial role in spearheading the violent separatist movement against the Indian state in the late 1980s. Women played a significant role in the initial phase of the movement when it had an indigenous character. They were the face of the militancy as they were at the forefront in mass protests, shouting anti-India slogans and shielding men. As captured by national and international media, their images of participating in protest marches and braving cane blows brought to focus their role in the struggle. Many women provided material and moral support to male militants engaged in direct combat. They carried out a variety of tasks ranging from intelligence work to nursing, from feeding combatants to providing shelters and from acting as couriers to fund raisers. They were actively engaged in enforcing civil curfew on calls of militant leaders and in defying administrative curfews. They sounded alerts for militants when the Indian security forces approached and blocked paths to let them escape. They took care of the injured militants in homes and hospitals and arranged for their medicines and food. Women negotiated with the local administration and security forces to ascertain the whereabouts of those who had disappeared and for the release of detained men. They transmitted militarist values to the youth to invoke passion for the community, the idea of revenge for the losses and the image of a future without suffering. Mothers of dead militants delivered speeches on the funerals of their sons, glorifying martyrdom. Stories of young women dreaming of marriages with militants were narrated with great passion to motivate young men to join militancy. Many women acted as messengers, informers, couriers and route facilitators for militants. There were instances when veiled women 'smuggled out' militants. In order to 'contribute' to the movement, some women publicly testified that they had been raped by the Indian security forces. Though a majority of the women were active in playing supportive roles in Kashmir, their direct participation in militant activities was not widespread as it has been in some other conflicts. This miniscule participation warrants the least comparison with separatist groups such as the Liberation Tigers of Tamil Eelam (LTTE) in Sri Lanka, where women formed a significant percentage of the fighting force, but indicates that the militant violence in Kashmir is not without its gender component.

At times it is argued that participation in conflict makes women feel liberated from household drudgery and thereby empowers them. A deeper analysis brings into picture the continuation of the overall patriarchal structure wherein women, irrespective of their role in conflict, remain subjugated to societal limitations. In Kashmir, women had to confront male dominated structures of militancy and the security apparatus of the state. There were instances when women supporters of militancy had to face societal rejection on grounds of not adhering to their gender specific responsibilities or crossing the limits imposed by society. The all-male separatist leadership used women in its propaganda war but failed to fight for justice for the raped, or to challenge the social stigma attached to women. The sacrifices of the *martyr's mother* and *martyr's wife* were barely acknowledged in the long term as these sacrifices appeared irrelevant in the highly masculinized peace making process. It is widely perceived that militancy in Kashmir could not have sustained for such a long time without women's support. Women multi-tasked during the militant movement but were not given due acknowledgment. On the pretext of women's inability to be part of combat operations, their responsibility towards the family and their 'preference' for remaining non-political, Kashmiri women have been denied recognition for their role in the movement. Though militant leaders agree that without the support from women militancy in the state could have faded much earlier, the general feeling is that women are good followers but not leaders. An ex-militant explained, 'women carry out the tasks assigned to them effectively but they are not able to lead or make strategies to make a movement successful.'[85] Non-recognition of the place of women in sustaining a conflict adversely impacts their position in the peace process. In India's immediate neighbourhood, both Nepal and Sri Lanka have emerged out of prolonged conflicts. In both these countries women played a crucial role as active combatants but in the post-conflict scenarios they have been relegated to invisibility with no major role in either peace or politics. This invisibility of women in Sri Lanka and Nepal posited a question – whether Kashmiri women will confront a similar fate or will they be accorded a place in peace making. My findings reveal that Kashmir is no exception and women, as elsewhere, have been pushed to the margins in both peace and reintegration processes. Militancy, that was at its peak in the mid-1990s, is in decline as can be seen in the decrease in the number of violent incidents in the region. In this overall scenario the Government of India has initiated a process of addressing separatism and alienation. It has taken steps to facilitate the reintegration of ex-militants into the mainstream by, amongst other things, offering them economic opportunities. More recently a policy has been adopted to facilitate the 'homecoming' of ex-militants residing on the Pakistan side of Kashmir to the Indian state of Jammu and Kashmir (J&K).[86] In this overall process for peace and reintegration, women are conspicuously invisible. The face of militancy in Kashmir has been denied the opportunity to become the face of peace.

An analysis of women's role in conflict helps in understanding conflict from an alternate perspective and also contributes to literature. Discourse on the issue of conflict and peace gets widened by understanding the whys and hows of women's participation. It helps to challenge the widespread 'understanding that women are irrelevant to the making and fighting of wars'.[87] Miriam Cooke suggests, 'recording women's presence and engagement at the front is crucial in order to counteract some of the distortions that have always been necessary to construct the age old story of war as men's business.'[88] The non-recognition of women's role in conflicts impedes their inclusion in peace politics and furthers their victimization and marginalization in post-conflict scenario. Understanding gendered dynamics of conflicts is of immense significance in charting out specific strategies and engendering policymaking in post-conflict rehabilitation and resettlement scenario. This book seeks to contribute to the growing body of literature on intersection of gender and war by focusing on Kashmir. Specifically, it examines the experiences of one particular section of women – who pose a challenge to conventional thinking on the gendered relationship of violence and peace, that is, women combatants. Starting with challenging the notion that women are necessarily peaceful, through an examination of theory and practice of women's participation in violence, the study goes on to establish that changed gender roles during times of violence do not necessarily revolutionize socially ascribed norms in long run. This becomes evident in post-violence peace and reintegration processes where women are relegated to their traditional socially ascribed roles with virtually no formal place in the overall process towards peace building. Women's role in conflict is not recognized and the direct corollary of this is no place for women in peace process.

This book examines women's role in the separatist movement in Kashmir and offers a nuanced picture of the processes that prompted them to outrightly support the violence initially, not only solely explained by ideological motivation but also by very mundane and immediate concerns partly endogenous to the conflict. It further emphasizes the necessity of crafting a gender inclusive peace making process. In the course of analysis, the following questions are addressed: In what ways do women contribute to violence? What factors act as motivators? What are the factors that may compel women to distance themselves from the violent struggle that they once zealously supported? Does participation in conflict provide women an opportunity to challenge gender stereotyping? Is there an element of real empowerment and liberation in this participation? Why are women denied recognition of their role in conflict? And why is it essential to make the peace making process gender inclusive?

Anecdotes from the Field

Cynthia Enloe raised the question several years ago, 'where are the women?' This study posits this question in the context of conflict and peace in Kashmir. It aims to fill the knowledge gap about women's role in militancy in Kashmir using their reflections collected through interviews. Keeping in view the sensitivity of the situation and the scope of the study I chose not to adhere to any particular research methodology. With merely 12 open-ended sample questions I attempted to formally or informally interact with the maximum number of women. This unconventional method of studying an under-researched issue did help to overcome hesitation on the part of the respondents. I do not claim that this study reflects the experiences of all Kashmiri women but I anticipate that this study will generate a debate for an inclusive peace making process. I also conducted unstructured interviews with women engaged in violence in other parts of India, where conflict has either subsided or is still raging including Maoist affected areas in central and eastern India, Manipur and Punjab. Interactions with female ex-combatants from Nepal and Sri Lanka, male ex-militants from Kashmir and retired and serving Indian security personnel in Kashmir, were highly informative and useful.

Interviewing women regarding their victimization, as part of some of my earlier studies, was easier than these interviews wherein I investigated women's role in violence. Most men and women I met were shocked to learn that I was interested in exploring not how conflict impacted women but how women impacted conflict. During interviews my first interaction was generally with a male member of a family and most of them did not shy away from admitting that women did play a crucial role in the militancy frequently in the words 'it was quite natural for them (women) to support their militant brothers, fathers and husbands.' It needed a patient and sustained effort to gain access to my respondents through 'their men' who were quite reluctant to allow 'their women' to be interviewed not as victims but as actors in conflict. Even the respondents had to be convinced unwearyingly. Being a frequent visitor to the field of research I was aware that I would be counter-interviewed not only by the respondents but also their family members, primarily male members. I clarified hundreds of times that the purpose of this study was neither to condemn nor to commend women's role; it was to highlight the role of women as actors in conflict towards making a case for their inclusion as actors in the peace making process. One of my respondents did not believe the focus of my research. She asked, 'Do you want to know about women or men?' despite being clearly informed that I intended to study women as actors in militancy. On being retold about my work she explained, 'I heard you rightly but got confused since when researchers interview women they want to know about our victimization. It is only when they interview men that questions such as how you (men) contributed to militancy and how you perceive the peace process are asked.'[89] This anecdote clearly indicates that the issue of women's existence in conflict and peace remain under-researched in the context of Kashmir.

I hope that this book will pave the way for further research on this subject and other gender and war related issues in Kashmir and beyond to ensure gender inclusive sustainable and positive peace in conflict ridden regions.

Endnotes

1. R. B. J. Walker, 'Gender and Critique in the Theory of International Relations', in *Gendered States: Feminist (Re)Visions of International Relations Theory*, ed., V. Spike Peterson, (Boulder and London: Lynn Reinner Publishers, 1992), 179–202.
2. V. Spike Peterson, 'Introduction', in *Gendered States: Feminist (Re)Visions of International Relations Theory*, ed., V. Spike Peterson, (Boulder and London: Lynn Reinner Publishers, 1992), 9.
3. Christine Sylvester, *Feminist International Relations: An Unfinished Journey*, (Cambridge: Cambridge University Press, 2002), 206.
4. Cynthia Enloe, 'Feminist International Relations: How to Do it; What We Gain', in *International Relations for the 21st Century*, ed., Martin Griffiths, (New York and London: Routledge, 2007), 6.
5. Cynthia Enloe, *Bananas, Beaches and Bases: Making Feminist Sense of International Politics*, (Berkeley: University of California Press, 1990).
6. Jonathan D. Wadley, 'Gendering the state Performativity and Protection in International Security', in *Gender and International Security: Feminist Perspectives*, ed., Laura Sjoberg, (London and New York: Routledge, 2010), 38.
7. See Nicole Detraz, *International Security and Gender*, (Cambridge: Polity Press, 2012).
8. Tricia Ruiz, 'Feminist Theory and International Relations: The Feminist Challenge to Realism and Liberalism'. Available at www.csustan.edu/honors/documents/journals/soundings/Ruiz.pdf (accessed on 23 September 2011).
9. Virginia Sapiro, *Women in American Society*, (Palo Alto, CA: Mayfield, 1986), 440.
10. Linda R. Forcey, 'Women as Peacemakers: Contested Terrain for Feminist Peace Studies', *Peace & Change*, 16, no. 4, (1991): 334.
11. Susan Okin, 'Is Multiculturalism Bad for Women?', in *Is Multiculturalism Bad for Women*, eds., Joshua Cohen, Matthew Howard, and Martha C. Nussbaum, (Princeton: Princeton University Press, 1999), 9–24.
12. Robert O. Keohane, 'International Relations Theory: Contributions of a Feminist Standpoint', *Millennium*, 18, no. 2, (1989): 245–53.
13. Sarah Brown, 'Feminism, International Theory, and International Relations of Gender Inequality', *Millennium*, 17, no. 3, (1988): 469.
14. Cynthia Cockburn, 'The Gendered Dynamics of Armed Conflict and Political Violence', in *Victims, Perpetrators or Actors? Gender, Armed Conflict and Political Violence*, eds, C. Moser and F. Clark, (New Delhi: Kali for Women, 2001), 15.
15. See, for instance, Mary Daly, *Gyn/Ecology: The Metaethics of Radical Feminism*, (Boston: Beacon Press, 1978) and Charlotte Bunch, *Passionate Politics: Feminist Theory in Action*, (New York: St. Martin's Press, 1987).

16. See Caroline Ramazanoglu, *Feminism and the Contradictions of Oppression*, (London and New York: Routledge, 1989) and Chandra Talpade Mohanty, 'Cartographies of Struggle: Third World Women and the Politics of Feminism', in *Third World Women and the Politics of Feminism*, eds, Chandra Talpade Mohanty et al., (Bloomington and Indianapolis: Indiana University Press, 1991).

17. Christine Sylvester, 'The Emperors' Theories and Transformations: Looking at the Field Through Feminist Lenses', in *Transformations in the Global Political Economy*, eds, Dennis Pirages and Christine Sylvester, (London: Macmillan, 1990), 235.

18. Diana Thorburn, 'Feminism Meets International Relations', *SAIS Review*, 20, no. 2, (2000): 2.

19. Laura Sjoberg, 'Introduction', in *Gender and International Security: Feminist Perspectives*, ed., Laura Sjoberg, (London: Routledge, 2010), 3.

20. Judith Lorber, *Paradoxes of Gender*, (New Haven: Yale University Press, 1994), 1.

21. Joan Wallach Scott, *Gender and the Politics of History*, (New York: Columbia University Press, 1988), 42.

22. J. Ann Tickner, *Gendering World Politics, Issues and Approaches in the Post-Cold War Era*, (New York: Columbia University Press, 2001), 15.

23. Wadley, 'Gendering the state Performativity', 49.

24. See Lewis A. Coser, *The Functions of Social Conflict*, (New York: Free Press, 1956); Donald L. Horowitz, *Ethnic Groups in Conflict*, (Berkeley: University of California Press, 1985); and D. G. Pruitt and J. Z. Rubin, *Social Conflict: Escalation, Stalemate, and Settlement*, (New York: Random House, 1986).

25. Håvard Strand et al., *Armed Conflict Dataset Codebook*, Version 2.1, (11 March 2004), 3. Available at http://www.prio.no/sptrans/-818603808/codebook_v2_1.pdf (accessed on 23 June 2011).

26. Strand et al., 'Armed conflict', 4.

27. ICRC, 'How is the Term "Armed Conflict" Defined in International Humanitarian Law?', *Opinion Paper*, (March 2008), 5.

28. Inger Skjelsbaek and Dan Smith, 'Introduction', in *Gender, Peace and Conflict*, eds, Inger Skjelsbaek and Dan Smith, (New Delhi: Sage Publications, 2001), 3.

29. Michael Klare and Peter Kornbluh, eds, *Low-Intensity Warfare: Counterinsurgency, Proinsurgency, and Antiterrorism in the Eighties*, (New York: Random, 1991).

30. Joshua S. Goldstein, *International Relations*, Fifth Edition, (Delhi: Pearson Education 2003), 214.

31. Mary Kaldor, *New & Old Wars, Organized Violence in a Global Era*, (Cambridge: Polity Press, 1999).

32. Wadley, 'Gendering the state Performativity', 39.

33. Elaine Showalter, 'Feminist Criticism in the Wilderness', in *Modern Criticism and Theory*, ed., David Lodge, (London: Longman, 1988), 345.

34. F. Ní Aoláin and E. Rooney, 'Underenforcement and Intersectionality: Gendered Aspects of Transition for Women', *International Journal for Transitional Justice*, 1, (2007): 342.

35. Jean Bethke Elshtain, *Women and War*, (New York: Basic Books, 1987), 232–33.

36. Christine Sylvester, 'The Art of War/the War Question in (Feminist) IR', *Millennium*, 33, no. 3, (2005): 855.

37. It is a matter of debate whether those directly involved in violence and those who support it can be treated at par. A ICRC report quotes a man from the southern Caucasus, 'somebody can hold a submachine gun and somebody only a ladle. But it doesn't mean a cook is less responsible than a soldier.' ICRC, *People on War*, (Geneva: ICRC, 1999), 24. In this book I have used the terms combatants, fighters and perpetrators of violence interchangeably.

38. Swati Parashar, 'Feminist International Relations and Women Militants: Case Studies from Sri Lanka and Kashmir', *Cambridge Review of International Affairs*, 22, no. 2, (2009): 251–52.

39. Francine D'Amico, 'Feminist Perspectives on Women Warriors', in *The Women and War Reader*, eds, Lois Ann Lorentzen and Jennifer Turpin, (New York: New York University Press, 1998), 119.

40. Ralph Pettman, 'Sex, Power, and the Grail of Positive Collaboration', in *The 'Man' Question in International Relations*, eds, Marysia Zalewski and Jane Parpart, (Boulder, CO: Westview Press, 1998), 174.

41. Jennifer Turpin, 'Many Faces: Women Confronting War', in *The Women and War Reader*, eds, Lois Ann Lorentzen and Jennifer Turpin, (New York: New York University Press, 1998), 32.

42. Chris Coulter, 'Female Fighters in the Sierra Leone War: Challenging the Assumptions?', *Feminist Review*, 88, no. 1, (2008): 54–73 and Kimberly Theidon, 'Gender in Transition: Common Sense, Women and War', *Journal of Human Rights*, 6, no. 3, (2007): 453–78.

43. Lauren Wilcox, 'Gendering the cult of the offensive', in *Gender and International Security: Feminist Perspectives*, ed., Laura Sjoberg, (London: Routledge, 2010), 75.

44. Wilcox, 'Gendering the Cult'.

45. Iris Marion Young, 'Feminist Reactions to the Contemporary Security Regime', *Hypatia*, 18, no. 1, (2003): 230.

46. Elshtain, *Women and War*, 140.

47. J. Ann Tickner, 'Why Women Can't Run the World: International Politics According to Francis Fukuyama', *International Studies Review*, 1, no. 3, (1999): 3.

48. Tickner, 'Why Women Can't Run the World', 4.

49. Sherry Ortner, 'Is Female to Male as Nature is to Culture', *Feminist Studies,* 1, no. 2, (1972): 5–31.

50. Diana Fuss, *Essentially Speaking: Feminism, Nature and Difference*, (New York: Routledge, 1989), xi–xii.

51. R. L. Cartwright, 'Some Remarks on Essentialism', *The Journal of Philosophy*, 65, no. 20, (1968): 615–26.

52. Elizabeth Grosz, 'Sexual Difference and the Problem of Essentialism', in *The Essential Difference: Another Look at Essentialism*, eds, Naomi Schor and Elizabeth Weed, (Bloomington: Indiana University Press, 1994), 84.

53. Inger Skjelsbaek, 'Is Feminity Inherently Peaceful? The Construction of Feminity in War', in *Gender, Peace and Conflict*, eds, Inger Skjelsbaek and Dan Smith, (New Delhi: Sage Publications, 2001), 49.

54. See Birgit Brock-Utne, *Educating for Peace: A Feminist Perspective*, (New York: Pergamon, 1985); Nancy Chodorow, *The Reproduction of Mothering: Psychoanalysis and the Sociology of Gender*, (Berkeley: University of California Press, 1978); and Carol Gilligan, *In a Different Voice: Psychological Theory and Women's Development*, (Cambridge, MA: Harvard University Press, 1982).

55. Rick Wilford, 'Feminism', in *Political Ideologies: An Introduction*, eds, Robert Eccleshall et. al., (London and New York: Routledge, 1994), 184–210.

56. Virginia Wolf, *Three Guineas*, (London: Hogarth Press, 1977 [1938]), 13–14.

57. Joshua S. Goldstein, *War and Gender: How Gender Shapes the War System and Vice Versa*, (Cambridge: Cambridge University Press, 2003), 41–52.

58. See Elshtain, *Women and War*.

59. Ruth Roach Pierson, *Women and Peace: Theoretical, Historical and Practical Perspectives*, (London: Croom Helm, 1987); M. K. Burguieres, 'Feminist Approaches to Peace: Another Step for Peace Studies', *Millennium*, 19, no. 1, (1990): 1–18; and Betty Reardon, *Sexism and the War System*, (Syracuse: Syracuse University Press, 1996).

60. Skjelsbaek, 'Is Feminity Inherently Peaceful? The Construction of Feminity in War', 61–62.

61. Elshtain, *Women and War*, 4.

62. Janet C. Wesselius, 'Gender Identity without Gender Prescriptions: Dealing with Essentialism and Constructionism in Feminist Politics', Paper presented at Twentieth World Congress of Philosophy, Boston, 10–15 August 1998. Available at http://www.bu.edu/wcp/Papers/Gend/GendWess.htm (accessed on 26 June 2011).

63. Andrew Sayer, 'Essentialism, Social Constructionism, and Beyond', *The Sociological Review*, 45, no. 3, (1997): 455.

64. Elizabeth Spelman, *Inessential Woman: Problems of Exclusion in Feminist Thought*, (Boston: Beacon P., 1988), 187.

65. Judith Butler, *Gender Trouble: Feminism and the Subversion of Identity*, (New York: Routledge, 1990), 3.

66. Robert Jackson and Georg Sørensen, *Introduction to International Relations: Theories and Approaches*, (Oxford: Oxford University Press, 2010), 166.

67. See, Jeffrey T. Checkel, 'The Constructivist Turn in International Relations Theory', *World Politics*, 50, no. 2, (1998): 324–48; Peter J. Katzenstein, ed., *The Culture of National Security: Norms and Identity in World Politics*, (New York: Columbia University Press, 1996); and Thomas U. Berger, *Cultures of Antimilitarism: National Security in Germany and Japan*, (Baltimore, Md.: John Hopkins University Press, 1998).

68. Alexander Wendt, 'Anarchy is What States Make of It: the Social Construction of Power "Politics"', *International Organization*, 46, no. 2, (1992): 391–425; and by the same author, *Social Theory of International Politics*, (Cambridge: Cambridge University Press, 1999).

69. Marianne Hirsch and Evelyn Fox Keller, eds, *Conflicts in Feminism*, (New York: Routledge, 1990); Kathy Ferguson, *The Man Question: Visions of Subjectivity in Feminist Theory*, (Berkeley: University of California Press, 1993); and Judith Butler, *Gender Trouble: Feminism and the Subversion of Identity*, (New York: Routledge, 1990).

70. Candace West and Don H. Zimmerman, 'Doing Gender', in *The Social Construction of Gender*, eds, Judith Lorber and Susan A. Farrell, (Newbury Park, CA: Sage Publications, 1991), 24.

71. Vivien Burr, *An Introduction to Social Constructionism*, (London: Routledge, 1995), 3.

72. J. S. Bohan, 'Regarding Gender: Essentialism, Constructionism and Feminist Psychology', *Psychology of Women Quarterly*, 17, (1993): 7.

73. Skjelsbaek, 'Is Feminity Inherently Peaceful? The Construction of Feminity in War', 51.

74. Simone de Beauvoir, *The Second Sex*, translated by H. M. Parshley, (London: Vintage, 1997), 295.

75. Enloe, 'Feminist International Relations', 3.

76. Skjelsbaek, 'Is Feminity Inherently Peaceful? The Construction of Feminity in War', 50–51.

77. Charlotte Hooper, *Manly States: Masculinities, International Relations, and Gender Politics*, (New York: Columbia University Press, 2001), 80–87.

78. Cynthia Enloe, *Maneuvers: The International Politics of Militarizing Women's Lives*, (Berkeley, CA: University of California Press, 2000), 237.

79. Tickner, 'Why Women Can't Run the World', 7.

80. B. Byrne, 'Towards a Gendered Understanding of Conflict', in Gender and Peace Support Operations. Available at http://www.genderandpeacekeeping.org/resources/3_Towards a_Gendered_Understandingof_Conflict.pdf (accessed on 11 March 2011).

81. Rosemarie Tong, *Feminist Thought: A Comprehensive Introduction*, (Boulder: Westview, 1989), 2.

82. Alison M. Jagger and Paula S. Rothenberg, eds, *Feminist Frameworks: Alternative Theoretical Accounts of the Relations Between Women and Men*, (New York: McGraw-Hill, 1984).

83. Francine D'Amico and Peter R. Beckman, eds, *Women in World Politics: An Introduction*, (Westport, CT: Bergin & Garvey, 1995); Barbara J. Nelson and Najma Chowdhury, eds, *Women and Politics Worldwide*, (New Haven and London: Yale University Press, 1994); Michael A. Genovese, ed., *Women as National Leaders: The Political Performance of Women as Heads of Government*, (Thousands Oaks, CA: Sage Publications, 1993); and Nancy E. McGlen and Meredith Reid Sarkees, *Women in Foreign Policy: The Insiders*, (New York: Routledge, 1993).

84. Linda Grant De Pauw, *Battle Cries and Lullabies: Women in War from Prehistory to the Present*, (Norman, Okla: University of Oklahoma Press, 1998); Linda Bird Francke, *Ground Zero: The Gender Wars in the Military*, (New York: Simon & Schuster, 1997); Judith Hicks Stiehm, ed., *It's Our Military, Too!*, (Philadelphia: Temple University Press, 1996); Elisabetta Addis, Valerie E. Russo and Lorenza Ebesta, eds, *Women Soldiers: Images and Realities*, (New York: St. Martin's, 1994); and Eva Isaksson, ed., *Women and the Military System*, (New York: St. Martin's, 1988).

85. Personal Interview, 26 May 2011.

86. The terms Kashmir and J&K have been used interchangeably in the book. Pre-partition Kashmir has been referred to as undivided Kashmir or as the princely state of Kashmir.

87. Laura Sjoberg, 'Gendered Realities of the Immunity Principle: Why Gender Analysis Needs Feminism', *International Studies Quarterly*, 50, no. 4, (2006): 897.

88. Miriam Cooke, 'Wo-Man, Retelling the War Myth', in *Gendering War Talk*, eds, Miriam Cooke and Angela Woollacott, (Princeton: Princeton University Press, 1993), 177.

89. Personal Interview, 13 June 2011.

Chapter 2

Women Making War in South Asia

Is war a male domain? Major responses may still be in affirmative but no longer does this notion remain unchallenged. Literature and mundane reality corroborate that war is not a male bastion and women are not necessarily peaceful. Women have played direct and indirect, organized and unorganized roles in combat operations throughout history, which is replete with evidences of how women formed part of state armies and played valiant roles in the battlefield. Recent decades, in which intra-state wars have surpassed inter-state wars, have witnessed women playing significant roles in non-state violent groups in challenging the might of the state. I focus on selective conflicts in South Asia as it is not feasible to analyse how women are impacting conflicts across the globe in a single chapter, and also the main argument of the book does not necessitate such a study. Instead I attempt an analysis of intersection of gender and conflict in the South Asian landscape with focus on two inter-related questions – what kind of roles do women play in conflicts and why they join violent non-state groups?

The Scholarship

Historically, women have participated in wars across the globe[1] though their involvement has been highly undervalued. Scholarship has accorded scant attention to this issue since usually women are either considered peaceful and apolitical, or a 'pacifying' impact on politics. The focus therefore has been on masculine violence in inter-state relations.[2] In recent years many analysts have brought into focus the intersection of women and conflict, with some also focusing on women making war.[3] Women resorting to violence have been traditionally considered a diversion from their perceived natural selves; indeed a perversion, a distortion. This is no longer the case. The intersection of gender and war is now analysed as 'elements of the politics and practices of war and peace, rather than cases of gender deviance, false consciousness or globalized militarization.'[4] Laura Sjoberg and Caron E. Gentry argue that since gender is visible in most of the areas of life such as in discussions on human rights and development, it is crucial to recognize its role in violence as well.[5] Joshua S. Goldstein has reviewed the historical performance of women combatants in war across history and regions in his work on war and gender. He points that the Dahomey Kingdom of West Africa in the 18th–19th centuries was a documented case where an all-women combat unit was part of the state army.[6] According to Goldstein, the women combatants were, 'armed with muskets and swords. They drilled regularly and resembled the men in dress and activities. They stayed in top physical condition and were fast and strong.'[7] Another well documented instance is of the Soviet Union that successfully mobilized women in the Second World War. This World War highlighted women's role, primarily in reserve or support units in the German and British forces, and their direct participation in the case of the Soviet Union constituting about 8 per cent of the total armed forces.[8]

The post-Second World War period has witnessed a sharp growth in internal conflicts across the globe including in South Asia. Women have become an almost inseparable component of many such conflicts wherein battle lines are drawn within human habitations. In fact, women's participation in violent activities has grown exponentially both quantitatively and qualitatively in these conflicts. They are increasingly becoming visible in violent non-state groups. This is revealed by a survey wherein out of 55 conflict-ridden countries women were involved as active participants in violence in as many as 38 countries.[9] Although women represent a fraction of the armed militants worldwide, their contribution to violence is far-reaching. The spectrum of roles that they play has expanded substantially. Generally women have been considered secondary players by both scholarship and militant leadership, typically relegated to support functions such as providing safe houses or gathering intelligence.[10] In conflict situations women are usually associated with nurturing roles and depicted as 'wives, girlfriends, and mothers, waiting for their soldiers to return and caring for wounded.'[11] Evidence, however, suggests that women form about one-tenth to one-third of non-state violent actors and play a greater role in supportive services. They fight and kill as well.[12] Women have participated as active combatants in many conflict-ridden regions such as Algeria, El Salvador, Eritrea, Mozambique, Namibia, Nicaragua and South Africa. They perform all tasks that directly or indirectly promote and sustain violence – ranging from nursing to spying, from raising funds to recruitment and from being active fighters to suicide bombers.[13] They become war leaders as was the case of Black Diamond in Liberia.[14] They 'founded and led militant groups, hijacked planes, served on all-female tank units, blown up buildings and assassinated national leaders.'[15]

The ethno-religious composition of South Asia is highly diverse. The countries in the region include many ethnic constituencies with divergent linguistic, religious and territorial aspirations, which enhance the proneness of the region as a theatre of conflicts. As state policies falter or prove inadequate at assimilating the diversities into a dynamic national idea, intra-state conflicts continue to challenge the integrity of many South Asian countries. Throughout the region, competing claims between the state and the insurgents are enormous. The aspirations of violent non-state groups are diverse: some of them struggle for recognition and participation in political affairs, while others seek greater autonomy or complete independence. Even within the insurgent groups, competing factions exist and may have different goals. In 1999, over 40 ethnic struggles were active in the region – ranging from being highly volatile to just simmering. While some of the internal conflicts have been resolved, at least for the time being, others continue. In many of these conflicts, the whole spectrum of roles, both direct and indirect, played by women is highly evident.

Wearing Combat Gear

Women in some of the South Asian conflicts have been direct participants – as active combatants and even as suicide bombers. Sri Lanka was characterized in some quarters as one of the most unstable countries until recently. The whole country, particularly its north eastern part, was engulfed in violence due to frequent clashes between the state army and the secessionist organization the Liberation Tigers of Tamil Eelam (LTTE), leading to heavy men and material losses. LTTE waged a violent movement demanding an independent state for Tamil people in 1983 by resorting to tactics such as suicide bombings and assassinations of civilian and political leaders, including that of incumbent President Ranasinghe Premadasa in 1993. The Sri Lankan conflict that led to a loss of thousands of lives and displacement of millions witnessed a large-scale presence of women contributing to this collateral damage. In the context of South Asia, LTTE women were visible the most in combat operations; this was unlike in other situations where they mostly performed support roles. Women enjoyed significant visibility in LTTE, and their large-scale participation in the conflict has been a theme of debate both within political circles and scholarship. It is difficult to gauge the exact number of female combatants in LTTE. The generally accepted estimates are about 15–20 per cent to one-third of the core combat strength of the organization though there are also claims that almost half of its members were women.[16] Being part of direct combat operations women suffered heavy causalities. As per a news report between 1985 and 2002 nearly 4,000 female LTTE cadres were killed.[17]

As soon as LTTE adopted violence as a strategy to put forward its demands in the early 1980s, it started enlisting women aggressively. Initially, women were involved in support activities including, but not limited to, propaganda, recruitment drives, fund raising, attending to the injured, intelligence gathering and couriering arms and messages. In 1983 an all-women group of LTTE called Vituthalai Pulikal Makalir Munani (Women's Front of the Liberation Tigers) was formed, headed by a woman, Colonel Vithusha.[18] In 1985 the first batch of female fighters was trained, setting the stage for scores of subsequent women-exclusive batches to prepare them not only to directly confront the Sri Lankan security forces but also to carry out suicide bombing. LTTE also had an all-women battalion of suicide bombers.[19] The organization carried out 378 suicide attacks from 1987 to 2008. While 274 of these were carried out by male suicide bombers as many as 104 were carried out by female suicide bombers.[20]

Sri Lanka is not an exceptional case as far as suicide bombing by women is concerned as this is visible in other conflict situations. Why women are increasingly being enlisted by violent non-state groups to carry out these perilous acts that kill them along with many other people? A major reason is that women are considered generally peaceful, which makes them a 'natural' choice for suicide bombing. Rohan Gunaratna argues that women are the preferred choice for this deadly task because, 'first, women are less suspicious. Second, in the conservative societies... there is hesitation to body-search a woman. Third, women can wear a suicide device beneath their clothes and appear pregnant.'[21] Mia Bloom points out that female suicide bombers bring in the element of surprise, unlike male suicide bombers:

> [First] people still don't expect women to be involved in violence. Second, women tend to infuse a movement with enthusiasm and a great deal of momentum. Third, a lot of movements use women's involvement to shame men when recruitment is sagging. They say, 'Your sisters are fighting for you.' Finally, acts perpetrated by women, particularly attractive women, get far more media attention.... Plus, the use of women and children is much more distressing to the other side. I did a study of soldiers returning from Iraq, and their levels of PTSD (Post Traumatic Stress Disorders) were much higher if they had had to shoot a woman or child, even if they knew the person was a suicide bomber.[22]

Bloom goes on to add that the success rate of female suicide bombers in terms of reaching targets and causing maximum damage is comparatively more, 'with a civilian target, female bombers tend to be more successful and cause more damage ... women are less likely to be stopped at the entrance. They get further inside, where they have a more deadly effect.'[23] Karla J. Cunningham contends that women are able to use their gender to avoid visibility on several fronts:

> [Their] non-threatening nature may prevent in-depth scrutiny at the most basic level as they are simply not considered important enough to warrant investigation; second, sensitivities regarding more thorough searches, particularly of women's bodies, may hamper stricter scrutiny; and third, a woman's ability to get pregnant and the attendant changes to her body facilitate concealment of weapons and bombs using maternity clothing, as well as further impeding inspection because of impropriety issues.[24]

The invisibility that helps women to aid and fuel violence with lesser effort however comes with its own gender specific disadvantages, including the extension of this invisibility to the peace making process; women are not accorded due place in the formal process of peace making. This issue of continuation of gender invisibility in peace is dealt in detail later in the book.

Women have been involved in direct warfare in other conflicts in the region, the foremost being Nepal where Maoists violence erupted in the mid-1990s as a reaction to prevailing poverty, underdevelopment and a feudalistic social order. In February 1996, the Maoists declared People's War, claiming that only a communist state could resolve the country's ills. Their promise of an equitable society and economic prosperity received considerable support, especially from the socially and economically disadvantaged sections. It is claimed that women constituted a significant percentage of active Maoists fighters – anywhere between 30 and 50 per cent.[25] The former Vice Chairperson of the Maoists party and ideologue, who later became Prime Minister of Nepal, Baburam Bhattarai revealed in 2003 that 50 per cent of the cadres at the lower level, 30 per cent of the soldiers and 10 per cent of the members of the central committee were women.[26] The United Nations' (UN) figures reveal that women constituted about 20 per cent of the total active combatants; out of the 19,602 combatants, 3,846 were women.[27] These figures may be small in comparison to what was earlier speculated, but are nonetheless significant.

In this discussion of women warriors, India requires special attention since it is confronting a number of conflicts within its boundaries in which women are involved. The trend of women directly participating in war is not new for India. One comes across scores of mythologies and historical narratives of women warriors. Though in Hindu religion, followed by a majority of Indian citizens, women are portrayed as embodiments of peace and tolerance they can also become power and strength personified, if needed. Hindu mythologies abound with depictions of women as a source of *shakti* (power). Goddesses Durga and Kali are worshipped as endowers of power to eliminate evil forces. Goddess Durga, portrayed as killing Mahishashura (the demon king) with a trident, and goddess Kali, as wearing a neck piece made of skulls and performing the dance of death, have been a source of inspiration for warriors, including women, to valiantly fight the enemy. Warriors sought blessings of these goddesses to achieve victory in the battlefield.

There are instances in Indian history of women becoming rulers and fighting wars. Raziya Sultana, who ruled the Delhi sultanate from 1236 to 1240 before being imprisoned by her enemies in fort Qila Mubarak in Bathinda in the state of Punjab, has become a part of folklore in India. India's freedom struggle proved to be an archetype of women's participation on a mass scale and many of them took up arms. The first war of Independence of 1857 perhaps could not have reached its zenith without participation of valiant women such as *rani* (queen) Laxmi Bai of Jhansi. Her popular image of straddling a horse with a raised sword in her hand and her infant son tied on her back still captivates Indian public memory. Storybooks and television soaps based on her life are read and viewed with great interest. Children grow up listening to bed time stories of her bravery along with the advice to become courageous like her. After decades, with the mounting intensity of the Indian independence movement in the 1930s and 1940s, Laxmi Bai's name was invoked to mobilize women. The Rani Laxmi Bai battalion was set-up in 1945 in the Indian National Army, formed by Subhash Chandra Bose. This all-women battalion was led by a young woman named Laxmi Sehgal, popularly called Captain Sehgal, who breathed her last in July 2012. In India, mythology and history are replete with such instances of goddesses and women taking up arms for defending right and confronting wrong. In current times the involvement of women in war is, however, far complex. It is not an easy task to outrightly acclaim or disapprove of modern day violent conflicts and women's involvement in them; these, thereby, cannot be juxtaposed with the above instances drawn from Hindu mythology and Indian history.

Among armed movements in post-colonial India, women are perceptible in the Maoist movement. The origin of this movement can be traced to the late 1960s, in the north of West Bengal, particularly to a place called Naxalbari (that is why the movement is also labelled the Naxal movement). It was initiated by a split group of the Communist Party in the form of a peasant uprising. The Maoists questioned the basis of the political system, the hierarchical social structure and exploitative economic arrangements. They sought to alter the entire socio-political structure by targeting the alleged exploitative system and its perpetrators. Maoists have emerged as a major internal security challenge to India. Labelled 'Red terrorism,' 'home grown terrorism' and 'Red menace', Maoist violence has spread to many parts of India. In 2011, Naxalites were active across approximately 83 districts in nine provinces of the country.[28] Despite being outlawed, Maoists have acceptance among rural masses and hence there seem to be no dearth of fighters and supporters for the violent movement.

It is not unusual to come across female Maoists dressed and armed as combatants in the Maoist affected areas. The involvement of women in Maoist violence is not a recent phenomenon. Since its commencement in the form of the Naxalbari armed peasant movement women have played a crucial role. They now form a significant percentage of Maoists. As per a 2011 estimate, a significant percentage of cadres in the Maoist affected Gadchiroli district and its adjacent areas of in Maharashtra, were women. Out of 290 hard core Maoists operating in the area as many as 74 were women, or nearly 25 per cent.[29] Media reports about female Maoists, directly involved in combat operations, are abundant. In a high profile Maoists attack, which led to the killing of 18 policemen in Gadchiroli on 8 October 2009, the leader of the group was a woman. Female cadres also played a major role in an attack on a camp of security personnel at Shilda in West Midnapore district in West Bengal on 15 February 2010. This group was also led by a female commander. The role of women in the Maoist affected state of Odisha has been reported prominently in the local media. Twenty-three year old Adari Murmu, alias Deepa, was involved in two cases of murder and one case of arson between April and July 2010. Similarly, the killing of a suspected police informer in Malkangiri district on 7 July 2012 by a group of Maoists included two women.[30] Seventeen-year-old Budhuni who joined the movement at the age of 15 in 2010, was involved in violent activities including fire exchanges between Maoists and police forces in Jajpur district in Odisha in January 2011.[31] Eighteen-year-old Sabita became a Maoist in 2009. She was involved not only in auxiliary roles such as cooking and making bombs but also in the attacks on Central Reserve Police Force (CRPF) personnel, a paramilitary force.[32]

Sikh women in Punjab too participated in the Khalistan movement, which aimed at carving out a separate state based on religion. The movement started in the 1960s to accord Sikhs, a religious minority in India, their 'due'. In early 1980s the movement turned violent with many youth taking up arms. In 1984 Indian security forces launched Operation Blue Star and entered

Golden Temple (a revered Sikh shrine in Amritsar, Punjab) to overpower
the armed militants hiding in the shrine. These militants led by Jarnail Singh
Bhindranwale were accused of indiscriminate killing of scores of Hindus
and even Sikhs. The operation was a success in the sense that the Indian
army was able to kill the militants. This strategy was, however, severely
criticized in many quarters as scores of innocent Sikhs, who were present
in the Golden Temple at the time of the operation, too were killed. During
my interviews in Punjab, many Sikhs contended that the operation in the
sacred shrine, for whatever reason, was an insult to their religion. The killing
of Indian Prime Minister Indira Gandhi by her Sikh bodyguards to avenge
the operation was followed by communal riots wherein hundreds of Sikhs
were killed in 1984. All these events of 1984 proved to be a turning point in
the history of the Khalistan movement because of which the militants gained
mass support. The strength of the militants grew exponentially. This was also
the time when many women joined the violent movement as after Operation
Blue Star 'women swore revenge and offered their sons for the Sikh cause'.[33]
One of my respondents who had joined the movement to avenge the atrocities
on Sikhs said:

> I supported the movement after witnessing the mass killing of Sikhs in 1984
> in New Delhi, capital of India. Sikhs were butchered mercilessly and there
> was no one to help us. This is not how we expected the Indian state to treat a
> minority community. I thought if Sikhs have a separate homeland things will
> be certainly better. I came to Punjab and joined a militant group active in my
> native place. My parents did not object to this decision since they too were
> horrified by the killings of innocent people. Many of my friends also supported
> the movement. Though ideology played a role in motivating us but the major
> factor, for me, was revenge.[34]

As I noticed in Kashmir, supporting a violent movement in patriarchal
societies is presumed to be a natural course for women if their men are
involved. In the context of the Khalistan movement, the case was somewhat
different. My respondents pointed out that Sikh women can be equally good
fighters being members of a community of warriors; Sikh men are called *singhs*
(lions) and women *singhnees* (lionesses). Hence, for many women supporters
of the Khalistan movement it was not merely the case of following men but
that of 'demonstrating the combat quality inherited from the ancestors'.[35]
Cunningham points out that Sikh religion 'neither precludes female combat
nor categorizes that role as uniquely masculine (or "unfeminine")'[36] and hence
the role of women in the movement was not religiously undermined; rather

it was acclaimed as proof of 'their ability to fight and die for the nation'.[37] On gender equality in Sikh religion Cynthia Keppley Mahmood writes:

> While it is obvious that the celebrated virtues of courage, bold action, and strong speech are consonant with masculinity as understood in the West, among Sikhs these qualities are treated as neither masculine nor feminine, but simply as Sikh, values. Women may be bound to the kitchen and may have babies in their arms, but they are still fully *expected* to behave as soldiers, if necessary.[38]

Historically women have been part of combat operations carried out by the Sikh community. Sikh women warriors of the 18th century such as Mai Bhago have been a source of inspiration for both female and male fighters. Stories of valiant Sikh women who fought against the Mughals are narrated with passion by members of the community.

Though most Sikh women supported militant activities from the back stage, some of them enlisted as formal members of militant groups and were directly involved in violent operations. A Sikh religious website says:

> Many Sikh women participated in the Sikh resistance movement as fighters. Like their sisters from past ages, Sikh women joined their brothers in the fight for freedom. Many brave Singhnees fought side by side with their Singhs and attained Shaheedee (martyrdom). The examples of Shaheeds (martyrs) Bhai (brother) Harvinderjit Singh Taini Babbar and Bibi (lady) Manjeet Kaur Babbar...Bhai Pritpal Singh and Bibi Harjeet Kaur, etc., are notable.[39]

Jasmeet Kaur played an active role in the militancy both before and after her marriage. She became a widow two years after being married to Satnam Singh Cheena of the Bhindranwale Tigers Force of Khalistan in 1991. Kaur details her journey:

> I was a proclaimed offender (PO) even before I got married. While in Khalsa College, Amritsar, I was annoyed at the attack on the Golden Temple. My links with the militant movement grew as did my desire for revenge....I was involved in the murder of Comrade Hardev Singh, and was in jail for a year, in Amritsar. After marriage I became PO again and was arrested and later bailed out. In 1995, I was arrested in Gurdaspur, where there was a case against me. The police would have hounded every family I stayed with. So till January 1996 I was in jail and when I was released, I decided not to be a PO because I had children to raise. I decided to attend the court hearings and to work. I can't say I returned to the mainstream, but can't even say I have given up the movement...that is in my blood by now. It is another matter that I have decided not to lift a gun, but will fight politically.[40]

In her autobiography *Bikhra Painda* Sandeep Kaur narrates her story as a fighter. She claims to be different from other women involved in the movement who only cooked and cared for the male militia. Although Kaur does not give details about the kind of operations she undertook, Laurent Gayer who has conducted extensive research on women's role in the Khalistan movement contends that women played an active role in the attacks perpetrated by militia groups against the Indian security personnel.[41] Gayer cites the example of another women militant Harneet Kaur who admitted of being involved in 'the kidnapping and subsequent decapitation of a communist activist'.[42]

In the north eastern region of India which comprises of eight states – Assam, Arunachal Pradesh, Manipur, Meghalaya, Mizoram, Nagaland, Tripura and Sikkim – a series of conflicts have been continuing. These conflicts have their origins in a set of diverse demands championed by variegated militant groups. These range from greater autonomy to a separate state within the Indian federal structure to complete independence from India. I look at Manipur which continues to confront a high number of incidents of violence with the conflict remaining intractable. The state has nearly 30 armed groups operating not only against Indian security forces but even against each other. Female cadres are present in considerable numbers in many militant groups active in the region.[43] In this conflict also some instances of women playing a direct role have been reported. There are cases of women militants being killed during combat operations.[44] On 22 January 2010 ten militants, including two women, were arrested for their involvement in the 6 January bomb attack at the residence of former Chief Minister Radhabinod Koijam.[45]

Back-up Roles

The support roles that women play in conflicts in South Asia encompass roughly all tasks that a human being can accomplish. As women's support roles in conflicts are not clearly defined, the activities can mean any task that can buttress the movement. These range from couriering to cooking, from being sentries to being propagandists and from nursing to spying. In the context of the Maoist movement in Nepal, Hisila Yami Parvati, a female Maoist, gives details of some of the roles played by the women:

> One of the historical achievements of the People's War was that it made a big leap in women's lives. Women joined all the fronts: the Party, United Front and the People's Liberation Army (PLA), the three instruments of revolution. For

the first time, women became professional full-time revolutionaries not in tens or hundreds but in thousands!.... Women became professional revolutionaries by joining PLA, militias, production brigades. They became policy makers; they worked as couriers, organizers, as barefoot health workers, as radio anchors.[46]

Women were quite visible in support roles in the Khalistan movement. They primarily acted as couriers of messages and arms and ammunition.[47] Narrating her experiences as the head of the women's wing of the once powerful Khalistan Commando Force, Gurvinder Kaur is quoted as recalling, 'myself and some other girlfriends had only one job: transportation of arms from one place to another'.[48] Rajinder Kaur, a respondent, gave details of her activities as a messenger and informer:

> I used to receive and dispatch messages. I acted as an informer. I utilized my vocal skills to extract information about police activities and about their informers by going from home to home in my village. Most women are fond of gossiping and hence I spent a substantial duration of my day conversing with women to seek information. It was a tiring and time-taking task. Sometimes for days together I could not get any crucial information. I had to be attentive all the time since at times apparently prosaic information could prove crucial for our militant brothers. For instance, once during conversation I came to know that one police official, who had killed four of our brothers (militants), was coming to the village to attend a wedding. I passed on this information to the militants. The officer was shot dead in the wedding hall itself. You may call it gruesome but I call it justice. He killed our brothers and revenge was necessary not only to bring him to justice but also to deter the Indian forces.[49]

Incidents such as those of preparing delicious dishes for the militants active around their *pind* (village) and taking care of ill or injured 'brothers and sons' were narrated with passion once women were comfortable enough to share their experiences with me. For women participating in militancy-related activities did not mean abandoning the normal life altogether, at least in the initial years of the militancy, as the militants lived in villages and towns, not in hideouts. Women carried out the tasks assigned to them by the militants while continuing their accustomed errands. Simran Kaur detailed:

> We women were largely assigned the tasks as supporters and this enabled us to successfully carry out our duties both as home makers as well as militancy supporters. This way, we had time to serve the family and our national cause simultaneously. If I had to carry a message from one place to another or weapons or had to cook, all these activities individually took only an hour or

so and thereafter I had adequate time to look after my family and children. But if I had to fight as a combatant then balancing the two roles could have been very difficult.[50]

Many Manipuri women have been trained to handle arms and perform other activities including bomb making. Many women have received training in militant camps outside Indian borders. On 24 May 2012 three female militants were apprehended, along with some male militants, by the Indian Border Security Force on the India–Bangladesh border. One of the detained women was the publicity secretary of a militant group and the other two were cadres.[51] Twenty-one-year-old Lily from Manipur studying in a Mumbai college revealed during an interaction that her elder sister was a militant involved primarily in spying and intelligence gathering tasks.[52] Indian security forces have arrested many women for their involvement in activities such as extortion and propaganda. To cite a few instances: In December 2009 two female militants, Laisham Bembem and Laishram Indu, were arrested for extortion of money from people. In July 2010, a woman was arrested for being involved in extortion and in August 2010 two female cadres were arrested on the same charges.[53] Mani, an Indian Maoist woman active in propagandist activities, was arrested for her role as an 'educator', which included teaching the local tribal people Maoist philosophy and imbibing in them an anti-state outlook.

In the violent Muttahida Quami Movement (MQM)[54] in Pakistan in the 1990s women were actively involved in demonstrations and protest movements. Anis Haroon points out that women raised funds for the movement and acted as 'couriers, protecting militants, running torture cells, transferring arms and hiding guns for their men in demonstrations.'[55] They even claimed the bodies and buried their dead.[56] In MQM women did not play an active militant role in terms of taking up arms but fully supported their armed men. Haroon notes:

> Even in the most violent phase of MQM it was not established that women were playing an active militant role. They were fully aware that their men used guns but they were not involved in any planning…[N]o women even admitted to being used to transfer arms…[There were] allegations of torture cells being run under their (women's) patronage…[They] fully supported the 'mission of their sons, husbands and brothers.' They themselves were convinced that the fight…was vital for their survival.[57]

In the Chittagong Hill Tracts (CHT) conflict in Bangladesh women performed the tasks of supporting the movement in all possible ways including going to markets to buy essentials (it is commonly asserted that in a conflict situation if men go out of their homes they are more vulnerable of being caught and may even get killed), taking care of families in the absence of male members and helping male militants as and when required. Hana Shams Ahmed writes, 'women, during that time played their dual role of being involved in the insurgency and taking care of their homes in absence of the male members of the family.'[58] Women significantly contributed to the movement by organizing themselves. The first all-women organization – the CHT Mohila Samiti (Women's Committee) – was formed as early as 1975, only four years after the independence of Bangladesh. Later the Hill Women's Federation (HWF) came into existence. These organizations were active in bringing human rights violations by the Bangladesh security forces to the forefront. Issues such as rape and harassment were raised by HWF by staging protests and demonstrations, petitioning and disseminating information on such issues among the international community through various forums. Meghna Guhathakurta elaborates the activities of the all-women organization:

> Despite…male dominance, the very nature of the struggle has brought forth the participation of women… in various periods of the struggle women members of the HWF were just as active and sometimes even more so than male colleagues. During the struggle the women of HWF have openly agitated against army rule and oppressive measures followed by the state. They have organised rallies and demonstrations against the genocide of the hill people propagating their message through posters, leaflets and other media such as art and songs. They have had an important role to play in bringing up the gender issue along with the rights of indigenous people. Several of the HWF members participated in international forums where they drew special attention to the problems faced by the [people of] Chittagong Hill Tracts. [59]

How and Why of Participation

The above discussion raises the problematique: why do women participate in conflict? Cunningham emphasizes the widening spectrum of women's involvement in violence 'ideologically, logistically, and regionally' and identifies several reasons for this trend:

> First, increasing contextual pressures (e.g., domestic/international enforcement, conflict, social dislocation) create a mutually reinforcing process driving terrorist organizations to recruit women at the same time women's motivations to join these groups increases; contextual pressures impact societal controls over women thereby facilitating, if not necessitating, more overt political

participation up to, and including, political violence; and operational imperatives often make female members highly effective actors for their organizations, inducing leaders toward 'actor innovation' to gain strategic advantage against their adversary.[60]

Bloom asserts that women are motivated by the 'five Rs: revenge, redemption, relationship, respect and rape'.[61] In his 2007 study on suicide bombing in Palestine, Tim McGirk argues that since 2002, 88 Palestinian women attempted suicide bombings and the motivation, besides 'religion and rage at Israeli occupation', included 'exit from personal despair...[and] for having broken taboos in strict Palestinian society'.[62] For some women becoming suicide bombers seems to be a better option than being married to persons not of their choice and for others it is necessitated 'to restore family's honour'.[63] Many women fall prey to a relationship trap of male recruiters while others to 'secret reasons that have little connection with religion and everything to do with private tragedy or shame'. [64] McGirk points out another crucial factor mentioned by a few of his respondents – promise of paradise, 'some women suicide bombers believe that in paradise they will become queens, while others are told by recruiters that no matter how old or grotesque they may be in this life, they will become the fairest of the 72 virgins that await each [male] jihad warrior.'[65] Lack of physical beauty or loss of it by accident (thereby lessening chances of marriage, considered the ultimate aim of all women in traditional societies) is another motivator. McGirk cites the example of Wafa Samir al-Biss, a 22-year-old burn victim from Gaza, who was recruited to carry out a suicide bombing on the pretext that 'she was disfigured [and] she would never get married and that she was better off becoming a martyr.'[66]

At times, acute personal suffering especially rape is projected as a humiliation to the whole community in conflict situations. In such cases, women are prompted to avenge the 'shame'. Socially ostracized raped women, prohibited from getting married and bearing children, that is, to lead a 'normal life' are motivated not only to avenge but also to make a sacrifice for their community by carrying out deadly attacks, such as suicide bombing, that would eventually make them martyrs, and help regain lost esteem. In case of Sri Lanka, martyrdom was an appealing factor for LTTE's suicide squad. By carrying out suicide bombings female members of the squad contributed to the cause of the violent movement, added to their family honour and avenged their victimization. The families of the slain combatants were publicly honoured as *maha viru* (most brave). The well known case of revenge by internalizing personal sexual abuse as humiliation of the whole community is that of Dhanu. Dhanu joined the LTTE suicide squad after being raped by personnel of the Indian Peace Keeping Force (IPKF). In 1991, she acted as a human bomb in assassinating Rajiv Gandhi, the former Prime Minister of India, who on the request of the Sri Lankan government had dispatched the IPKF in 1987 to suppress LTTE rebels. A respondent trained to carry out suicide bombings revealed:

> I along with my mother was raped by Sri Lankan security forces during a raid. We were mortified and villagers proclaimed that I would never get married. My father died due to this humiliation. I joined LTTE to save my family and myself from further disgrace. Once I decided to become a suicide bomber my family was honoured by the same villagers. My mother felt very proud. My younger brother was very excited at being called a martyr's brother. Killing Sinhalese would have helped me to revenge the humiliation that ruined my life. Also it was a life time opportunity to do something for the Tamil cause.[67]

In Nepal, vengeance was a crucial factor for many women to join the Maoist movement. Rights violations of women and their families prompted many to become Maoists. Savita was vocal in giving details of the atrocities that were committed by Nepalese security personnel during anti-Maoist operations. The affliction was acute for those families where a member had become a Maoist or was even suspected of being one. Families who were suspected of being sympathizers of the movement too had to suffer immensely. Savita narrated:

> My elder sister had joined the movement after being raped by an upper caste boy. There was no help from the administration. She was threatened of gang-rape and even murder if she continued her attempts to get the case reported in the police station. There was too much humiliation since her naked photos were pasted on our walls. After one week she joined the movement. Next month a group of Maoists came to our village and they delivered justice by killing the rapist. He was shot dead by my sister who had undergone training for handling a gun. My sister took her revenge but the family had to pay a big price. My parents and we four siblings were kept in police custody for four days. There we were given rationed water and no food at all. My youngest brother was only six years old but even he was not spared. My father was beaten mercilessly and mother was sexually abused in front of all of us. After four days a group of Maoists, led by my sister, attacked the police station and saved us. We did not return to our village thereafter. My parents and younger brother settled in a Maoist ruled village. The rest of us joined the ranks. I rose to the level of commander and killed seven security personnel. For me it was survival though for my sister it was revenge that forced us to join the movement.[68]

In India, human rights violations by security personnel, exploitation of poor tribal people by outsiders with vested interests in natural resource rich areas and lack of an effective administration prompted many men and women to become Maoists. Preetam Jain explains:

> There are many girls who join the Maoists to avenge exploitation by outsiders and the police. The poor adivasi (tribal) can't approach any system – political or judicial – where they can plead their plight or seek redress against injustice. Maoists have that system, so the villagers naturally support them....If a woman complains of her exploitation to the police, she may not even get heard, or she may get quite delayed justice....In contrast, if she approaches the Maoists for justice, she gets it immediately. This also appeals to her.[69]

The narrative of my respondent Sukanta, who surrendered before Odisha police in 2006, sums up this issue:

> My father was brutally tortured by police on suspicion of being a Maoist. My mother and we three siblings were mute spectators to his suffering. We were poor and hence had to take a loan from a money lender who was not a native. He bought crops from villagers at throwaway prices and sold them at exorbitant rates in urban areas. Despite the fact that we were regularly paying the interest the money lender was pressurizing us to hand over our land to him where he intended to set up an industrial unit. His men threatened my father that I will be kidnapped, raped and killed if he did not listen to them. My father went to the police but they did not pay attention. He was told 'when your daughter gets raped and killed then come to us and we will take action.' Thereafter we approached the Maoists. They asked the money lender at gun point to leave the village at once and he abided. This was the power of the gun. There was poverty, exploitation and discrimination on the one hand and money, gun power and equality on the other hand. I chose the latter option. I surrendered only because I was pregnant and my Maoist husband was killed in a police encounter.[70]

Under the Armed Forces Special Powers Act, 1958 (amended in 1972) Indian security personnel have unrestricted powers to carry out anti-militant operations in Manipur. There have been large-scale human rights violations in the region as there is no appropriate mechanism to check the conduct of security forces personnel. This has prompted many Manipuri women to enlist in the militant movement. Similarly, in the Khalistan movement many women supported militant violence to avenge their losses, as was the case of Paramjit Kaur who enlisted 'to kill the murderers of her parents, killed during anti-Sikh riots in Delhi'.[71]

In Manipur the nationalism and ideological appeal of fighting 'for the motherland' inspired many to enlist in militant groups. Nationalist ideology played a crucial role in the Sri Lankan conflict as well. Sumantra Bose argues, 'Tamil nationalism, in its radical form, had been transformed into a mass phenomenon and women of the younger generation of Tamils were as alienated from the state, and as inspired by the vision of a liberated Eelam, as their male counterparts.'[72] A Sri Lankan respondent reasoned that 'Tamils have been deprived of their rights and there was no other option but to grab the rights by resorting to violence.'[73] Simran Kaur who was an active member of the Khalistan movement believed, 'Sikhs are being discriminated in India and they should have a separate homeland to fully enjoy their rights as citizens of a free country.'[74] In the MQM movement, women internalized its ideology by exhibiting it in their attire. They were 'exhilarated and adorned themselves with dupattas (a variety of scarf that women wear over head or on shoulders) and glass bangles in the white, red and green colours of the MQM flag.'[75] Many women enrolled as Maoists in Nepal because they were impressed by the goal of a communist and classless society. Propaganda speeches for an egalitarian society devoid of oppression and injustice persuaded the Nepalese people to believe in the cause and to join or at least sympathize with the movement. The Maoist ideology was propagated through various means including cultural programmes with revolutionary music, dance and drama. An ex-combatant from Nepal, Radha, recalled:

> I came to know through a cultural programme of drama that so many problems had afflicted the Nepalese society and a classless society would help overcome all of them. It was such a noble thought! Maoists were fighting for the betterment of the people and not for personal gains. Any right thinking person would have been inspired by such performances. I therefore enlisted and my parents supported my decision.[76]

At times, women join violent struggles in order to escape feudal socio-economic conditions. For many South Asian women suffering from caste discrimination and poverty, joining a non-state armed movement emerged as a better option. For them enrolment in a militant group was a panacea for all their problems. Dharmi, a Nepalese ex-Maoist, said:

> We had to suffer exploitation in both public and private. As a lower caste Hindu I was not allowed to attend school or even to walk on the roads used by the upper caste people. I lived along with my family on the fringe of the village with no easy access to wells or shops. Being poor we did not have enough to eat. My father was getting pressurized to solemnize my marriage with a 67 year

old man. Despite my opposition my father was considering this proposal as he was promised a hefty amount of money by that old man. My mother had no say in family decisions. It was horrifying. Even my younger brother thrashed me twice for refusing to get married to that old man. I ran away from home and joined the movement. I did not understand the ideology fully then but it was the best decision of my life. In the camps we were never differentiated on gender basis and there was enough to eat and drink. There was no caste based segregation. We were fighting for equality across gender, caste and class. In that sense it was a dignified life. It was a perfect life both on personal and professional fronts with few difficulties.[77]

Dharmi pointed out that looting and extortion were widespread in Nepal. These activities contributed significantly to the financial resources of the individuals as well as the group, making Maoists of Nepal one of the richest rebel groups in Asia.[78] Thus, economic prospects lure many to join rebel struggles. Seventeen-year-old Basuda, who looked too young to be called a combatant or a mother though she was both, joined the Maoist movement in India at the age of 14 due to economic compulsions.[79] Radha became a Maoist to earn money that helped her family live a modest life. Within a year of enlisting she had three encounters with Indian forces and killed as many as seven security personnel. She later married a fellow Maoist and when she became pregnant she took 'leave' from her 'duties' for about a year. Radha returned to the fighter group leaving her newborn son with her mother 'to earn for family and son'.[80] A serious leg injury in a fight with security forces forced her to 'retire' from active combat. Interestingly, while being interviewed Radha talked more about human rights violations carried out by Indian security forces and less about her life as a combatant. When at the end of the interview I brought this to her notice she said, 'it is my way of contributing to the fight for our rights.'[81]

In Nepal, by publicly opposing patriarchal suppression and practices such as polygamy, early marriages, domestic violence, gambling and alcoholism, Maoists elevated their status to that of admirable heroes for many young women who later followed their role models and became combatants. Maoists' fast track courts helped them to widen their base among women folk. In these courts justice was speedy and many men were 'reformed' by punishments for crimes such as domestic violence.[82] Parvati, a Nepalese Maoist, argues in one of her writings that the revolution positively impacted Nepalese women since:

For the first time they were taught to target the feudal state apparatus as an instrument of class and gender oppression....For the first time they got the opportunity to compete on an equal footing with men combatants on war fronts. For the first time they could get married or remarried irrespective of caste, class, region and ethnicity, choosing a partner on the basis of love and ideology. For the first time the women's mass front was geared not only to addressing women's oppression but also...for running cottage industries, producing soldiers and leaders for the Party, militias and the PLA, running communes, co-operatives etc....In villages declared 'woman model villages,' it was forbidden to beat women, women practiced special rights and exercised equal rights to parental property, women were involved in constructing trekking trails, martyr gates, running people's courts etc. [83]

Maoists in India have chronicled biographies of slain female cadres that provide an account of their gender based subjugation. This chronicling provides details of how these women, inspired by the promise of the eradication of a patriarchal structure, became Maoists. One of these documents reads:

The history of oppressed women is the real history of the dearest daughters of our beloved country which is an inseparable, vital component of the history of oppressed people. And no success in the revolutionary war or the final victory of the revolution is imaginable or possible without women. Hence, the need to study their history. These life histories are an inseparable part of peoples' history....The reasons for their joining the movement may vary but one common feature we find in them is their aspiration to be liberated from patriarchy and to liberate all women from patriarchy. Most of them were themselves victims of patriarchy and some of them though not as oppressed had consciously joined as they felt Maoism provided the answer to the eradication of patriarchy.[84]

There is the additional attraction of gender equality in many of the rebel groupings. For the success of a movement, even though violent, creating a common identity beyond the divides of gender, caste and class is considered crucial. The promise of equal treatment to male and female cadres, if not in practice but at least in proclamations by militant leadership, plays a crucial role to attract women. My interactions with women ex-combatants of Nepal and Sri Lanka reveal that all those who intended to be active fighters had to undergo rigorous training irrespective of gender. All those enlisted had to carry out daily chores such as cooking and washing, and activities such as advocacy programmes, making bombs, gathering information and even fighting. Maneesha, a Nepalese ex-Maoist said:

Men and women were equally assigned all the responsibilities. There was no difference in terms of training or even duties. If we lifted guns, boys washed clothes. Cooking for the group was not only women's job. Everyone in the group had to be part of the cooking team on a weekly basis. There were teams to not only cook but for other chores such as washing clothes and cleaning the camp. Even the teams for playing outdoor games comprised of both women and men. Also during combat operations there was no gender differentiation. When I was at home I never imagined this kind of equality. From childhood I had seen my mother and elder sister performing all household chores from cooking to taking care of cattle. My father and brothers never entered the kitchen.[85]

In LTTE, gender neutral military training was adheared while assigning tasks in battalions. Rajni who received military training in 1990 said:

Once I completed training along with 30 other women I was assigned the job of an information gatherer but during the counter operations against the Sri Lankan security forces we all had to fight. We had no differential treatment in terms of dress or even work load. It was a highly disciplined life. Our leadership did not believe in gender based privileges for either men or women. It was altogether different from the life that I had lived in my village. [86]

Vasudha echoed Rajni,

Gender equality was not at all an issue once we joined LTTE. Every fighter was called a Tiger irrespective of gender. What can be better proof of equality? We were trained equally and carried out all the activities that our male counterparts did – from fighting the security forces to becoming suicide bombers.'[87]

Many respondents from Nepal claimed that there was no gender based discrimination even in promotions. 'Women had equal opportunities to get promoted to higher ranks and become commanders to lead a whole brigade. The promotion was solely based on performance, hard work and capability,' asserted Neelam.[88] This assertion notwithstanding, few women were visible in higher ranks. Majority of the women I interviewed remained cadres throughout their tenure as combatants. When I asked Neelam why she did not reach a higher rank, her response was 'because I was not capable of leading a group'.[89] A study on women combatants in Nepal quotes a male commander who offered an odd reason for the invisibility of women in the higher ranks, 'I am working for the party for 16 years; I did not see women comrades working for higher position. I think it's because of lack of self-confidence, not believing in them [selves], and [being] unwilling to take more responsibilities.'[90] In the Maoist movement in India women are 'privileged' to attain leadership positions, though on a limited basis. They are not only cadres but also commanders, area commanders and deputy commanders. Jain, focusing on the Maoist movement in Maharashtra, finds that woman 'account for three Divisional committee members, nine Commanders, three Area commanders and two Deputy Commanders….[In fact] men are outnumbered by women as commanders and deputy commanders.'[91]

At times, women join armed groups to experience being empowered and privileged by stepping out of their restrictive traditional roles. In Manipur women are normally visible in lower ranks but Princy, an active Manipuri militant, was excited to talk about her empowerment even as a cadre:

> I joined the group at the age of 20. Since then I have led a life of equality. There is freedom and liberation from all patriarchal norms. Women enjoyed full freedom including in marital affairs. Women could marry outside the grouping but preferred to marry a militant man or a man who sympathized with the movement. I do not intend to marry and am happy that I do not have to confront any societal pressure. We are mainly assigned support tasks such as collecting money and gathering information because we carry out such tasks more efficiently. But we are fully trained to fight. I am skilled to make low-intensity bombs though so far I have not made one as we have enough supplies.[92]

Many LTTE female combatants felt that they had achieved personal liberation which made them feel 'exactly like men'.[93] A newspaper report on Maoist women in India points out, 'these women find peace in their fight against the State. No matter the risk to their lives or the sacrifices they make, these women are almost fierce in asserting that this is the chosen way of life.'[94] Some women combatants do not wish to abandon this life. 'I would never have been happy raising children and tending the fields. I have greater control over my life here. Working for the party, for the people, is the life I enjoy,' Janila has been quoted as saying.[95] This issue of being empowered by joining a militant movement remains contested. Recent times have witnessed a large number of female Maoists in India surrendering with many of them alleging abuse by male leaders, ranging from beating to sexual abuse. One of my respondents, an ex-Maoist in Odisha, alleged that she was sexually abused many times while being an active combatant. 'Though we performed all tasks including fighting that our male counterparts performed, sexual services were required from us. If we did not agree to these demands we were raped and beaten,' she revealed.[96] Claims of equality and empowerment need to be further interrogated keeping in view the global reality of the near absence of these 'empowered' women in the formal peace making process. I have elaborately dealt with this argument in the concluding chapter.

Many women in Manipur joined armed groups or supported them due to the presence of a relative particularly husband or a son in the group. On

14 December 2009 a woman militant, identified as Sagolshem O. Ebemcha Devi, was nabbed by Manipur police. During interrogation she revealed that she joined the movement because of her militant husband.[97] Many single or socially ostracized women too have joined militancy. Indian security personnel have reported that militants enlist widows, divorced and HIV positive women to mainly carry out extortion activities. These women are lured by male militants into relationships and are enlisted thereafter. On 10 May 2009 Manipur police arrested two widows who were allegedly involved in extortion for money. Both claimed to be in relationships with militants. A news report gives the following details:

> The two widows identified as Maibam Thoibi Devi alias Echantombi…and Thangjam Bala Devi alias Ngamkheingakpi…were apprehended by a team of Imphal east district police commandos….A 9mm pistol with two live rounds of ammunition was also recovered from the possession of one of the widows, Bala Devi, during an operation at Lamlong Bazar under Porompat police station Sunday at around 10.30 a.m. The two were rounded up by police acting on a tip off that some militants were collecting money from government officers by summoning them at a shop in the Bazar. Thoibi has two children and was arrested earlier as an active member…[of a militant group] in October 2008. It was reported that Thoibi was having a relation with one Pamen….Bala who has no children had been trained and inducted into the…cadre. She obtained training at 3rd batch (Women wing)….She…[had] relationship with one Chaoba Singh of Imphal. This is not the first time that widows, women living with HIV/AIDS and from broken families were nabbed by the police in the state allegedly for engaging in militancy related activities.[98]

In the case of the Khalistan movement, most women enlisted following marriages to militants. Gayer notes:

> Most female recruits of the movement for Khalistan went underground on the morning that followed their wedding night. Since their husband was already involved in the militancy, and thus wanted by security forces, their wedding itself was a clandestine event…weddings were…brief and took place under the cover of the night, in a secure area….In several cases, parents could not even attend the ceremony….The presence of armed fighters and commanders among the guests also infused these events with a militant touch that could not be missed by the participants….These militant weddings should therefore be seen as moments of radicalisation, both for the bride and for the participants.[99]

For some Sikh women marrying militants was a matter of personal choice and for others it was a family decision. Love marriages are not approved traditionally in the Sikh community.[100] There are instances when women married militants by choice. While some of them confined themselves to household boundaries and helped their husbands from a distance such as by cooking a meal or couriering weapons, many others lived with their militant husbands in hideouts. Hardeep Kaur, who had a love marriage with a militant and lived with him for nearly six years until he was killed in an anti-militancy operation, recalled:

> I was fascinated by the romanticized image of a militant; a tall handsome man with a gun in his hand and backpack with arms and ammunition. I married Kartar Singh after we met in a wedding. He came to the wedding with his gun and his parents proudly introduced him as a fighter. I married him against the wishes of my parents who despite believing in the ideology of Khalistan did not want their daughter to lead an uncertain life. After marriage I lived with him and his group in a big house. It was a comfortable life for nearly one year. In that one year I cooked meals for the group and occasionally went out for marketing. I was trained to handle a gun and always had a pistol hidden in my clothes. The husband's group sometimes went out for a day or so for work such as abduction or killing. I also once went with them for killing an informer. After one year we were constantly on the move for the next five years. I gave birth to two children while regularly changing our hideouts. When my husband was killed by police in an operation I moved to the house of my in-laws. We all now live here [in Amritsar], far away from my husband's native village. My in-laws do not want anyone here to know that I was involved in militant activities. It can adversely impact the reputation of our family since the euphoria of Khalistan has faded. I never talk about my past with anyone but cherish the memories of those glorious times.[101]

Gayer reveals that the women who joined militancy following arranged marriages had two major reasons for doing so. Some of them belonged to families with a 'tradition of resistance'; hence they were deliberately married to militants to demonstrate solidarity with the secessionist movement. In other cases the prospective groom joined militancy after his marriage was fixed. In this case despite knowing that the would-be groom had become a militant and even though the family was not a 'sympathizer' of the movement, the marriage was solemnized to protect family honour. There were, however, exceptional cases when single women enlisted. Gayer cites the example of two of the interviewees, out of 10, who joined the ranks of militancy when they were single. One of them was escorted by her mother all the time. The other woman who enlisted at the age of 17 later married a fellow fighter who 'provided her with protection against predatory sexual behaviours from other militants'.[102]

There are instances when women were coerced into violence not only by indirect methods but also by direct ones such as abduction. The best-known example of a large-scale abduction is that of 'comfort women' during the Second World War. Increasingly, women have been recruited into fighting forces by abductions, as evident in Sierra Leone, Liberia and Colombia where they are forced to play a dual role – sex slaves and combatants.[103] South Asia is no exception to this trend. In Manipur militant groups reportedly kidnap minor boys and girls to groom them as cadres.[104] A male Manipuri militant who had laid down arms in 2006 said during an interview that it is 'not only easy but advantageous' to recruit children. 'Children are like a clean board. Being at an impressionable age they can be easily motivated. Young boys and girls are indoctrinated easily and become more committed to the cause. Also they are too young to be scared of being killed,' he reasoned.[105] A letter recovered from a slain LTTE woman revealed the helplessness of many women who were forced to become violent. The letter addressed to her mother read, 'Amma (Mother), what can I do? When all those at home in the area were taken away, I too had to go with them (LTTE).'[106] A respondent echoed this saying, 'there was no other option but to join LTTE. There was so much fear.'[107] In Nepal, Maoists had drafted a recruitment policy that besides allowing voluntary enlistment had the provision for forcible enlistment. A policy of 'one house, one person' was imposed in many areas. People were threatened with dire consequences if they refused to adhere to this diktat. A study quoted a female combatant saying, 'when Maoists announced one house one person to join party (Maoist movement), I had to join party at the age of fifteen to save my old parents from physical punishment and seizure of the small piece of land that they had.'[108] Interestingly, women were part of these recruitment groups entrusted with the task of forced enrolment.[109] In some Maoist dominated areas in India parents have to 'donate' their one child, be it a girl or a boy, to the movement. 'This is being practiced for quite some time. If we have to save ourselves and our other children then there is no escape from this practice,' said Baruna Prasad who 'donated' her daughter 12 years ago and has not met her since then. He said,

> Nobody knows about her whereabouts though many other children of our village visit their families occasionally. May be she got killed by security personnel or may be by Maoists. She was reluctant to join the movement but we had to force her to go. May be, she tried to escape and got killed.[110]

When there is a possibility that the person joining a violent movement may get killed, people prefer to send daughters if they have a choice. Patriarchy thus plays a decisive role in this preferential treatment of girls, as this is a question of death rather than life. Pradhan Jena, a respondent from Odisha, had twins, one son and one daughter, and hence a choice to 'donate' either of the two. He preferred to send his daughter to kill or get killed. Like elsewhere, Maoists in India do not rely merely on this enlistment tactic as they, many times, force young boys and girls to join their ranks and these young apprentices later follow the same tactic of coercion to convert innocent children into dreaded Maoists. Manjhi, who was forced to join the movement at gun point, recalled,

> Seven boys and girls, including myself, were selected by comrades from my village. We were not asked about our preference. We were ordered to pack a small bag of essentials. Initially I enjoyed this life of freedom. We dressed like boys and had guns to scare or even kill.[111]

Manjhi later deserted the group. She now lives far away from her native place where no one is aware of her past. She did not disclose the reason why she left the life she 'enjoyed' initially.

Several generalizations can be drawn from this analysis of the how and why of women's involvement in violent movements. Nationalist sentiments or identifying with the ideology of the movement generates a sacrificial element, motivating women to sacrifice in person (as suicide bombers or fighters) or in relations (by sending husbands and sons to fight). Revenge for sufferings such as the killing of a kin or rape is another crucial factor that pushes women to the brink of violence. The relationship factor, which underlies the significance of a woman's associations in the family and beyond, plays an important role in kindling in women a 'natural' urge to join violence. Prospects of financial gains, socio-economic (caste and class based) deprivation and patriarchal set-up further contribute to this trend.

Endnotes

1. See, for instance, Linda Grant De Pauw, *Battle Cries and Lullabies: Women in War from Prehistory to the Present*, (Norman, OK: University of Oklahoma, 1998); David E. Jones, *Women Warriors: A History*, (Washington DC: Brassey's, 1997); Jessica Amanda Salmonson, *The Encyclopedia of Amazons: Women Warriors from Antiquity to the Modern Era*, (New York: Paragon House, 1991); Mary-Ann Tetreault, ed., *Women and Revolution in Africa, Asia and the New World*, (Columbia, SC: University of South Carolina Press, 1994); and Elisabetta Addis, Valeria E. Russo, and Lorenza Sebesta, eds, *Women Soldiers: Images and Reality*, (New York: St. Martin's Press, 1994).

2. Laura Sjoberg and Caron E. Gentry, *Mothers, Monsters, Whores: Women's Violence in Global Politics*, (London: Zed Books, 2007), 2 and Idem, eds, *Women, Gender, and Terrorism*, (Athens, GA: University of Georgia Press, 2011).

3. See, for instance, Jennifer Turpin, 'Many Faces: Women Confronting War', in *The Women and War Reader*, eds, Lois Ann Lorentzen and Jennifer Turpin, (New York: New York University Press, 1998), 3–18 and Olivia Bennett, Jo Bexely, Kitty Warnock, eds, *Arms to Fight, Arms to Protect: Women Speak out About Conflict*, (London: Panos, 1995), Annika Kronsell and Erika Svedberg, eds, *Making Gender, Making War*, (London: Routledge, 2011), Carol Cohn, *Women and Wars*, (London: Polity Press, 2013), Kathleen Kuehnast, Chantal de Jonge Oudraat, Helga Hernes, eds, *Women and War: Power and Protection in the 21st Century*, (Washington DC: United States Institute of Peace Press, 2011), and Sandra I. Cheldelin and Maneshka Eliatamby, eds, *Women Waging War and Peace, International Perspectives on Women's Roles in Conflict and Post-Conflict Reconstruction*, (New York: Continuum, 2011).
4. Christine Sylvester, 'Tensions in Feminist Security Studies', *Security Dialogue,* 41, no. 6, (2010): 609, see by the same author, *War as Experience: Contributions from International Relations and Feminist Analysis*, (London: Routledge, 2013).
5. Sjoberg and Gentry, *Mothers, Monsters, Whores*, 2.
6. Joshua Goldstein, *War and Gender: How Gender Shapes the War System and Vice Versa*, (Cambridge: Cambridge University Press, 2003), 60–64.
7. Goldstein, *War and Gender,* 61.
8. For details see, Françoise Krill, 'The Protection of Women in International Humanitarian Law', *International Review of the Red Cross*, no. 249, (1985): 337–63.
9. Frances Stewart, 'Women in Conflict and Post-conflict Situations', Paper presented at the Economic and Social Council's 2010 Thematic Discussion of 'The Role of Women in Countries in Special Situations: Africa, LDCs, LLDCs, SIDS, Post-conflict and Post-crisis Countries,' 30 June 2010. Available at http://www.un.org/en/ecosoc/julyhls/pdf10/frances_stewart.pdf (accessed on 22 June 2011).
10. Karla J. Cunningham, 'Cross-Regional Trends in Female Terrorism', *Studies in Conflict & Terrorism*, 26, no. 3,(2003): 173.
11. April Carter, 'Should Women be Soldiers or Pacifists?', in *The Woman and War Reader*, eds, Lois Ann Lorentzen and Jennifer Turpin, (New York: New York University Press, 1998), 33–41.
12. Goldstein, *War and Gender,* 127.
13. Miranda Alison, 'Women as Agents of Political Violence: Gendering Security', *Security Dialogue*, 35, no. 4, (2004): 447–63.
14. Sylvester, 'Tensions in Feminist Security Studies', 609.
15. Jessica Stern, 'When Bombers are Women', *The Washington Post*, (18 December 2003).
16. Miranda Alison, 'Cogs in the Wheel? Women in the Liberation Tigers of Tamil Eelam', *Civil Wars*, 6, no. 4, (2003): 39.
17. *The Hindu*, (10 March 2002). Malathy was the first female 'martyr'. The propagandist celebration of her death anniversary on 10 October every year as Tamil women's day motivated several Tamil women to join the LTTE.
18. For details see Adele Ann Wilby, *Women Fighters of Liberation Tigers*, (Jaffna: LTTE Publication Section, 1993).

19. Cynthia Cockburn, 'The Gendered Dynamics of Armed Conflict and Political Violence', in *Victims, Perpetrators or Actors?: Gender, Armed Conflict and Political Violence*, eds, Caroline O. N. Moser and Fiona C. Clark, (New Delhi: Kali for Women, 2001), 21.

20. 'Humanitarian Operation – Factual Analysis, July 2006 – May 2009', *Report*, Ministry of Defence, Government of Sri Lanka, (1 August 2011), 22.

21. Rohan Gunaratna, 'Suicide Terrorism: A Global Threat', *Jane's Intelligence Review*, (April 2000), 53.

22. 'Mia Bloom in Conversation with Kate Fillion', 24 January 2011. Available at http://www2.macleans.ca/2011/01/24/macleans-interview-mia-bloom/ (accessed on 16 March 2012) and Mia Bloom, *Dying to Kill: The Allure of Suicide Terror*, (New York: Columbia University Press, 2005).

23. 'Mia Bloom in Conversation with Kate Fillion'.

24. Cunningham, 'Cross-Regional Trends in Female Terrorism', 172.

25. See M. Sharma and D. Prasain, 'Gender Dimensions of the People's War. Some Reflections on the Experiences of Rural Women', in *Himalayan 'People's War' Nepal's Maoist Rebellion*, ed., Michael Hutt, (London: Hurst & Company, 2004), 152–65.

26. Quoted in Sharada Khadka, 'Female Combatants and Ex-combatants in Maoist Revolution and Their Struggle for Reintegration in Post-war Nepal', Unpublished Master's thesis, (University of Tromsø, 2012), 37.

27. 'JMCC 61st meeting signs off on verification figures', United Nations Mission in Nepal. Available at http://un.org.np/unmin-archive/?d=activities&p=activity_detail&aid=54 (accessed on 26 March 2011).

28. *The Times of India*, (23 June 2011).

29. Preetam Jain, 'The Kitchen or the Battlefield', *Indian Streams Research Journal*, 1, issue 4, May 2011. Available at http://www.isrj.net/May/2011/Political_Science_The_Kitchen_or_the_battlefield.aspx (accessed on 12 January 2012).

30. *The Samaja* (Oriya newspaper), (8 July 2012).

31. *The Samaja* (Oriya newspaper), (17 July 2012).

32. Personal Interview, 26 October 2011.

33. Harinder Baweja, 'Living by the Gun', *Seminar*, no. 398, (October 1992): 30.

34. Personal Interview, 15 June 2012.

35. Personal Interview, 20 June 2012.

36. Cunningham, 'Cross-Regional Trends in Female Terrorism', 180.

37. Cunningham, 'Cross-Regional Trends in Female Terrorism', 181.

38. Quoted in Cunningham, 'Cross-Regional Trends', 181.

39. 'Atrocities on Sikh Women in Punjab', Undated. Available at http://www.sikhlionz.com/atrocitiesonsikhwomen.htm (accessed on 14 June 2012).

40. Quoted in 'Atrocities on Sikh Women in Punjab.'

41. Laurent Gayer, '"Princesses" among the "Lions": The Activist Careers of Khalistani Female Combatants', *Sikh Formations*, 8, no. 1, (April 2012): 11.

42. Gayer, '"Princesses" among the "Lions"', 17.

43. Anuradha M. Chenoy, 'Resources or Symbols? Women and Armed Conflicts in India', in *The Impact of Armed Conflicts on Women in South Asia*, eds, Ava Darshan Shrestha and Rita Thapa, (New Delhi: Manohar, 2007), 194.

44. Cited in Chenoy, 'Resources or Symbols', 195.

45. 'Manipur Terrorist Outfits: People's Revolutionary Party of Kangleipak', Undated. Available at http://www.satp.org/satporgtp/countries/india/states/manipur/terrorist_outfits/Prepak.htm (accessed on 22 June 2012).

46. Hisila Yami, 'Women's Role in the Nepalese Movement: Making a People's Constitution', 8 March 2010. Available at http://mrzine.monthlyreview.org/2010/yami080310.html (accessed on 12 January 2012).

47. Satyapal Dang, *Genesis of Terrorism: An Analytical Study of Punjab Terrorists*, (New Delhi: Patriot Publishers, 1988), 145.

48. Testimony quoted in Dang, *Genesis of Terrorism*, 72–76.

49. Personal Interview, 16 June 2012.

50. Personal Interview, 19 June 2012.

51. *The Telegraph*, (25 May 2012).

52. Personal Interview, 9 September 2011.

53. 'Manipur Terrorist Outfits: People's Revolutionary Party of Kangleipak'.

54. For details on this conflict, see Mohammad Waseem, 'Ethnic Conflict in Pakistan: The Case of MQM', *The Pakistan Development Review*, 35, no. 4, (1996), 617–29 and Feroz Ahmed, 'The Rise of Mohajir Separatism in Pakistan', *Pakistan Progressive*, 10, no. 2/3, (1989), 8–13.

55. Anis Haroon, 'They Use Us and Others Abuse Us: Women in the MQM Conflict', *Women War and Peace in South Asia: Beyond Victimhood to Agency*, ed., Rita Manchanda, (New Delhi: Sage Publications, 2001), 185.

56. Haroon, 'They Use Us and Others Abuse Us', 189.

57. Haroon, 'They Use Us', 187.

58. Hana Shams Ahmed, 'Women in the CHT: The Violent Hills', *Forum*, 5, issue 3, (March 2011). Available at http://www.thedailystar.net/forum/2011/march/women.htm (accessed on 2 January 2012).

59. Meghna Guhathakurta, 'Women's Narratives from the Chittagong Hill Tracts', in *Women War and Peace in South Asia: Beyond Victimhood to Agency*, ed., Rita Manchanda, (New Delhi: Sage Publications, 2001), 279–80.

60. Cunningham, 'Cross-Regional Trends in Female Terrorism', 172.

61. 'Mia Bloom in Conversation with Kate Fillion'.

62. Tim McGirk, 'Moms and Martyrs', *Time*, (3 May 2007). Available at http://www.time.com/time/magazine/article/0,9171,1617542,00.html (accessed on 16 March 2012).

63. Ibid.

64. Ibid.

65. Ibid.

66. Ibid.

67. Personal Interview, 15 February 2012.

68. Personal Interview, 22 July 2011.
69. Jain, 'The Kitchen or the Battlefield'.
70. Personal Interview, 28 October 2011.
71. Personal Interview, 18 June 2012.
72. Sumantra Bose, *States, Nations, Sovereignty: Sri Lanka, India and the Tamil Eelam Movement*, (New Delhi: Sage Publications, 1994), 111.
73. Personal Interview, 17 February 2012.
74. Personal Interview, 25 June 2012.
75. Sheen Farrukh, 'Women and Ethnic Identify: Case of MQM', in *Locating the Self: Perspectives of Women and Multiple Identities*, eds, Nighat Saeed Khan, Rubina Saigol and Afiya Shahbano Zia, (Lahore: ASR Publications, 1994), 207.
76. Personal Interview, 24 July 2011.
77. Personal Interview, 22 July 2011.
78. Dhruba Kumar Shrestha, 'Consequences of the Militarized Conflict and the Cost of Violence in Nepal', *Contributions to Nepalese Studies*, 30, no. 2, (July 2003): 184.
79. Personal Interview, 27 October 2011.
80. Personal Interview, 26 October 2011.
81. Ibid.
82. María Villellas Ariño, 'Nepal: A Gender View of the Armed Conflict and the Peace Process', Peacebuilding Paper No. 4, 4 June 2008, 8. Available at http://escolapau.uab.cat/img/qcp/nepal_conflict_peace.pdf (accessed on 18 January 2012).
83. Yami, 'Women's Role in the Nepalese Movement'.
84. Quoted in Uddipan Mukherjee, 'The Women Guerrillas', *Geopolitics*, (May 2012): 72.
85. Personal Interview, 21 July 2011.
86. Personal Interview, 17 February 2012.
87. Personal Interview, 15 February 2012.
88. Personal Interview, 23 July 2011.
89. Ibid.
90. Quoted in Khadka, 'Female Combatants and Ex-combatants', 104.
91. Jain, 'The Kitchen or the Battlefield'.
92. Personal Interview, 12 December 2011.
93. Margaret Trawick, 'Interview with Sita in Reasons for Violence: A Preliminary Ethnographic Account of the LTTE', *South Asia*, 20, Special Issue, (1997): 153–80.
94. *The Times of India*, (22 February 2009).
95. Ibid.
96. Personal Interview, 26 October 2011.
97. 'Manipur Terrorist Outfits: People's Revolutionary Party of Kangleipak'.
98. Nagaland Post (online), 11 May 2009. Available at http://www.nagalandpost.com/ShowStory.aspx?npoststoryiden=UzEwMTIwNjM%3D-josDuqRc6Ek%3D (accessed on 22 June 2012).
99. Gayer, '"Princesses" among the "Lions"', 4–5.

100. In fact many women were expelled from militant groups for marrying by their own choice. Dang, *Genesis of Terrorism*, 72–76, 145.
101. Personal Interview, 28 June 2012.
102. Gayer, '"Princesses" among the "Lions"', 8.
103. Radhika Coomaraswamy, 'Girls in War: Sex Slave, Mother, Domestic Aide, Combatant', *UN Chronicle*, nos. 1&2, (2009): 50–53.
104. Kaushik Deka, 'Manipur Mothers Want Children Back', *India Today*, 28 May 2012. Available at http://indiatoday.intoday.in/story/manipur-militants-recruiting-children-as-cadre/1/189360.html (accessed on 14 June 2012).
105. Personal Interview, 14 December 2011.
106. Cited in *The Times of India*, (30 January 2008).
107. Personal Interview, 18 February 2012.
108. Quoted in Khadka, 'Female Combatants and Ex-combatants', 46.
109. For details, see Hisila Yami, *People's War and Women's Liberation in Nepal*, (Raipur: Purvaiya Prakashan, 2006).
110. Personal Interview, 28 October 2011.
111. Personal Interview, 26 October 2011.

Chapter 3

Conflict within Contested Kashmir

Kashmir was one of the 500 odd princely states of British India on which colonial control ended on 15 August 1947. As per the terms of British withdrawal and Partition of India, the rulers of all the princely states were offered the option of joining either of the emerging independent states – India and Pakistan – while factoring geography and popular sentiment. Both these considerations, however, were not easily applicable in case of the princely state of Kashmir, a Muslim majority region ruled by a Hindu king and bordering both India and Pakistan. The possession of this Muslim majority state had specific significance both for India as well as Pakistan due to divergent conceptions of nation-building.[1] India was committed to secularism and Pakistan to the creation of an Islamic state. While Kashmir's accession to India could have strengthened its secular credentials; the two nation theory,[2] implying that Hindus and Muslims cannot live together as citizens of a single country, could have been strengthened had Kashmir acceded to Pakistan.

The Contestation

The Kashmir issue acquired complexity due to the political situation within the state. Its ruler, Maharaja Hari Singh, was confronting significant opposition from his population against his autocratic rule. The discontent had been politically organized with the establishment of the All J&K Muslim Conference (MC) in 1932. This organization, initially representing Muslim interests, gradually became secularized under the leadership of Sheikh Mohammad Abdullah. Abdullah changed the name of the party in 1939 to the All J&K National Conference (NC) by replacing the word 'Muslim' with 'National'. Inspired by the Quit India Movement of 1946, the NC launched the Quit Kashmir Movement to dislodge the monarchy from power. Abdullah appealed to the people of the state to rally behind him for freedom from an 'irresponsible rule'.[3] Gradually, NC became a mass movement with the goals of freedom from autocracy and establishing popular rule. Abdullah made pronouncements such as, 'Sovereignty is not the birthright of Maharaja Hari Singh', and 'Quit Kashmir is not a question of revolt. It is a matter of right' which had wider appeal for the people.[4] While in the state, the Maharaja was facing a formidable challenge from the local people, at the external level both India and Pakistan were pressurizing him to take a decision on accession in their favour. The ruler appeared to be in no hurry to take a decision about accession of Kashmir to either of the independent states. He solicited standstill agreement with India and Pakistan in order to buy time to decide the future course of action. As per the terms of the agreement 'the existing arrangements (governing the relations between the two independent countries and princely state of Kashmir) should continue pending settlement of details.'[5] While India asked for further negotiations, Pakistan accepted the agreement and assumed control over, among other things, the supply of foodstuffs and other essential commodities to the kingdom. Pakistan used the newly gained advantage as leverage to pressure the Maharaja to accede to Pakistan by intermittently discontinuing the supply of agreed commodities to Kashmir. As a result of this, relations between Kashmir and Pakistan worsened. Hari Singh's move in releasing Sheikh Abdullah on 29 September 1947, who was in jail for leading Quit Kashmir Movement against the dynasty rule, further soured the relations. This step of the king was noted with disapproval by Pakistan due to Abdullah's proximity to the Indian leadership.[6]

The uprising in Poonch region of the princely state against the ruler and infiltration of armed groups from Pakistan added fuel to fire. The armed groups included Hazara and Afridi tribesmen, paramilitary forces such as the Muslim League National Guards and even regular Pakistani army personnel.[7] India considered Pakistan's move as one to 'grab J&K by force'[8] by sending its troops disguised as local tribesmen. Pakistan took the stand that the atrocities perpetrated by the Maharaja's forces against the Muslim population of Poonch provoked spontaneous reactions within the princely state and from kinsmen in Pakistan. Amidst competing claims, the invaders occupied Muzaffarabad in the princely state of Kashmir on 22 October 1947 and subsequently progressed towards Srinagar, the winter capital of the state.[9] This development forced Hari Singh to send his troops who proved to be incapable of impeding the onslaught. He then requested help from the neighbouring Maharaja of Patiala who sent an infantry battalion, which too could not stall the advances of the invaders. Hari Singh then appealed to Lord Mountbatten[10] for help. Along with Prime Minister Jawaharlal Nehru and Home Minister Vallabh Bhai

Patel, Mountbatten decided that sending Indian troops for help could be committed only if the princely state acceded to India. There was introduced a key caveat – the people of the state would ratify the accession as soon as law and order was restored. Complying with the stipulations, the Maharaja sent a letter to Mountbatten, which read,

> with the conditions obtaining at present in my state and the great emergency situation exists, I have no option but to ask for help from the Indian Dominion. Naturally, they cannot send the help asked by me without my state acceding to the Dominion of India. I have accordingly decided to do so.[11]

He signed the Instrument of Accession on 26 October 1947. The legality of this accession became an enduring source of contention between India and Pakistan. India claimed legal right to the whole of pre-1947 Kashmir because Hari Singh had signed the Instrument of Accession with it. It argued that Pakistan sponsored military aggression was a provocation designed to overthrow a legally binding agreement by force.[12] Pakistan on the contrary held that the accession of Kashmir to India was illegal since it violated the standstill agreement. It also labelled the accession illegitimate on the ground that the Maharaja had abandoned his throne before signing the document; hence, he had already relinquished his authority to decide the future of the state.

On 27 October 1947 India dispatched troops to Kashmir, which curbed further advancements by invaders towards Srinagar. There started a full-blown war between India and Pakistan within the princely state. As the conflict escalated, the Indian political leadership apparently realized that the war would drag on indefinitely unless Pakistani support for and involvement with the insurgents ended. To achieve this, India had to expand the scope of the conflict for which it was not prepared.[13] India's Prime Minister, Jawaharlal Nehru preferred a peaceful resolution of the crisis, for which the newly found international body the UN appeared most appropriate platform to the Indian leadership. India, which had just emerged from colonial rule, did not evince interest in a protracted war as it would not only have complicated the Kashmir issue but also led to diversion of national resources for armed preparedness. In pursuit of this approach, India filed a complaint against Pakistan in the UN on 1 January 1948. The UN Security Council (UNSC) resolution 39 created the UN Commission for India and Pakistan to investigate facts concerning the dispute. Subsequently in April 1948, UNSC passed resolution 47 noting that both states had agreed to determine the question of accession through plebiscite.[14] On 1 January 1949, the UN negotiated a ceasefire. The UN Military Observer Group for India and Pakistan was set-up to monitor the Ceasefire Line,[15] later rechristened in 1972 as the Line of Control (LoC). The ceasefire left a considerable portion of the territory of the princely state of Kashmir in the possession of Pakistan[16] and hence divided Kashmir into two parts – one with India and the other with Pakistan. Later years witnessed a further division.[17]

The embroilment of Kashmir at the UN, particularly due to the contested positions of the major players in the international body, widened the scope of the conflict. Developments in international politics, as the cold war was raging and each bloc was attempting to expand its influence, also impacted the course of the conflict. The emergence of India and Pakistan as independent states on the international scene, dominated by the two blocs led by the United States of America and the United Soviet Socialist Republic striving to consolidate their respective positions worldwide, complicated the situation in the region. Dependence on major powers for military supplies, economic assistance and diplomatic support made newly independent states vulnerable to external pressures. In later years India's non-aligned status and Pakistan's membership of regional security alliances such as the Central Treaty Organization and the South East Asia Treaty Organization impacted the politics over Kashmir and also Indo-Pak relations.[18] The simmering differences brought the two neighbouring states to the brink of war in 1950, further compounded by the raging communal violence in the Indian border states of West Bengal and Tripura and in the eastern wing of Pakistan.[19] Another war scare emerged in 1951 due to Pakistan's allegations about concentration of Indian troops along the Ceasefire Line in Kashmir.

India and Pakistan fought the second war in 1965. The Rann of Kutch issue preceded the outbreak of formal hostilities. Victoria Schofield argues that the withdrawal of the Indian army, leaving behind 40 miles of marshland in the Rann of Kutch encouraged Pakistan to assess that the Indian army was still suffering from the after effects of defeat in the India-China war of 1962.[20] Pakistan considered it an opportune time to resolve the issue of Kashmir militarily. In the first week of August 1965 under codename Operation Gibraltar the Pakistani military began infiltrating forces in Kashmir across the 470-mile-long Ceasefire Line.[21] The first major engagement between regular armed forces of the two countries took place on 14 August 1965. India's early gains prompted Pakistan to mount Operation Grand Slam on 1 September to capture Akhnoor bridge and cut off supplies to the southwest of the Indian side of Kashmir. On 5 September 1965, the Pakistani army launched a major assault and penetrated 14 miles in J&K. Indian forces counter-attacked from Punjab and crossed the international border.[22] By mid-September 1965, the war had reached a stalemate. The UNSC unanimously passed a resolution on 20 September 1965, calling for a ceasefire, which ended the impasse on 23

September 1965. Indian Prime Minister, Lal Bahadur Shastri and Pakistani President Ayub Khan met in Tashkent on 4 January 1966 to negotiate a settlement. Under the terms of the Tashkent Agreement the two sides agreed to maintain status quo and resolved to abjure from violence to settle outstanding disputes including Kashmir.

India and Pakistan engaged in the third war in December 1971. This war was not directly fought over Kashmir, but the battle eventually engulfed the region. The fight ensued following a civil war in East Pakistan (now Bangladesh) over the issue related to regional autonomy. In Pakistan, since independence, there had been a tussle between the Punjabi dominated, Urdu speaking elite of West Pakistan (currently Pakistan), and the Bengali dominated, Bengali speaking people of East Pakistan (currently Bangladesh), notwithstanding the fact that people from both the parts shared a common religion. The people of East Pakistan had a sense of deprivation and under-representation in the decision-making process as well as in the resources of undivided Pakistan. The unrest became violent in 1970 as people of East Pakistan demanded independence. Under codename Operation Searchlight, the Pakistani army on the night of 25 March 1971 began a crackdown on Dhaka, the capital of East Pakistan. Although estimates of casualties vary, it is commonly agreed that thousands of Bengali rebels including university students, intellectuals and professionals were killed within the first week of the crackdown. Hundreds of thousands of refugees fled from East Pakistan to West Bengal, Assam and Tripura, the adjacent Indian provinces. Despite repeated appeals to the international community to take cognizance of these developments, the Indian government could not garner requisite support. Several diplomatic attempts towards the return of the refugees notwithstanding, their numbers continued growing. Under such circumstances, the Indian Prime Minister, Indira Gandhi, decided in April 1971 to aid Bengali rebels fighting for the liberation of East Pakistan. By November 1971, the rebels were attacking Pak military installations from bases along the Indian border. On 3 December 1971 a full-scale war commenced between India and Pakistan. Pakistan's defeat in the war led to the creation of Bangladesh. India and Pakistan signed the Shimla Pact on 2 July 1972, which stipulated settlement of disputes between the two through dialogue and bilateral negotiations.

Since the Shimla Agreement, India has adopted a principled position against the involvement of any third party towards the resolution of the Kashmir dispute. It further argues that the UNSC resolution regarding plebiscite is no longer binding.[23] Pakistan contends that the Shimla Agreement does not restrain the parties to rake up the Kashmir issue at international forums and that the UNSC resolutions on Kashmir remain valid.[24] Though the Shimla

Agreement has not been able to resolve the Kashmir issue so far, it has provided a comprehensive framework for stabilizing relations. Notwithstanding occasional tensions, a major clash between India and Pakistan did not occur till 1999, when the Kargil war took place.

Nuclear tests by India and Pakistan in 1998 added to the debilitating scenario with concern in international quarters that the Kashmir conflict might turn into a nuclear flashpoint.[25] This development brought international pressure on the governments of both the countries to resolve contentious issues peacefully. Partly due to this pressure, and also owing to the changing realities of the post-cold war world in which the rigidity of contentious borders was questioned, India's and Pakistan's leaders appeared to realize the imperative of a peaceful South Asia. Under the initiative of then prime ministers of India and Pakistan, Atal Bihari Vajpayee and Nawaz Sharif, the historic peace bus rolled from New Delhi to Lahore on 20 February 1999 with Vajpayee and other prominent Indian personalities on board. During the meeting, India and Pakistan signed the Lahore declaration, in which both sides expressed readiness to intensify their efforts to resolve all contentious issues, including Kashmir. The development could be termed as the realization of the emerging imperative of the post-cold war world order in which the rigid conflict paradigm was moderated by a framework of mutual understanding and cooperation. Political analysts, however, could not predict that this sanguine development and related euphoria would be sabotaged by the Pakistan army within a short span of three months in the form of Kargil war, the most violent Indo-Pak military engagement since 1971. Pakistan infiltrated regular troops and militants into J&K and on 6 June 1999 the Indian Army launched Operation Vijay (meaning victory), which included air strikes in the Kargil and Drass sectors. The war ended on 14 July 1999, partly due to intense international pressure.[26] The war led to loss of hundreds of lives on both the sides, further buttressed old memories of animosity and hatred, nullified the peace capital generated by the Lahore bus and added to the protracted nature of the Kashmir conflict.[27] The dividing line in Kashmir continued to remain tense due to rigid realistic approaches of India and Pakistan. Debidatta Aurobinda Mahapatra notes:

> In Kashmir, the realistic paradigm of inter-state relations in terms of sacrosanct borders, as markers of sovereignty and independence of India and Pakistan, remained largely intact even after more than six decades of artificial divisions. Hence, the haphazardly drawn border in Kashmir is a unique example in the border discourse. The all-pervasive security apparatus in terms of observation towers, strict border surveillance, landmines and electrified fencing is testament to the impregnable nature of this border.[28]

Both the countries view the conflict from a zero-sum perspective, which in turn has guided their policymaking. The dominance of offensive realism[29] has led to suppression of indigenous peace potential and other flexible approaches to conflict transformation.

The protracted engagement over Kashmir witnessed an intricate dimension with the rise of armed militancy in the Indian state of J&K. The conflict within J&K needs to be factored in the light of this discussion due to two reasons: first the role of Pakistan in sustaining militancy and relatedly India's claim that the armed unrest in J&K was 'proxy war of Pakistan'. The emerging scenario adversely affected Indo-Pak relations. India accused Pakistan of interference in its internal affairs and repeatedly called Pakistan to discontinue its support to various militant groups operating from Kashmir under its control. Pakistan, in turn, persistently accused India of denying Kashmiris their right to self-determination and of systematic human rights violations.[30] These acute differences led to an apprehension of another war in 1986–87 when India conducted a military exercise close to the Indo-Pak border. In 1990, the two countries again reached the brink of another war. This was the time when militancy, supported by Pakistan, was countered by India by deploying forces along the dividing line in Kashmir. Though the crisis was eventually defused, the developments added to the atmosphere of hostility and suspicion. Subsequently, armed militancy in J&K brought the two countries to the brink of a war twice. Attacks on the Indian Parliament and J&K's Legislative Assembly in 2001 and 2002 respectively led to two consecutive war scares with India alleging the role of Pakistan sponsored militants in these attacks.[31]

Pakistan's role in militant violence in J&K cannot be brushed aside as Indian rhetoric. Stephen P. Cohen notes, 'Pakistan's role was not the decisive factor in starting the uprising, although a critical one in sustaining it.'[32] Mahapatra and I, in an earlier study, argue that,

> The Indian policies in J&K to address popular concerns such as economic development, alienation of local people from mainstream politics and human rights abuses may be questioned on different grounds, nonetheless, without the terrorist infrastructure across LOC supported by Pakistan, the popular discontent in J&K, especially the Kashmir valley, could not have assumed such a violent proportion.[33]

Some influential sections in the Pakistani establishment support the network of violence in J&K as 'an obligation towards their co-religionists'[34] and towards concluding the 'unfinished agenda of partition'. Pakistan has not only supported militant groups morally, as claimed by it, but also monetarily, logistically and in all other ways that can foster violence in J&K. Major militant groups that are active in J&K operate from Pakistan and from Kashmir under its control. An International Crisis Group report, 'Kashmir: Confrontation and Miscalculation' (2002) notes:

> Notwithstanding its denials, however, the...[Pakistan] government has continued its proxy war in Kashmir as part of a broader long-term strategy to make the costs of controlling the territory untenable for India. Intending to bleed its larger neighbour – economically, politically, and militarily – the...government backs Pakistan-based, violent Islamist extremists in hopes of securing Kashmir's integration into Pakistan or at least its independence from India.[35]

In an interview to a news channel in September 2009, former Pakistani ruler, Pervez Musharraf admitted that Pakistan under his rule had diverted the US military aid to strengthen defences against India.[36] Pakistan cannot be termed the sole source of internal tumult in J&K though. Conflict in Kashmir cannot be explained without factoring India's ostrich like attitude to the core concerns of the state, the accumulated alienation of the people and a slew of half-hearted measures from New Delhi to address popular grievances. The subsequent section focuses on the factors that contributed to the estrangement between J&K and India, and the consequent challenge to the Indian state and its legitimacy to rule the state.

Catalysts for Internal Conflict

The people of Kashmir valley who had initially supported the accession of the state to India and had in fact resisted Pakistan's attempt to take control of their state by force[37] in due course of time stood up for secession from India and demanded freedom.[38] Kashmiris who were largely apathetic towards the India-Pakistan conflict became dynamic players in this internal dimension of the conflict. A publication of the Carnegie Endowment for International Peace (1995) summarized this development 'before 1989, India and Pakistan fought over Kashmir. Since late 1989, it is Kashmiris who have done [most] fighting.'[39] The onset of militancy marked the transition of the Kashmir conflict 'from a stubborn dispute over real estate between two adversarial neighbours to a much more complex and multidimensional problem.'[40] A variety of factors, at times overlapping, led to the rise of the violent separatist movement within J&K. The reasons for this ranged from dilution of the special powers accorded to the state to lack of democracy.

Constitutional privileges and safeguards guaranteed to the state under the Indian Constitution were gradually eroded by constitutional amendments or executive orders from New Delhi. Following accession, the state was granted special status under Article 370 of the Constitution, under which partial applicability of the Constitution of India and the governance of the state by its own constitution defined J&K's relations with India. The arrangement provided for a restrictive jurisdiction of the Indian legislature within the scope of the Instrument of Accession. In accordance with the Instrument, powers of the Indian Parliament in J&K were limited to defence, external affairs and communications. Under the provisions of Article 370, the Government of India was entitled to legislate on these three subjects only in consultation with J&K and on the other subjects in the Union List[41] only with the final concurrence of the J&K Assembly. Gradual erosion took place in this autonomous character of the state despite the Indian leadership's assurance to uphold its special status. Emphasis was placed on the constitutional integration of the state instead of its autonomy and special status. I now give some instances of how the Indian government gradually geared its policy mechanism to erode the state's autonomous status, thus not only diluting the constitutional promise to the state but also weakening its position as a genuine protector of the rights of the Kashmiri people. A constitutional order of May 1954 superseded the previous proclamation of 1950 related to the state's statutory autonomy and extended New Delhi's powers to the state with only a few exceptions and modifications. It accorded the central government at New Delhi the power to legislate in a majority of the subjects in the Union List regarding the state. The state's financial relations with the central government were brought on the same footing as those of other states of the Indian union. The Supreme Court of India was granted full jurisdiction over the state. In December 1964, another constitutional order from New Delhi brought the state under the purview of emergency Articles 356 and 357 of the Indian Constitution.[42] The control of the Indian union was further strengthened when in March 1965 the state Assembly passed a constitutional amendment. This amendment made the provision for a governor in the state to be appointed by the central government and substituted the title of *sadar-i-riyasat* (prime minister) with chief minister, the practice followed in other units of the Indian federation. The order had the provision for direct elections for representatives of J&K to the lower house of the Indian Parliament called Lok Sabha, instead of the earlier practice of nomination. All these developments aided the process of discontent in J&K, particularly in the Kashmir valley. The people of Kashmir were disgruntled with New Delhi's integrative tactics. They perceived these steps as an assault on their identity and self-rule.[43] One respondent said:

> We people of Kashmir are very conscious of our distinct identity. At least initially, India respected our sentiments by according special status to our state. Gradually through direct and subtle ways an attempt was made to do

away with this special status and bring J&K at par with other states of India. In theory India continued with our special status but in practice it denied all the privileges under the Constitution. What does it signify? First you give the privileges and then take away them when you wish to do so, implying you are the master and we are slaves. This was not acceptable to us.[44]

People were not provided a democratic outlet to vent their frustrations. While Kashmir was a source of contention between India and Pakistan even after its formal accession to India, New Delhi crafted policies to suit the exigencies of the situation instead of addressing the core differences between the two countries or ensuring the local people a fair share in the democratic process. Lack of a long-term vision in handling the affairs of J&K gradually dented India's democratic and pluralistic credentials in Kashmir and fuelled popular discontent. New Delhi was neither persistent nor firm in its policies towards the state. The Indian leadership was more concerned about the state's position within the union rather than about the sensitivities, wishes and even rights of its people.[45] Hasty attempts to integrate Kashmir to the Indian federation and bringing it at par with other provinces of India proved costly as later developments revealed. While discontent was mounting due to dilution of special powers, the denial of democratic rights to people to elect the state government added to popular dissatisfaction and compelled the people to search for other means to express their frustrations. The poor record of democracy in J&K was characterized by the constant manipulation of elections, suppression of voices of opposition and dissent as also stringent laws restraining civil liberties.[46] In the elections conducted in the state, New Delhi followed a policy of ensuring victory of only those candidates who abided by its diktats. The electoral history of the state has been marked by manipulation and malpractices. New Delhi aided these malpractices and also planned them to retain its territorial integrity, even at the cost of alienating the people of the state.

Manipulation of electoral machinery to win elections had started in 1951, the year when elections to the state constituent assembly were held. The NC candidates won all the available 75 seats unopposed. In Kashmir valley and the Ladakh region of J&K, 43 NC candidates won unopposed and non-NC candidates who had filed for the other two seats withdrew. In the Jammu region, Praja Parishad Party candidates decided to contest 28 out of the 30 seats but 13 of its candidates were disqualified on the pretext of irregularities. Parishad considered this move as undemocratic and in protest, withdrew the candidature of its other 15 contenders. Non-NC candidates who had filed nominations in the remaining two seats dropped out. Complaints of opposition groups against rigging were dismissed by New Delhi. Many analysts argue that the results of the 1951 elections were accepted only because of widespread support for Sheikh Abdullah.[47] This manipulated election set the trend for the state electoral process with three major implications: first, it undermined the democratic right of the people to choose their representatives. Second, it led to neutralization of opposition to NC. Third, following the dictum 'first impression lasts long', all the elections until 1996, except those in 1977, were marred by allegations of being neither free nor fair. 'Only the degree and technique of manipulation varied from election to election'.[48] In subsequent elections the NC could not win all the seats in the state as it faced competition from other political parties in the Jammu region. This provided, at least on a small scale, representation to the people of Jammu region but representation of Kashmir valley was still monopolized by NC.

Elected governments in J&K remained in power as far as they enjoyed confidence of New Delhi. Balraj Puri observes:

> There has been a persistent policy of denying Kashmir a right to democracy: one-party rule has been imposed on the State through manipulation of elections, opposition parties have been prevented from growing and elementary civil liberties and human rights have been refused to the people. This refusal to integrate Kashmir within the framework of Indian democracy has proved to be the single greatest block to the process of Kashmir's emotional and political integration with the rest of India. The basic premises of this policy are that the Kashmiris are unfit for democracy, or do not deserve it and that democracy and national interest are incompatible. These premises are not only an insult to the people of Kashmir but to all democratic sensibility.[49]

New Delhi continued to intervene in local politics of Kashmir even after 1951 as it dismissed elected leaders on flimsy grounds and groomed candidates of its choice. Sheikh Abdullah was New Delhi's choice to lead the state in 1951 but before long he lost favour as he demanded greater autonomy for the state and occasionally referred to Kashmir's right to self-determination. This elected leader was dismissed on 9 August 1953 and was placed under indefinite detention. He was again arrested and detained for 30 months on suspicion of supporting a separatist agitation after release in 1964. The dismissal and the arrest of Abdullah, a popular leader, impacted the psyche of the people and conveyed to them that New Delhi could intervene in J&K politics any time and dismiss as well as impose a government on them. The undemocratic move proved to be a turning point in undermining the faith of the people of Kashmir valley in the Indian government. Yusuf Malik asserted:

> Abdullah was soliciting more autonomy for our state. For this not only was he dismissed but also imprisoned. India should not have forgotten that Abdullah had played a crucial role in the accession of the state to India. His arrest

conveyed a message that our elected leaders were controlled by an external power that could intervene in our political affairs any time. New Delhi's interference in J&K politics continued, as a result of which we lost faith in the Indian democracy.[50]

Bakshi Ghulam Muhammad, who advocated complete integration of the state with India, was made the Prime Minister of J&K following Abdullah's ouster. The process of sidelining detractors and installing puppet governments did not stop there. In October 1963, Muhammad was replaced by Khwaja Shamshuddin.

In 1975, following prolonged negotiations and signing of an accord with the Indian government, Abdullah was restored to power.[51] The 1975 Indira-Sheikh accord, signed by Indian Prime Minister Indira Gandhi and Sheikh Abdullah, authorized the Indian Parliament to formulate laws to prevent 'activities directed towards disclaiming, questioning or disrupting the sovereignty and territorial integrity of India or bringing about secession of a part of the territory of India from the Union or causing insult to the Indian national flag, the Indian national anthem and the constitution.'[52] Sheikh Abdullah proclaimed that, 'the accession of Jammu and Kashmir to India is not a matter at issue. It has been my firm belief that the future of Jammu and Kashmir lies with India because of the common ideals that we share.'[53] After death of Sheikh Abdullah in 1983, his son Farooq Abdullah became the Chief Minister. Within a year, in July 1984, Farooq government was dismissed. This move led to increased discontentment among the people. For months, the Kashmir valley remained tense. Mass demonstrations, civil curfews and occasional violence marred public life. Notably, in many protest movements anti-India slogans were raised. Violent clashes took place between Indian security forces and demonstrators leading to several casualties. According to Puri,

'[Sheikh] Abdullah's dismissal signalled a message that even if the Kashmiri people did not wish to remain within India, they would not be allowed to secede. Whereas the dismissal of Farooq conveyed that even if the people wished to remain within India, they would not be free to choose their own government.'[54]

Sabeena Begum echoed this argument:

It was the turning point. We were not satisfied with the rule of NC but at least they were our own people. We could not time and again reconcile with the fact that few people sitting in New Delhi decide who will be at the helm of affairs in J&K. We thought that with the passage of time Indian obsession with Kashmir will lessen and people here will be able to live peacefully in a democratic state. But we were wrong. We felt betrayed when Farooq was dismissed. We protested but there was no one to listen to our grievances. Rather New Delhi used force to suppress non-violent protests.[55]

To make things worse, in 1986 NC formed an alliance with the Congress, which had been in power in New Delhi since independence, to win the forthcoming elections. This alliance not only revived memories of the interventionist policy of the central government but also led to erosion of the credibility of the NC to a large extent. People's loss of faith in the NC created a political vacuum in the Kashmir valley to be filled by the extremist political parties that had remained at the fringes of state politics till that time. In 1986 religion based parties, including the Jamaat-i-Islami, the Ummat-i-Islami and the Anjumane-i-Ittehad-ul-Musalmeen, formed a coalition called the Muslim United Front (MUF), which challenged the secular politics of NC, particularly in the Muslim majority Kashmir valley. It needs to be emphasized that Kashmir cherished a rich history of secularism in which people across religious divides, particularly Islam and Hinduism, shared an integrated identity called Kashmiriyat.[56] This integrated culture witnessed rapid decay in the late 1980s and early 1990s when a large section of native Hindus of Kashmir, called Kashmiri pandits, were forced to flee from the valley.[57] Assembly elections of 1987 and their outcome proved to be the final catalyst for the eventual radicalization of the socio-political set-up in the state. The NC-Congress alliance swept the polls but the outcome was contested due to excessive rigging. Instance may be cited of Amirakadal constituency in Srinagar where MUF's Yusuf Shah was initially declared the winner by presiding electoral officers. Within hours, he was declared defeated and NC candidate Ghulam Mohammed Shah, was confirmed the winner. Shah and his polling agent were thereafter imprisoned for several months. This process of rigging was repeated in several constituencies.[58] Life in the Kashmir valley in the post-electoral period was paralysed by mass protests. All allegations of electoral malpractices were rejected by New Delhi, reinforcing the feeling that the people of Kashmir would never get a fair deal through democratic means. Consequently, there developed a general sense of disillusionment not merely with the electoral politics but with the entire framework of the democratic structure imposed on J&K by New Delhi. The complete state of alienation set the stage for armed militancy in the late 1980s, headed by some MUF leaders.[59] Abdul Ghani Lone, the leader of the All Party Hurriyat Conference (APHC), an amalgamation of separatist groups in J&K, told veteran journalist, Kuldip Nayar in 1990, 'you did not allow them to rule themselves. You did not allow them even to win some seats in the assembly elections. They thought that going across the border and getting the arms was the only way out.'[60]

The Crescendo

The late 1980s were a turning point as popular frustration reached a crescendo and Kashmir was exposed to a storm of revolt not by any outside force but by its people. The onset of militancy was marked by a mass upsurge called *tahrik* (movement),[61] closely followed by an armed struggle led by the Jammu and Kashmir Liberation Front (JKLF). Armed militants challenged Indian claim on Kashmir by resorting to violence with complete support from the disenchanted people who not only sympathized with them but also contributed to their activities in multiple ways. Separatist sentiments had the advantage of having complete synchronization between armed militancy and popular response and of monopolizing the political space by discrediting mainstream political parties including NC. By early 1990s, the political and electoral process had totally collapsed in the Kashmir valley. The state administration appeared paralysed to control the situation and even essential services including postal and banking remained completely paralysed for a long time.

Kashmir valley witnessed a series of civil curfews, strikes and numerous demonstrations that turned violent many times. During numerous curfews imposed by the state, the people remained defiant. With people becoming increasingly rebellious there was virtual collapse of the state authority. Kashmiris came out in the streets and joined huge processions, shouting pro-independence slogans. 'Nearly every day a procession of lawyers, women, teachers, doctors marched through the streets of Srinagar,' notes Victoria Schofield.[62] Anti-India sentiments were so ensconced in the popular mind that all detested events were considered to be constructions at India's behest. Protests on local or religious issues such as a hike in power tariff and the demand for a ban on Salman Rushdie's book, *Satanic Verses*, eventually turned into anti-India protests. A civil curfew, with a complete shutdown, was observed on India's Independence Day on 15 August 1988. The Indian flag was burned and black flags hoisted. In contrast, Pakistan's Independence Day was celebrated with fanfare on 14 August 1988. A public condolence meeting was organized on the death of Pakistan President Zia-ul-Haq on 17 August. The day of accession, 26 October, was mourned as the day of occupation.[63] India's reaction was kneejerk as it deployed thousands of security personnel in the valley to suppress the indigenous movement by force; more than a decade of protracted and deadly violence ensued that led to the killing of thousands of civilians, armed militants and Indian security personnel.

The mass-based armed militancy reached its zenith in the mid-1990s, after which it witnessed a perceptible recession. This decline could mainly be attributed to four factors. First, unlike earlier, this later phase witnessed Pakistan's active involvement in armed militancy. The controversy regarding the timing of Pakistan's involvement in the movement notwithstanding, it is evident that though the separatist movement had gained roots internally, Pakistan's systemic support to militant groups expanded and prolonged the scope, duration and intensity of the militancy.[64] The unrest by the Kashmiris was offered a violent outlet by militants trained in Pakistan. India's neighbouring country ensured steady supply of arms and cash to the militants to continue operations against Indian security forces. By the mid-1990s Pakistan had explicitly started instigating violence in J&K. The second factor was the rise of a sharp internal rivalry among local militant organizations, JKLF and Hizb-ul-Mujahideen (HM), leading to the weakening of the indigenous movement. The two organizations had opposite goals. While JKLF aimed at the independence of Kashmir, HM was in favour of accession of the state to Pakistan.[65] JKLF was shunned by Pakistan in favour of HM headed by Syed Salahuddin, who is currently based in Pakistan controlled Kashmir and directs anti-India militant operations from there. This group was provided full support by Pakistan in arms, training, logistics as well as funding. The ascendancy of this Pakistan backed organization eventually led to the decline of JKLF. JKLF laid down arms in 1994, leading to a substantial erosion of the local element in the movement. The third factor was the arrival of foreign militants from countries such as Pakistan, Afghanistan, Sudan, Lebanon, Turkey and Saudi Arabia.[66] Ali Mohammad (a teenager in the 1990s) recalled,

> Tall people with long beards, some fair and others dark, arrived by crossing the LoC. We were told that these people from as far as Arab and Africa had shouldered the noble mission to help us in our fight against Indian oppression. They commanded respect and obedience from us. They addressed congregations, though discreetly, and promised to help us in remaking our Kashmir a paradise on earth and in building a state and society without any corruption and criminalization.[67]

These militants operated mainly through three organizations – Harkat-ul-Mujahideen (HUM), Lashkar-e-Toiba (LeT), and Jaish-e-Mohammad (JeM), which have bases in Pakistan or Pakistan-controlled Kashmir.[68] According to an ICG report,

> Pakistan's military has always kept a fairly tight grip on its militant "clients" operating in Kashmir, going so far as to create, merge and eliminate militant

organisations to better suit its purposes. Indeed, to ensure unity of command and control over the militants, the military created an umbrella group, the fourteen-member United Jihad Council.[69]

Foreign militants landed in J&K to aid local rebels but in due course they took over the control of the movement, and put forward their extremist agendas ahead of the goal of independence for Kashmir. With a self-professed goal of establishing an Islamic state, these foreign militants did not agree with the indigenous ideology of the ultimate goal of armed militancy being the independence of Kashmir. For them, Kashmir was only a stepping stone towards establishing an Islamic state for all Muslims and not only for Kashmiris. To establish a Nizam-e-Mustafa (Islamic Caliphate) these foreign militants attempted to correct the 'distortion' in the culture and society of Kashmiri Muslims due to the impact of Hinduism. These militants, being alien to the socio-cultural ethos of Kashmiri society, completely discarded Kashmiriyat on the plea that Islam does not recognize territorial nationalism or co-existence with non-Muslims. With the arrival of these foreign militants called *mehmaan mujahideen* (guest fighters) or jihadis (holy warriors) the Kashmir valley not only lost its symbiotic culture of Kashmiriyat but also witnessed attempts at imposing an extremist version of Islam, thereby negatively impacting the movement that had the objective of freedom of Kashmir from India. They discarded indigenous secular culture of Kashmir and propagated religious extremism. These militants in due course of time became the prime force in the state, seizing the initiative from the local people and adding a fundamentalist flavour to the conflict. The fourth factor impacting militancy was the entry of anti-social elements. The admission of these elements in the ranks changed the nature of militancy as they took up arms not for Kashmir's independence but for personal gains and hence did not share a common ideological outlook with local militant groups. The new phase of militancy lost legitimacy among common people who could no longer identify with either the foreign elements[70] or the new breed of local militants. Most of the local militants who shared the common goal of Kashmir's independence gave up arms and various local militant organizations came together to form a political group, the APHC in March 1993. The separatist politics of APHC remains quite limited, as it could not attain a representative character in terms of accommodating voices from all over the state of J&K. Its support base is largely confined to the Kashmir valley and even there it has failed to gain popular support. The assemblage has not succeeded in putting forward a unified solution to the Kashmir problem.

Recent years have witnessed shrinking space for violence though this development does not imply that sentiments of alienation and separatism among the people of Kashmir have withered away. Any stagnation and relative calm in the region cannot be construed as the dawn of peace. Separatism remains a dominant force. People have renounced violence but not the cause. There have been sporadic incidents of mass protests, a major one in 2010 when violence erupted following the killing of a Kashmiri, Tufail Ahmed Mattoo, by Indian security personnel. Within a span of about three months, the Kashmir valley witnessed deaths of nearly 90 people who had joined street protests openly defying curfews. A protest calendar was published, detailing the date and time of the protests to enable mass participation. These protests were different from the protests of the early days of militancy on two major accounts.[71] The protesters followed the Palestine *intifada* model wherein they were involved in extensive use of stone pelting against security forces to express their discontent. In the past, the protesters did not resort to stone pelting in such a massive and well organized manner. Besides, in recent protests the youth participated actively. My informal interactions with students in the valley revealed that many of the participants were supplied bags full of stones and were paid in the range of ₹ 100 to 200 (USD 2 to 4) on a day of protest.[72] Besides monetary gains, for some young Kashmiris, participating in the protests was 'a kind of fun activity'.[73] A respondent said, 'We threw stones as if practicing bowling for a game of cricket.'[74] Even if the Indian establishment's claim that the 2010 violence was sponsored by Pakistan is accepted, what cannot be overlooked is that all those involved in stone pelting were primarily local youth who did not come out on the streets for only fun and money but also to give vent to a simmering discontent. The mass protests of 2010 serve an indication that alienation continues to be a strong force in the Kashmir valley.

Endnotes

1. Sumit Ganguly, *The Crisis in Kashmir: Portents of War, Hopes of Peace*, (New Delhi: Foundation Books, 1997), 8.
2. The two nation theory was elaborated upon by the founder of Pakistan, Mohammad Ali Jinnah. According to him, Hinduism and Islam

   are not religions in the strict sense of the word, but are, in fact, different and distinct social orders, and it is a dream that the Hindus and Muslims can ever evolve a common nationality, and this misconception of one Indian nation has troubles and will lead India to destruction if we fail to revise our notions in time. The Hindus and Muslims belong to two different religious philosophies, social customs, and literatures. They neither intermarry nor interdine together and, indeed, they belong to two different civilizations which are based mainly on conflicting ideas and conceptions. Their aspect on life and of life are different. It is quite clear that Hindus and Mussalmans (Muslims) derive their inspiration from different sources of history. They have different epics, different heroes, and different episodes. Very often the hero of one is a foe of the other and, likewise, their victories and defeats overlap. To yoke together two such nations under a single state, one as a numerical minority and the other as a majority, must lead to growing discontent and final destruction of any fabric that may be so built for the government of such a state.

Quoted in Ainslie T. Embree and Stephen N. Hay, *Sources of Indian Tradition: Modern India and Pakistan, Volume 2,* (New York: Columbia University Press, 1988), 230.

3. Alastair Lamb, *Crisis in Kashmir: 1947 to 1966,* (London: Routledge and Kegan Paul, 1966), 28.
4. Quoted in M. J. Akbar, *India: The Siege Within: Challenges to a Nation's Unity,* (Harmondsworth: Penguin, 1985), 227–28.
5. See 'Standstill Agreement with India and Pakistan', in *The Story of Kashmir: Yesterday and Today,* Volume 3, ed., Verinder Grover, (New Delhi: Deep and Deep Publications, 1995), 106.
6. On release, Sheikh sent G. M. Sadiq to Pakistan to convey the sentiments of the people of Kashmir who were unwilling to be coerced in any way. Afsir Karim, *Counter Terrorism: The Pakistan Factor,* (New Delhi: Lancer International, 1991), 139.
7. M. Akbar Khan, *Raiders in Kashmir,* (Islamabad: National Book Foundation, 1975). In his book the Pakistani army officer, M. Akbar Khan, who played a crucial role in military operations during the first Indo-Pak war, gives details of how Pakistani soldiers joined the tribal invaders in Kashmir.
8. Jagmohan, *My Frozen Turbulence in Kashmir,* (New Delhi: Allied Publishers, 2000), 85.
9. George Cunningham noted in his diary on 20 October 1947,

   I am afraid the Kashmir situation is going to be a serious crisis. Heard this morning that 900 Mahsuds had left Tank in lorries for the Kashmir front…about 200 Mohmands are also reported to have gone. They were soon to be joined by Wazirs, Daurs, Bhittanis, Khattaks, Turis and some Afridis for Tirah as well as Swatis and men of Dir. At dawn on 22 October 1947, they crossed the Jhelum river into Kashmir.

   Quoted in Victoria Schofield, *Kashmir in the Crossfire: India, Pakistan and the Unending War,* (New Delhi: Viva Books Pvt. Ltd., 2004), 50.
10. Lord Mountbatten was the last Governor General of British India as well the first Governor General of independent India. This position was abolished within three years of independence of India on 26 January 1950, when India was declared a democratic republic.
11. Cited in Verinder Grover, ed., *The Story of Kashmir: Yesterday and Today,* (New Delhi: Deep and Deep Publications, 1995), 105.

12. Schofield, *Kashmir in the Crossfire*, 70–72.

13. Raju G. C. Thomas, *Indian Defense Policy*, (Princeton: Princeton University Press, 1986).

14. Subsequently, the plebiscite question emerged as a bone of contention between India and Pakistan with Pakistan arguing that India did not abide by its commitment to refer the matter of accession to the people of Kashmir. The Indian rejoinder to this argument was that Pakistan had not abided by the preliminary conditions for the plebiscite including, among others, withdrawal of its forces from the Kashmir under its control.

15. The ceasefire line was delineated on maps during the Karachi Agreement of 27 July 1949, formally known as the Agreement between Military Representatives of India and Pakistan Regarding the Establishment of a Ceasefire Line in the State of Jammu and Kashmir.

16. For details on Pakistan controlled Kashmir see, Debidatta Aurobinda Mahapatra and Seema Shekhawat, *Kashmir Across LOC*, (New Delhi: Gyan Publishing House, 2008).

17. The total area of the Kashmir region is 2,22,236 sq km, including 1,01,387 sq km with India and 78,114 sq km under the control of Pakistan. Another part of Kashmir is with China that it occupied following Indo-China war of 1962. China control 42,735 sq km of territory of Kashmir and out of this, 5,130 sq km was gifted to it by Pakistan. Available at http://www.jammu kashmir.com/basicfacts/tour/regions.html (accessed on 25 March 2012).

18. Pakistan's decision to cede some territory from its part of Kashmir to China in March 1963, further exacerbated Indian fears of the emergence of another alliance against India. C. Dasgupta, *War and Diplomacy in Kashmir 1947–48*, (New Delhi: Sage Publications, 2002), 9.

19. These riots forced hundreds of Hindus to flee from Pakistan and about the same number of Muslim refugees from Bengal and Tripura in East Bengal took refuge in Pakistan. There were apprehensions of full-scale war since the flight of refugees stirred communal passions. Declarations issued by Indian Prime Minister Jawaharlal Nehru and Pakistani Prime Minister Liaqat Ali Khan led to easing of tensions.

20. Schofield, *Kashmir in the Crossfire*, 107.

21. Sumit Ganguly, 'Avoiding War in Kashmir', *Foreign Affairs*, 69, no. 5, (1990–1991): 57–63.

22. Gulab Mishra Prakhar, *Indo-Pakistan Relations: From Tashkent to Shimla*, (New Delhi: Ashish Publications, 1987), 117.

23. The announcement of the UN Secretary General Kofi Annan, during his visit to India in March 2001, that the resolution on plebiscite might not be applicable in the changed circumstances reinforced the Indian stand. For details of the Kofi Annan visit to India in March 2001 see, http://www.un.org/News/Press/docs/2001/sgt2270R.doc.htm (accessed on 2 January 2012).

24. Interestingly, in a significant statement, while in office former Pakistani ruler Pervez Musharraf had announced that his country was prepared to set aside the

demand for the settlement of the Kashmir issue through UN resolutions. Later Pakistan backtracked and it was claimed that Musharraf was quoted out of context.

25. 'Perched between three nuclear powers India, Pakistan and China the Kashmir is really a difficult issue to resolve', argues Mahapatra. Debidatta Aurobinda Mahapatra, *World Order, Multipolarism and Terrorism: The Indian Approach*, (New Delhi: New Century Publications, 2011), 168.

26. US President Bill Clinton had played a crucial role by summoning Pakistani Prime Minister Nawaz Sharif to Washington on 4 July 1999 and pressuring him to withdraw forces from the Indian side of the LoC.

27. The well-known cliché about this war is that while Vajpayee and Sharif were shaking hands in Lahore, then Pakistani Army Chief, General Pervez Musharraf, was training his soldiers for the Kargil war.

28. Debidatta Aurobinda Mahapatra, *Making Kashmir Borderless*, (New Delhi and Colombo: Manohar Publishers and Distributors and Regional Centre for Strategic Studies, 2013), 20.

29. For the theory of offensive realism see, John J. Mearsheimer, *The Tragedy of Great Power Politics*, (New York: W. W. Norton & Company, 2001).

30. Inder Malhotra contends that Pakistan raised the issue of human rights violations in Kashmir believing that 'foreign countries, unwilling so far to rake up Kashmir on the strength of outdated U.N. resolutions, might do so if the question of human rights is brought to the fore', Inder Malhotra, 'One False Step', *Sunday*, (16–22 June 1991), 18.

31. Both the countries reached the verge of a war in December 2001 after India, followed by Pakistan, mounted its largest ever military build-up on the Indo-Pak border. Beginning May 2002, for almost a year, the armies of the two countries remained deployed on the border in a state of high alert.

32. Stephen P. Cohen, *India: Emerging Power*, (Washington DC: Brookings Institution Press, 2001), 217.

33. Debidatta Aurobinda Mahapatra and Seema Shekhawat, *Conflict in Kashmir and Chechnya: Political and Humanitarian Dimensions*, (New Delhi: Lancer's Books, 2007), 39.

34. 'Kashmir: The View from Islamabad', *Asia Report No. 68, International Crisis Group*, (4 December 2003), 3.

35. 'Kashmir: Confrontation and Miscalculation', *Asia Report No. 35, International Crisis Group*, (11 July 2002), 6.

36. *Indian Express*, (15 September 2009).

37. Many Kashmiris were outraged by the Pakistani attempt to secure accession first by wooing the oppressive ruler, and later by using force. Balraj Puri, 'Kashmiriyat: The Vitality of Kashmir Identity', *Contemporary South Asia*, 4, no. 1, (March 1995): 57.

38. Here it will not be out of context to mention that amongst the three distinct regions of J&K – Jammu, Kashmir valley and Ladakh, only the Sunni Muslim dominated Kashmir valley had remained the epicentre of the violent separatist movement with sporadic outbursts in the two other regions particularly in the

areas of Poonch and Rajouri in Jammu. Buddhist and Shia Muslim dominated Ladakh and Hindu majority Jammu largely remained apathetic to militancy and even opposed the movement for independence.

39. Paula R. Newberg, *Double Betrayal: Repression and Insurgency in Kashmir*, (Washington: Carnegie Endowment for International Peace, 1995), 74.

40. Sumantra Bose, *Kashmir: Roots of Conflict, Paths to Peace*, (New Delhi: Vistaar, 2003), 4.

41. The Union List details the items on which only the Indian government has legislative powers. The Constitution provides two other lists namely the State List in which the states of the Indian federation have jurisdiction and the Concurrent List in which both the central government and the states have jurisdiction as detailed by the Constitution.

42. While Article 356 authorizes the centre to dismiss state governments in the event of breakdown of law and order, Article 357 enables it to assume a legislative role.

43. Balraj Puri, *Kashmir: Towards Insurgency*, (New Delhi: Orient Longman, 1993), 31 and by the same author, *Kashmir: Insurgency and After*, (New Delhi: Orient Blackswan, 2008).

44. Personal Interview, 18 June 2011.

45. Debidatta Aurobinda Mahapatra, 'Viewing Kashmir Conflict through the Prism of Dignity and Humiliation', paper presented at International Workshop on Conflict and Humiliation, Columbia University, New York, (11–12 December 2008).

46. Rekha Chowdhary and Nagendra Rao, 'Elections 2002: Implications for Politics of Separatism', *Economic and Political Weekly*, 38, no. 1, (4 January 2003): 15.

47. Abdul Jabbar Ganai, *Kashmir: National Conference and Politics*, (Srinagar: Gulshan Publishers, 1984), 16; Ashutosh Varshney, 'Three Compromised Nationalism: Why Kashmir Has Been a Problem', in *Perspectives on Kashmir: The Roots of Conflict in South Asia*, ed., Raju G. C. Thomas, (Boulder: Westview Press, 1992), 212.

48. Puri, *Kashmir: Towards Insurgency*, 45.

49. Puri, *Kashmir: Towards Insurgency*, 52.

50. Personal Interview, 25 May 2012. It needs to be added that on 30 October 1947, an emergency government was formed in J&K with Sheikh Abdullah as its head. This government supported the Maharaja's decision to join India and helped Indian security forces to impede advancing Pakistani forces.

51. Rekha Chowdhary, 'Political Alienation in Kashmir', *Indian Journal of Political Science*, 62, no. 2, (June 2001): 164–65.

52. Jagmohan, *My Frozen Turbulence in Kashmir*, (New Delhi: Allied Publishers Pvt. Ltd., 2007), 795.

53. Kuldip Nayar, *Wall at Wagah: India-Pakistan Relations*, (New Delhi: Gyan Publishing House, 2003), 168.

54. Puri, *Kashmir: Towards Insurgency*, 34.

55. Personal Interview, 21 May 2011.

56. M. J. Akbar argues that Kashmiriyat 'became ideological fountainhead of the modern Kashmiri mind, gave a unique quality to the Kashmiri identity, provided a conviction which long preserved Kashmir from the unspeakable and unbelievable

bloodshed which Indians have inflicted upon each other in this century in the name of religion', M. J. Akbar, *Kashmir: Behind the Vale*, (New Delhi: Viking Penguin India, 1991), 7. For a detailed analysis of the concept see, Robert G. Wirsing, *Kashmir in the Shadow of War: Regional Rivalries in a Nuclear Age*, (New York: M. E. Sharpe, 2003) and M. Ishaq Khan, *Kashmir's Transition to Islam: The Role of Muslim Rishis*, (Delhi: Manohar, 2002).

57. The issue of pandits leaving the valley, after living together with Muslims amicably for centuries, is controversial. Most displaced Kashmiri pandits residing in camps claim that they were forced to leave. They contend that an intense vilification campaign was launched by militant organizations against them. There were rumours that a hit list of non-Muslims was prepared. They were threatened through letters, posters, pamphlets, telephones and advertisements in the press. An ultimatum from Hizḅ-ul-Mujahideen published in *Alsafa* on 14 April 1990 read, 'All pandits should leave from here (Kashmir valley) in two days.' Religious slogans such as *Nara-i-Taqbir, Allah-o-Akbar, Yahan kya chalega ?- Nizam-i-Mustfa*, (what kind of law will prevail here?- The Islamic law), *Mussalmano jaggo , kafiro bhago, jihad aa raha hai* (Arise and awake Muslims, run away infidels, jihad is approaching) and *Agar Kashmir mein rehna hoga, Allah Allah kehna hoga* (If you wish to continue living in Kashmir, you will have to pray to Allah) were raised by militant organizations. Some selective killings of pandits led to a panic situation. This passage is adapted from Seema Shekhawat, *Conflict and Displacement in Jammu and Kashmir: The Gender Dimension*, (Jammu: Saksham Books International, 2006), 138–43. For details on the displaced lives of pandits see my following publications, 'Resettlement of Displaced Pandits', *Journal of Internal Displacement*, 2, (2012): 49–65; 'Displacement in Kashmir', *Conflict Trends*, Issue 4, (2009): 31–37; and 'Return and resettlement of the displaced Pandits in Jammu and Kashmir', Report, Internal Displacement Monitoring Centre, Geneva, 2010.

58. Bose, *Kashmir: Roots of Conflict, Paths to Peace*, 47–50.

59. In an earlier study, Mahapatra and I summed up the major catalysts for the alienation and consequent militancy as,

The follies committed by the centre have contributed to the dismal scenario. Reliance on one party and one leader, negligence of the popular feeling, sidelining of the issue of such a huge magnitude, adopting an ostrich-like attitude to inherent problems further complicated the issue…distance (both material and psychological) from the main power centre, too contributed to the problem…. Support by the establishment across the border, the religious colouring of the issue, and the coincidental international events have contributed to the alienation. The flickering flame of alienation was also fuelled by the events in Afghanistan (the Soviet retreat, thus supplying the Mujahideen to the valley), the results and conduct of 1987 elections and the belief in some segments of the people in the valley that violence and its methods can be used to profit (the Rubiya Sayeed abduction case in 1989 was the beginning in the chain), led the disenchantment of the people to extremes.

Mahapatra and Shekhawat, *Conflict in Kashmir and Chechnya: Political and Humanitarian Dimensions*, 34–35.

60. Nayar, *Wall at Wagah: India-Pakistan Relations*, 148.
61. Navnita Chadha Behera, *State, Identity and Violence: Jammu, Kashmir & Ladakh*, (New Delhi: Manohar Publishers, 2000), 164–65.
62. Schofield, *Kashmir in the Crossfire*, 150.
63. Puri, *Kashmir: Towards Insurgency*, 55–56.
64. See A. G. Noorani, 'The Betrayal of Kashmir: Pakistan's Duplicity and India's Complicity', in *Perspectives on Kashmir: The Roots of Conflict in South Asia*, ed., Raju G. C. Thomas, (Columbia: Westview Press, 1992), 254–75 and Sumit Ganguly, 'The Islamic Dimensions of the Kashmir Insurgency', in *Pakistan: Nationalism Without a Nation*, ed., Christophe Jaffrelot, (New Delhi: Manohar Publications, 2002), 179–94.
65. Sumantra Bose, *The Challenge in Kashmir: Democracy, Self-Determination and a Just Peace*, (New Delhi: Sage Publications, 1997), 59.
66. *International Encyclopedia of Terrorism*, (New Delhi: S. Chand & Company, 1999), 502–03.
67. Personal Interview, 15 June 2011.
68. Foreign presence in Kashmir became public when in March 1995 Master Gul, a former shopkeeper from Pakistan's North West Frontier, occupied the mosque at Charar-e-Sharif about 25 miles from Srinagar which is revered for its association with Nund Rishi, the patron saint of the valley. Gul had been trained during the war in Afghanistan and amongst his followers were 70 mercenaries.
69. *Kashmir: Confrontation and Miscalculation*, 6.
70. In a survey by MORI, a British pollster, a majority of the respondents in Kashmir (65 per cent) argued that foreign militants had damaged the Kashmiri cause. Further, 68 per cent respondents believed that Pakistan was not genuinely concerned with the plight of the people of Kashmir. *Financial Times*, 1 June 2002.
71. For details see Debidatta Aurobinda Mahapatra, 'Apotheosis of Kashmir', *Strategic Culture Foundation*, online magazine, 22 September 2010. Available at http://www.strategic-culture.org/news/2010/09/22/apotheosis-of-kashmir.html (accessed on 26 March 2011).
72. A Kashmiri student conceded that he received 'sufficient money to account for his pocket money for six months', for participating in the protests. Personal Interview, 30 May 2012.
73. Personal Interview, 28 May 2012.
74. Personal Interview, 26 May 2012.

Chapter 4

Engendering the Conflict

The Indian freedom struggle provided women the opportunity to shed those customs that limited their mobility and to take part in public protests and other pro-independence activities. Undivided Kashmir, a princely state, was not exempt from this phenomenon, where the protesters had two major goals: to obtain freedom from the oppression of the monarchy as well as from the colonial rule. Women's visibility in Kashmir as a mobilized group could be traced to this era as they came out of their homes and participated in anti-monarchy protests in large numbers.[1] This indicated that Kashmiri women were historically conscious of public protest as a means to put forth their demands. Decades later this technique was again put into practice during the anti-India movement in late 1980s. The *azadi* (freedom) movement was initially indigenous and enjoyed widespread support from all sections of people including women. The goal of *azadi* was shared by a majority of Kashmiri people. For them the cause was just and hence the movement received wide support for the realization of the objective: independence of J&K from India. There were instances when women organized and addressed protesters; most of them were also visible as participants in marches, shouting anti-India and pro-independence slogans.

Protestors and Caretakers

Women were the face of the militancy in its initial phase being visible at the forefront of protest movements. As one prominent Indian news daily reported on 3 September 1990:

> More and more Kashmiri Muslim women – mainly college and school students – are decrying the 'Indian occupation' of Jammu and Kashmir and alleged atrocities by security forces against local people. Thousands of them,

in separate groups, poured onto streets in Srinagar on three days last week and clashed with police or made a determined bid to march to the United Nations Military Observer's office seeking the world body's intervention to help solve the Kashmir dispute.[2]

Women usually took front stage during protests to receive cane blows and thereby protect men. Sometimes during demonstrations they engaged in fierce arguments with Indian security forces or resorted to abusing them. At times they pelted stones at security personnel in full media glare to provoke them to resort to violence. 'We used to engage security personnel in a number of ways, including stone pelting. It was an appropriate strategy to provoke them. They would fire tear gas shells and cane charge,' recalled Sabeena.[3] Nafeeza elaborated on this strategy:

> Independence was a sacred goal for us; hence it needed our full commitment. We had to avail all possible options to attract international attention. Indian security forces were at times reluctant. They resorted to cane charge sparingly so it was crucial to provoke them to resort to violence. When they got provoked and used violence, our movement received worldwide attention. We abused them shouting publicly *hindustani kutte* (Indian dogs), *namard* (impotent) and *kutton Hindustan bhag jao* (dogs go back to India). Our men could not do all this as they could have been arrested, so we performed all these activities. It may not be a good tactic, but you must have heard the saying: all is fair in love and war, and for us it was a total war against India.[4]

It was clear to the male militant leadership that for any movement to be characterized a mass movement, the involvement of women was crucial. The movement could not have received international attention on such a large scale had Kashmiri women not supported it.[5] The visibility of Kashmiri women in the struggle enhanced its credibility and disseminated the message globally that the struggle is just. It conveyed that the Indian state had deprived Kashmiris of their fundamental rights and resorted to force to restrain the unarmed men and women from demanding their rights. A male ex-militant recalled:

> Without women's participation how could our movement receive sympathy from national and international quarters? Just like in a family, everyone has to contribute to the movement for independence. I remember guiding women on how to carry out protest movements, how to confront and provoke security forces, and how to behave when the media was around. Women played their part quite well. They were very enthusiastic to shoulder any responsibility. They

simultaneously managed houses singlehandedly and participated in militant activities. It was not an easy task but it is said that women are naturally capable of multi-tasking and our women proved this in those days.[6]

Women rejoiced at the attention they received even though they were not in control of the movement. With directives coming from the male militant leadership, women were not entirely on their own, but they had the intermittent space to chart out their own strategies, for instance, while they were on the protest ground without a male leader around to direct them. The space that women negotiated with the militants and the Indian security forces in those times was unprecedented. It brought to women an empowering experience. Zeenab explains:

Men have more experience of dealing with public life. We had remained indoors and hence needed guidance from the leaders. But, we had the space to take decisions and feel powerful. We led the protest movements, while men were either absent or followed discreetly. Though when and how a protest had to be organized was decided by male militant leaders, we were assigned the duty to fill in the details to make the protest successful. It was a very different experience.[7]

Women enforced civil curfews under the direction of the male militant leadership. When the state imposed curfews, women were at the forefront to defy them. During crackdowns or when Indian security personnel chased militants, women sounded alarms and blocked the narrow alleyways to help the militants to escape. Many respondents vividly recalled how they protected militants from security personnel. Nusrat Begum claimed being part of an all-women group that saved a militant from arrest:

We four women were enjoying sunlight outside our houses when a young Kashmiri boy came running towards us with a gun in hand, and following him were Indian security forces. In seconds I sensed the whole story and decided what to do. I snatched the gun from his hands and hid it in my *firan* (long gown worn by Kashmiri women). Then I started scolding him as if he was my son and had not performed well in the examination. The other women acted as if they were mediating between mother and son. When the security personnel reached the spot, I confidently asked what they wanted. Though they wanted to whisk away the boy for interrogation I intervened and told them he was my son who had performed poorly in his examination and that I was going to lock him up in the house. Convinced or confused or whatever, the security people left.[8]

Many respondents narrated being passionately involved in tracing the whereabouts of missing men, seeking the release of detained ones and collecting donations to ensure bail of detainees. Shazia said:

> At the behest of militants, we went to military camps to look for missing men. Sometimes we did all possible drama to enable the release of detained Kashmiris. Outside military camps we shouted and abused armed security personnel. We cried and claimed that the person detained was my son or my husband and that he was innocent. Sometimes this drama continued for days. We would regularly go in the morning and remain there, sometimes shouting, sometimes crying, in order to force the security personnel to release the detainee. At times the tactic worked and security personnel, succumbing to our pressure, released the person.[9]

Sheltering militants, preparing food for them and taking care of them as guests were some other activities that women supporters of militancy performed competently. Tabassum recollected her experience in accommodating the combatants:

> Sheltering fighters in our homes was quite risky since security personnel could raid a house any time. But militants were fighting for all of us so we had to take their utmost care. During our leisure time we proudly counted how many times we had accommodated militants in our homes and for how many days. Yes, it was a difficult thing to do. With no men around, we women had to multi-task. We had to prepare food for the militants, look after other household chores and keep an eye on what was happening outside the home. The militants did not trust anyone even though they had popular support. Women had to manage both tasks – taking care of them and also keeping them safe from security personnel.[10]

When security personnel raided a house where armed men were hiding, they at times had to leave empty handed because of the intervention of women who opened the door and confronted them with abuse or made the excuse that they were alone at home and therefore the men could not search the house. This engagement of 5–10 minutes provided the militants enough time to escape. Rehana told me how once a group of five militants were present in her house when security people knocked on her door at around 11 pm. She said, 'I dared them (security personnel) to catch the fighters and not to threaten an unarmed woman who was alone in the house. Then I started crying. They did not know how to react. After 20 minutes they left and I saved my guests (militants).'[11] At times godowns and animal sheds were converted into meeting rooms where the combatants discussed strategy while sipping tea and eating the snacks prepared by the women of the house. Zeenab recollected:

> All preparations had to be done instantly. There would be a knock on the door and a group of fighters would come in and inform us that they were going to have a meeting in this house. No questions were entertained. We had to guide them to a place in the house where they could be secure and comfortable. We were not allowed to enter that part of the house until the meeting was over. We prepared refreshments and even meals, depending on the length of the meeting.[12]

Violent encounters between security personnel and the rebels swelled the number of injured militants who could not be taken to hospitals for fear of arrest. Tabassum recalled that women attended to wounded militants, and, if required, arranged for doctors and medicines:

> Nursing comes naturally to women but looking after an injured person is not easy. At times there was a bullet in the body. We were not trained nurses but we did everything we could, from first aid to calling a doctor if necessary. Once I had to threaten a doctor to come along and attend to an injured fighter who had two gun shots in his right leg. The doctor was hesitant to attend to him. I threatened him with a butcher knife and only then did he agree to treat the wounded man. I could not trust the doctor since he might have gone straight to the police and informed them of the militant's presence in my house. With the help of my 12-year-old son I tied him up and kept him in custody until the militant was shifted to a safe place by his associates. There are scores of such instances where we did not take orders from the leadership. We took our own decisions.[13]

Nusrat Begum vividly summed up the participation of women in the early phase of militancy:

> Those days (1989–90) were a time of pride for Kashmiri women. We used to come out of our homes almost every day to participate in protests. We shouted anti-India and pro-independence slogans with excitement. Sometimes we did not cook at home. Community meals were arranged to set us free from household errands and ensure our involvement in the protests. When a majority of men retreated due to crackdowns by security forces or went to Pakistan for training, we carried on the movement. When our men returned and anti-India demonstrations were replaced by armed militancy we changed our strategy. We marched to courts and camps of Indian security forces to protest against detentions and negotiate the release of our men. We collected money

to arrange bail for the detained. We visited the detainees and provided them food and clothes. We invented tactics to keep our armed men protected such as blocking the way of the security forces and delaying their entry into our houses by engaging them in arguments. We sheltered and cooked for fighters even if we did not know them personally. All armed men were our sons and brothers. Making them comfortable in every possible way, even at the cost of our suffering, was our duty. Sometimes the security forces cracked down and tortured us for helping militants but that did not deter us from supporting the freedom fighters who praised us enormously. It was a life time experience. We enjoyed that moment of glory. [14]

Facilitators

Rebellious movement against a state cannot be carried out without funding. Once militancy gathered momentum, financial support became a crucial issue to sustain the movement. Besides receiving funding from across the border, it was deemed necessary by the militant leadership that the local people should contribute. Taxes were imposed by the militants and collected by volunteers. The collection then had to be deposited with a person designated by the leadership, who in turn had to transfer the amount to the leaders. Many women not only willingly paid the tax, but also played an active role in collecting money for, as Nayla said, 'a just political cause'.[15] Several women acted as route facilitators, by identifying safe infiltration routes for militants coming from Kashmir across the LoC. Sneaking through the LoC was not an easy task due to an inhospitable terrain and the permanent presence of security personnel on the Indo-Pak dividing line in Kashmir. Dodging security personnel and helping militants sneak into J&K was a task that scores of respondents admitted to have performed, especially in the militancy-infested Poonch and Rajouri districts. The assignment did not end with facilitating crossing of LoC; women had to help the militants reach their destinations by guiding them through short cuts and less risky paths. Shamshad Begum was arrested in October 2001 by J&K police for carrying out such activities. She was accused of playing a key role in a large number of infiltration operations into J&K from across the dividing line.[16] Women also participated in reconnaissance missions and gathered intelligence in order to monitor troop movements and conduct operations against security forces. They used their 'feminine qualities' to honey trap security personnel to collect information.[17] A news report explained, 'women were...being used to trap Army officers and jawans (lower rank officers) to monitor troop movement and operations so that... [militants] gain vantage positions during encounters.'[18] Shereen conceded 'befriending' an army official of the rank of Colonel with the intention of extracting information from him:

> I was friend of a Colonel who lived inside a military camp. I had unobstructed passage to the camp thanks to him. Once I was told by the Colonel during a casual talk that they would be carrying out a military operation around a place where fighters were hiding. I passed the information to the militants. They escaped even before the operation started. Befriending an army official was both difficult and risky but we were clever enough to make out who could be an easy target.[19]

Cash, messages and other items were transported through women. One respondent recalled carrying messages from one hideout to another more than ten times. 'If the message was verbal then there was no problem, but if it was written then we had to be more careful. At times messages were noted down as prescriptions on a doctor's letterhead. That way even if we were frisked the message remained safe,' revealed Shamshad.[20] Some women were arrested in the process of transferring money and even arms. In March 2002, Shamima Khan was arrested with US $ 70,000 handed to her by a Hurriyat activist in Kathmandu to be delivered to Yasin Malik, a separatist leader in Kashmir.[21] In another case, Anjum Zamrooda Habib was arrested in February 2003 from outside the Pakistan High Commission in New Delhi with ₹ 300,000. The money was to be delivered to Abdul Gani Bhat, a Kashmiri separatist leader.[22] Ameena disclosed this strategy, 'we women were trusted couriers. I have performed this task on many occasions. Sometimes I knew what amount I was supposed to deliver, but most of the times I was just handed over a packet and address where it had to be delivered. I had to chart out the strategy of when and how to deliver it.'[23] In January 2006, Shreen Jaan was arrested by J&K police on the allegation that she was a small arms courier for LeT. There were also instances when women smuggled militants by using veils. In such an operation, a group of veiled women would walk with a militant, also wearing a veil, to hoodwink security personnel. Smuggling militants was a high risk task in comparison to delivering money but the veil acted as a shield against possible detection.

Motivators

Misrepresentation of human rights violations was employed as a part of a ferocious propaganda war by both the security forces and the militants as each attempted to denigrate the other in the national and international media.

Militants usually had the upper hand because Kashmiri women were at the forefront of this propaganda war. If it was the case of injuries caused by tear gas shells and cane charges, or deaths from gunfire, each campaign launched by the militants featured women. Whether it was a genuine case of human rights violation, or propaganda, the drive helped not only to attract international attention but also to mobilize the youth to join the ranks of militants and avenge the victimization of 'their' women. In most cases, allegations of rape against the security forces were made publicly. Mehrunissa told me that she, along with three other women, was handed a written statement by a male militant leader, which was to be read before a camera, about their rape by security personnel of a particular battalion active in their area. She averred:

> The statements were recorded on camera. The recording was dispatched to many countries to garner support, and to receive funding to counter the Indian state. It required a lot of strength since in Kashmir rape is considered a dishonour that should never be discussed publicly but this was our way of aiding militancy. Such public disclosures provoked many Kashmiri men to revenge the dishonour of their women by becoming militants.[24]

Social constructions of sexuality, femininity and motherhood are significant in deciphering women's participation in armed struggles wherein these may be utilized for aiding violence. These constructions shape women's functions such as mobilizers, who, besides performing other activities, impart militarist virtues to the uninitiated and marry combatants to boost their morale. Several respondents narrated their activities as transmitters of militarist values to infuse passion among Kashmiri men. In social events such as marriages young women sang couplets praising the militants such as *kalashnikov lagai balayai yenav ladayat path fairaleh* (don't give up this fight for freedom, I shower my life on this Kalashnikov), and *main mujahidov behan praraie hideoutas* (O my beloved militant, I will wait for you at the hideout).[25] Raheema remembered how as a child she attended festivities where women 'not only sang traditional songs appropriate to the occasion but also boosted the morale of the fighters'.[26] There was competition among women supporters to use their creativity to compose pro-militancy couplets. A woman whose couplet was appreciated by a majority of participants felt a victor though no award was given. Several former male militants that I interviewed admitted that they joined the militia after being motivated by their female relatives. An ex-militant revealed:

> My mother and sister asked me to take up a gun for the independence of Kashmir. I was hesitant since I was the only earner in the family, but they

agreed to shoulder all the responsibilities. I was also charmed by the stories that made the rounds among youth that young girls were keen to marry militants and they dreamt about a man with a gun in his hand. I attended a couple of social events where songs and couplets dedicated to the bravery of militants were sung. When I became a militant and came back from Pakistan after training, my mother proudly distributed sweets in the neighbourhood. I received proposals of marriage from three beautiful girls. I felt very special.[27]

Naseema married a militant when she was only 16-year-old. She recalled with much pride how her marriage was celebrated by the whole village:

All those present at the wedding praised me profusely and some said that I will definitely go to heaven for this action. After the marriage I stayed with my mother-in-law. My husband visited us every month until he was killed in 2003. I was aware that he may be killed any day. I mourn, but have no regrets. I had chosen an uncertain life. But in those days marriage was not for settlement but to motivate young militants to fight and die if needed.[28]

Besides motivation, nuptial ties with militants served the purpose of producing and preparing a future generation of fighters to fight for the cause of independence. Patriarchal militant leaders urged women to give birth to as many sons as possible. To prompt women to produce sons, Banat-ul-Islam, the women wing of a militant group, proclaimed women to be 'life givers, so they [women] should not kill their unborn children…[and should] sacrifice their sons for the sake of the cause.'[29] Swati Parashar in her study on Kashmiri women deconstructed a slogan which was popular during the early days of the militancy and is indicative of women's enthusiasm for attaining motherhood:

Pakistan jayenge, do roti khayenge, pet mein mujahid leke aayenge! (We shall go to Pakistan; we shall eat two chapattis [flat bread]; we shall get *mujahid* [fighters] in our wombs!) Pakistan is part of the nostalgia women feel especially those who have an affinity with its Islamic identity. Pakistan is also thought of (in this slogan), as the land of the *mujahid* (militants) as most of the early militants received training and instructions in Pakistan and came from there. *Do roti khayenge* is a reminder of the hardships and difficulties in the liberation struggle. Most significant is the last line of this slogan which combines issues of sexuality, nationalism and motherhood. For women to shout slogans about who they would mate with so as to best serve the movement marks a departure from the asexual, private and invisible women-gendered norms but this is tempered by reinstating the gender norm through ideal mothers who would carry *mujahid* in their wombs.[30]

Those killed during skirmishes with Indian security personnel were called *shahid* (martyr) and their mothers delivered emotional speeches glorifying martyrdom before the commencement of funeral processions. Through slogans such as *Ae mard-e-mujahid jag zara, waqt e shahadat aa gaya* (awaken, O holy fighter, the time for martyrdom has come!), *Hame apne beton par garv hai* (we are proud of our sons), and *Hamare bete kya banenge mujahid banege, mujahid banenge* (what will our sons become? They will become fighters, they will become fighters) women implored militants to fight and attain martyrdom, if needed.

In conflict situations, the construction of motherhood serves a dual purpose – to mobilize and get mobilized. Appealing to widely held beliefs about motherhood is one of the most effective strategies that enables the combatants to garner the unquestioning support of women. Laura Sjoberg and Caron E. Gentry suggest, 'the mother narrative describes women's violence as a need to belong, a need to nurture, and a way of taking care of and being loyal to men.'[31] Militant leaders talked about valiant and courageous mothers who were powerful enough to impact the struggle. Their appeal to maternal sacrifice for independence served as a major motivator. Funerals of slain militants were publicly celebrated to forge solidarity and honour the mothers of martyrs.[32] Narratives of brave mothers adorning their sons as bridegrooms and asking them to bring independence as their bride and of mothers of martyrs celebrating rather than mourning death of their militant sons were popular. One respondent recalled an incident in 1989 when her neighbour's son was killed by the police during an anti-India demonstration. 'He was put to eternal rest following a public procession in which people shouted slogans praising his martyrdom. His mother sang a song and danced to show her pride in being a martyr's mother,' Fareeda recollected.[33] Naseema's first-hand experience too is instructive:

> I was quite convinced by the ideology of the movement. I had heard stories how many mothers were sending their sons to become freedom fighters. My son was only sixteen at that time but I persuaded him to go for arms training to Pakistan and then fight for our rights. He had the *jazba* (valour) to do something for his mother. Once everything was finalized, we had a night long celebration with food and dance. Guests made speeches showering blessings on him and applauding my bravery. Everyone praised me so much that I thought I was the bravest mother. Once my son returned, the celebrations went on for about a week before he left the house to carry out anti-India operations. He got killed in a fight with Indian security forces after three months. His funeral was again a public celebration. I was asked to wear the best clothes and deliver a motivating speech so that other women could be motivated to sacrifice their men. I did not cry for my son. I have a guaranteed place in heaven and I will meet him again in *jannat* (heaven).[34]

Rationale for Support

Multiple overlapping reasons, as discussed in an earlier chapter, arising out of personal, religious, ideological, economic and socio-cultural obligations need to be looked into in order to map the multi-faceted support of women to armed struggle in Kashmir. Indoctrination (a debatable term as some might call it consented participation) was a significant driver. Involving women was a relatively easy task because they were mobilized as part of a specific ethno-religious community. Multiple strategies were charted out to garner women's support. These included the construction of heroic images of militants and valiant mothers who sent their sons to fight and who rejoiced at their martyrdom. Militants were projected as responsible Kashmiris who took all possible care to minimize civilian casualties during encounters with security forces and provided financial assistance to the needy. The combatants set-up courts for the speedy delivery of justice. Stories of how judges in these courts persuaded a man to accept his raped wife and another to refrain from domestic violence were recalled by Shaukat Begum, although she herself did not witness those incidents. Said she, 'the holy fighters were highly respected so it was hard to disbelieve stories of their great deeds. Their concern not only for independence but also for social reforms won them our total support.'[35] The militants emphasized on the justness of the movement on both ideological and religious grounds. Averred Shazia, 'we often heard in the speeches of our leaders that India was an aggressive occupier and we all had to get united to oust India from our land. Most of us were convinced by these statements.'[36] Ameena recollected:

> I supported the movement because we all had to fight and make sacrifices for independence from India. I listened to speeches of militant leaders who said that they had given their lives for the sake of the whole community and hence they had a right to ask us to support the movement. It was projected as a movement of every single Kashmiri. We were all excited about freedom. Our leaders were rich. They could have settled in foreign countries but they stood for the rights of common Kashmiris. Independence was their dream and it became our dream.[37]

'*Wo zamana aur tha, wo jazba alag tha* (that time was different, that passion was different),' averred Anjum, who was active during the initial phase of the militancy.[38] The ideologues mobilized women by promises not only of freedom, but also of better lives and living standards. Ruqaiya elaborated:

> It was a fair deal for all of us. Freedom would have brought, among other things, non-discrimination and equality in society. Everybody would have had a fair

chance to get the best available education and job opportunities. There would have been a government responsive to people's grievances and committed to bringing development and providing better infrastructure in terms of electricity, water supply and connectivity. What else do common people aspire for? [39]

Though Kashmir was a liberal society wherein both Muslims and Hindus had lived together for centuries, during the height of the independence movement the Islamic identity was invoked to garner support. Slogans such as 'Islam is in danger' and 'Kashmir is being discriminated against as a Muslim majority region' were raised to woo people into the militancy fold. 'After listening to the leaders I was convinced that the Islamic way of life should be compulsory for all Muslims and that Hindu culture was being thrust upon us to destroy our distinct identity. The only way out was independence,' explained Shamima.[40]

The absence of a neutral space pushed several women to support violence. Caught between Indian security forces and Kashmiri militia, some respondents felt that they had no choice but to support the militants, with whom they could relate better. The policy followed by both warring parties was 'you are either with us or against us'. Rabiya explained that there was no alternative but to support the militants since, 'Indians were fighting against Kashmiris. The militants were fighting for us hence naturally our sympathies were with them.'[41] It is debatable whether women choose to support an armed struggle or they are coerced to do so. Isn't the claim of choice a contested one? Aren't there good reasons to believe that the participation is partly due to the lack of a neutral space? Also it has to be analysed if the claimed choice is genuine, made by self-will or if it is veiled coercion. This debate about choice necessitates a deeper socio-psychological analysis of women's motives in joining armed movements. However, there are instances when direct coercion compels people to abide by the commands of the armed groups. Saleema disclosed that she supported violence for familial safety:

> Those not supporting militants were punished. The punishment ranged from thrashing to even killing. Performing the assigned tasks guaranteed both money and safety. The fighters used to come to our house, demanded food or asked us to deliver a message. We just abided by their command though at times we did not wish to cater to their demands. There was a rumour that two women were killed in a nearby village for refusing to obey. I did not verify this but the hearsay was lesson enough to never say no to militants.[42]

Generally in separatist struggles there is intense pressure on men 'to take up arms and for women to loyally support brothers, husbands, sons and lovers to become soldiers.'[43] In patriarchal Kashmiri society the participation of male members in militancy implied support from all the members of the family, including women and children. A male ex-militant explained, 'my wife and daughters supported militancy because I believed in the justness of the movement. Once I decided to join the freedom struggle it was but obvious that they would follow.'[44] Nasreen's son went to Pakistan for arms training without informing her. It was only when he returned after nearly six months with a gun and ammunition that she came to know that he had become a combatant. Nasreen said she had no option but to support him:

> I was shocked but what could I do? He kept sending his militant friends for food and shelter until he was killed in an encounter. I had to support my son. May be he chose a wrong path, but as a mother I could do nothing but to take care of him in all possible ways. I do not know if I supported violence or not. All I know is I supported my son who was a militant.[45]

People affected by conflict situations tend to be considered a part of collateral damage and hence termed victims. This victimization may fuel further violence by prompting the victims to become perpetrators; hence there is a vicious circle of violence reinforcing further violence. The Indian government's failure to check the excessive and indiscriminate use of force by security forces added to the alienation of Kashmiri people and pushed them to support militancy. Crackdowns, torture, arbitrary arrests and killings fostered a desire among many to counter violence with violence. Some respondents claimed to have supported the movement to avenge personal and familial sufferings. Raheema Begum recollected how the killing of her son prompted her to support the violent struggle:

> I had no interest in this (movement). My family was totally apathetic to this struggle. We never allowed our teenaged son to mingle with boys of his age who talked about fighting India. I do not know on what basis my son was dragged out of my house in the wee hours of one night by Indian security forces. He was arrested along with some neighbourhood boys who were allegedly involved in a case of firing on a military camp. For five days I went to the army camp and pleaded his innocence, but there was no one to listen. On the sixth day I was informed by the security personnel that my son had been set free the previous night. But he never returned. I know he was killed by the Indian forces. That was the turning point. I became an active participant. I did not do it for independence. I did it to avenge the death of my innocent son.[46]

Sabina Begum narrated a similar story:

> I was somewhat uninterested in this violent movement. Indian security forces
> picked up my innocent husband and his body was found the next day in a field
> near our home. I was told that he had tried to snatch a gun from a security
> official and got killed in the scuffle. I wanted to protest against this brutality.
> Freedom or no freedom my support for militancy was for fighting all these
> atrocities committed against innocent Kashmiris.[47]

Victims of the pervasive violence 'became easy prey for militants looking
for soft targets to swell their ranks and supporters,' claimed an Indian security
official.[48] The promises of revenge prompted many to support militant
activities. Sameera, who was raped by three Indian security personnel, recalled:

> I wanted to take revenge. I neither had the opportunity nor the guts to take a
> gun in hand, so the easy course was to facilitate attacks on Indian troops. The
> fighters sympathized with me and vowed to take revenge for my humiliation.
> This motivated me to help those who stood by me in that hour of distress
> despite not knowing me personally. They attacked the camp of the security
> personnel who had raped me and killed five troops. I do not know whether
> the culprits were killed, but at least their colleagues were.[49]

Whether victimization pushed women to enlist or they supported militancy
willingly can be debated, but indubitably intended and unintended human
rights violations by Indian security forces further fuelled the violent movement
against the Indian state. Asiya Andrabi, a female separatist leader, has been
quoted expressing gratitude to Indian security forces for violations of human
rights, stating that otherwise the struggle would not have achieved mass
support. 'We are thankful to the Indian security forces for the atrocities they
commit. The more excesses they commit, the more women will be willing to
join the cause of freedom,' she argued.[50]

Even by conservative estimates, thousands of people lost their lives in
the conflict and hundreds are missing. The number of Kashmiri widows is
estimated to be about 33,000.[51] These women had to face numerous problems
including, 'financial difficulties, psychological downfall, emotional stress,
denial of due inheritance rights, sexual harassment, physical insecurity and
social undesirability.'[52] Absence of men pushed many women into the public
sphere to negotiate with both the state and society for their survival as well
as of their families on an almost daily basis. For some, supporting militancy
for monetary gains was an easy option. There are reports from Dardpora in
Kupwara district, which is commonly known as 'the village of widows' that

a commonly pursued livelihood by women was acting as guides for armed men infiltrating from across the LoC.[53] Ameena elaborated:

> It was primarily for the survival of my family that I supported militancy. My husband died in an encounter and I had to look after my two children and parents-in-law. It is difficult for a semi-literate woman like me to get a job. Doing small tasks for the fighters helped me earn money. If I had not earned this way Allah knows how we could have survived.[54]

Sabiya, whose husband had been missing for six years in 1998, agreed to provide the militia food and shelter for three nights in exchange of ₹ 3,000. Said she, 'four militants came to our house in January 1998 and asked for food and shelter. I told them I could not afford their stay. They agreed to pay me. Later I accommodated many other groups of militants in exchange for money. Look, now we have a house to stay in and I have married my two daughters with fanfare.'[55] Several respondents claimed that they participated in the violent struggle to deal with societal and familial problems.

> Membership in a militant group saved women from many problems. My involvement in militancy related activities helped me to effectively counter my in-laws who wanted me to leave the house when my husband died. They did not wish to give my children a share in ancestral property. Now I have no problem. My children have grown up here, in their fathers' house, said Nusrat.[56]

'It was shield to save myself from prying eyes of men,' asserted Shabnam. She explained:

> My father died even before the onset of militancy. I was young when the violence started. It was chaos all around and there were many people who tried to take advantage of that situation. I joined a militant group and carried out multiple tasks to facilitate the group's anti-India operations. After I joined the militancy I did not face any gendered remarks from men. My younger sister never confronted anything odd since everybody around was aware of our relationship. You have to negotiate your own space to survive as a young woman and I did that by supporting anti-India violence.[57]

Shazia asserted that becoming a supporter of militancy enabled her to save not only herself, but also her two neighbours, who were abused and beaten by their husbands:

> Kashmiri men in general are not very aggressive but maybe because of the all-prevailing tense scenario, they became very restless and violent. Every day men had to negotiate with both militants and security forces. As they could

not confront either of the armed groups, they vented their frustration on women and children at home. After one long month of suffering daily abuse and beating I approached a militant relative. He came to our house with his group armed with guns. My husband realized his fault without even a single word of threat from my relative. That day I understood that when a gun speaks, everyone listens. I did not take up a gun, but I helped the militia and thereafter life changed for good. My two neighbours who used to beat their wives got a good lesson when I told them about my militant relative who believed in gender equality. I felt powerful.[58]

Shazia's assertion resonates the wider concern for gender equality and empowerment, also emphasized by the respondents from other South Asian conflicts.

The Retraction

Within a decade of its inception popular support for the violent movement started waning. Women, once the backbone of the struggle, gradually withdrew from being its active supporters. A perceptible change in both the quantity and quality of women's participation became obvious. Several respondents did not outrightly reject or disown the struggle but revealed that their vigorous support for violence no longer existed. While some of them refused to shelter armed men in their homes at a risk of their own lives, others admitted abiding by their diktats due to fear. Haseena narrated her experience of refusing to pay the monthly 'war tax' to the group active in her area.[59] Defiance had its fallouts including forced displacement of many families.

The perceptible shift in the popular response to the armed struggle cannot be attributed to a single factor, but to an array of overlapping factors. War fatigue played a crucial role in creating a sense of disillusionment. The armed struggle, which was projected to achieve success within a few months, dragged for years with few visible outcomes apart from death and destruction. The protracted nature of the movement led to weaning of the passion that had been all-pervasive in the initial years. The general population became weary when independence remained a distant dream after years of struggle. As the Indian government resorted to excessive violence to contain the movement, it eventually became comprehensible that it would not be an easy task to achieve the goal of independence. 'We lost our enthusiasm. We thought we would be an independent country by 1990 but as the war dragged on we realized it is not as close as we perceived,' reasoned Haleema.[60] 'The longer the battle lingered, the more destruction we suffered. Everyone wanted to be independent, but the pain outweighed the advantages of a freedom yet to be attained,' said Tabassum.[61] Several respondents denounced the violent methods that caused them immense sufferings. They were convinced from personal experiences that guns do not offer a viable solution to political problems. Some raised questions about the projected independence bringing normalcy to lives that had been shattered by years of violence. Sabeena Begum, who lost her militant husband in 1998, symbolizes the victims' grief and struggle for survival: 'What has this struggle given me? Widowhood. I have four children and have to do menial jobs to feed them. Even if we Kashmiris become independent now I do not know how my life will become better.'[62] Here it would not be out of context to point out that a majority of the respondents who spoke passionately about *azadi* could not put forward a coherent definition of the term. A male ex-militant residing in Surankote area of Poonch district pointed out, 'what *azadi* we were supposed to fight for I did not know. We were informed that we would get a monthly salary if we crossed the LoC for training and later fought the Indian security forces. For me it was a means of earning. Actually I do not know what *azadi* implies.'[63] On being asked about *azadi* a young respondent studying in Kashmir University offered an interesting reply:

> *Azadi*, as of now, means independence from India. First we are fighting for freedom of this part of Kashmir (J&K) from India. Then we will fight with Pakistan for independence of Kashmir that is under its occupation. I am sure we Kashmiris will be able to manage our own affairs once we are free. If that does not happen then we would ask USA or China to help us to run the country. So we will have freedom to invite any country to help us both politically and economically, if needed.[64]

There were equally ambivalent responses regarding the potential impact of independence on the lives of Kashmiris. 'We were told that once independence was achieved our lives would change for good. I am not sure what that meant, may be better jobs and infrastructure. We never asked our leaders about this,' said Shaheen.[65]

Insensitivity and neglect about the concerns of common Kashmiris by the militant leadership played a significant role in generating popular disenchantment. Despite promises by the ideologues, lack of support to those who lost family members in the conflict disappointed many. The indifference towards personal losses especially that of widows, half widows and raped had a particular impact on the psyche of women. Raped women provided public testimonies as a contribution to the struggle. The separatist leaders exploited the victimized women for propaganda but failed to fight for justice for them or to challenge the associated stigma. The most often narrated case concerned Kunan Poshpura village, where, at the insistence of separatist leaders, raped women testified in front of cameras only to be later abandoned not only by their families but also by those who had urged them to publicly provide details of their suffering. Following the incident, the village witnessed some married women being abandoned by their husbands, while many single women could not find bridegrooms. Similarly, the public honouring of the mothers and wives of martyrs remained symbolic and later these families suffered from apathetic attitude of the militia leaders towards their distress. 'Honouring the mothers and widows of martyrs and delivering emotional speeches to fight for justice for raped women were for anti-India propaganda and for garnering mass support. Everyone was dumped later,' lamented Shabnam.[66] The separatist leaders appealed to the people to actively participate in the struggle but several of them did not allow their own family members to join it. Some others enjoyed police protection which was interpreted by many Kashmiris 'as a mockery of the struggle'.[67] 'Hurriyat does not represent us though earlier our family supported the JKLF. What have the leaders done apart from enjoying luxurious lives at the cost of our suffering?,' was Ameena Begum's response on being questioned about the role of separatist leaders.[68]

The turning point was the change in the character of militancy. The initial indigenous popular uprising turned into a criminalized and radicalized movement at a later stage. Many respondents characterized the initial phase of the militancy as 'pure and justified', and the later one as 'impure and unjustified'. Militants' new cohorts were not concerned with the popular aspirations for independence. They instead took up arms for reasons such as settling personal scores, forcefully marrying a girl of choice, monetary benefits, power and spreading religious fundamentalism. According to Raheema, 'these militants had their own agenda. Many were extremists who wanted to use Kashmir as a pawn in pursuit of the dream of a pan-Islamic state. For some it was a key to prosperity and for yet others it was an excuse to indulge in immoral activities.'[69] A male JKLF ex-militant summed this up:

Once our local leadership decided to shun violence we backtracked. It was expected that negotiations would commence. But, it did not happen. Guns were taken up by many of our young boys who had their personal aims and not independence as an objective. They had no sense of social responsibility and no high aim. If someone wanted to marry a girl of his choice, he took a gun and married her by force. If somebody was unemployed he used gun for extortion. Foreign militants who had arrived on the pretext of helping us attain independence worsened the situation. It became a mess and caught in between were common Kashmiris who had borne the brunt of the violence from all sides and in the end gained nothing.[70]

Some respondents revealed that their disillusionment with the movement was partly a consequence of Pakistan's active involvement, as in later years the movement became more violent and extremist under its direct guidance. 'Pakistan played with our emotions for its own agenda; we had been fooled by Pakistan,' lamented Rabiya Sayeed, who lost three male members of her family to violence. One of her brothers was killed by foreign militants. 'He had threatened to leave the group after becoming disillusioned with Pakistan's role in our independence movement,' added Sayeed.[71]

The new class of militants used violence indiscriminately, directly targeting civilians merely on the basis of suspicion or refusal to comply with their demands. In August 2004, a 'divisional commander' of a militant group, Barkat Ali, kidnapped, Tahira Bano, the daughter of one Mohammed Din Sheikh of Doda district. She was taken to a remote place where the armed men forcibly conducted her marriage with Barkat Ali.[72] I came across numerous such narratives during the survey. In 1999 Hameeda was shot dead publicly by militants who alleged that she was a police informer. In 2001 militia went to Jameela's home and asked for shelter. Jameela's daughter, Parveena, recalled the horrifying story of her mother's murder when she refused to accommodate the militants. 'In the old days she had helped them. But times had changed. The militants were no longer our people (Kashmiri), fighting for us. So she refused. They barged into the house and shot her and took away all our savings,' she said.[73] Sameena echoed the same sentiment, 'the popular character of the *azadi* movement was later replaced by a struggle that was violent and extremist in character. The moral justness of the *azadi* struggle was abandoned. The guns that had initially been taken up for us were ultimately aimed at us. Eventually, the early enthusiasm that had attracted us faded away.'[74] Women suffered the consequences of this changed character of the movement in gender-specific ways. Rita Manchanda in her study of women in the Kashmir conflict notes:

> Overnight, it (the new phase of militancy) opened up for poor unemployed boys access to the leather jacket and boots culture and the power to extort, abduct and rape. A cook in a middle-class home picks up a gun and demands the daughter of the house in marriage. Middle-class mothers who had sheltered militants, even disguising them as sons-in-law discovered to their horror that is exactly what they wanted to be, by force if necessary.[75]

Abhishek Behl highlights how the militants indulged in sexual abuse:

> Every time that a militant hideout is busted in Jammu and Kashmir, along
> with routine arms and ammunition, two things that security forces recover
> without fail are packets of condoms and narcotics. The militants spreading
> violence in the name of *jihad*, particularly those from foreign countries, have
> been indulging in rape and molestation as well as consensual sex with the
> local girls....Foreign militants have many times sodomized boys and killed
> girls who became pregnant....Coercion and sexual abuse by the militants
> has become the bane of Kashmiri women living in terrorism-infested parts of
> Jammu and Kashmir.[76]

While documentation of human rights abuses by Indian security personnel
is available, it is difficult to obtain reliable information regarding atrocities by
militants. In an interview, Madam Bakhtawar, leader of the Muslim Khawateen
Markaz (MKM), a Kashmir based women's separatist organization, admitted
that women suffered at the hands of militants but because of fear no one
held militants publically responsible. According to her, it was much easier to
criticize the security forces.[77]

The atmosphere of fear and intimidation forced many Kashmiri Muslims
to escape from their native places to save lives and protect the 'honour'
of their women. Haseena, a displaced Kashmiri Muslim woman has been
living in a two-room rented accommodation in Jammu city along with her
family comprising husband, father-in-law, three daughters and one son since
2001. Her family fled in the middle of the night from Srinagar when she was
informed by militia to make preparations to welcome a bridegroom for her
then 16-year-old daughter the next day. She narrated:

> I had heard that the new breed of militants was cruel and did not care for the
> common people, but that day I experienced it personally. A militant leader
> of our locality who was not a native Kashmiri had sent the marriage proposal
> for my daughter through a group of armed men. I was handed a bundle of
> rupees (Indian currency) for the marriage that I was informed would take
> place the next day. I was shocked and did not know how to react. Their tone
> was threatening. In the afternoon I left with my daughters, informing our
> neighbours that we are going for shopping. My husband joined us later with
> my son at a designated place. My father-in-law was already in Jammu. We left
> our native place forever in a hired vehicle. My mother-in-law remained at home
> in Srinagar so that we could leave the valley safely. She had planned to leave
> for her brothers' house in a neighbouring village the next morning. Somehow
> the mercenaries sensed our plan. They killed my mother-in-law when she did

not tell them our whereabouts. We did not even go back for her funeral. We had fled Srinagar nearly empty-handed. Here we started our life from scratch. It is a difficult life with such a small house and no steady income, but at least we all are alive and my daughters are safe.[78]

The armed men who perpetrated heinous crimes had no qualms about dictating a code of conduct and dress for common people. They did not hesitate to dictate how the people of Kashmir should lead their lives. Women have borne the brunt of these processes in specific ways since most of the diktats impacted them directly. Extremist campaigns led to closure of cinema halls, video libraries and beauty parlours in all militancy-infested areas of J&K. Women were ordered to quit education and jobs and not to venture out of their homes without a male relative. Family planning, contraception and abortion were banned. At times such restrictions brought serious health complications for women – 23-year-old Zenab died in 1998 owing to a complicated pregnancy. 'The doctors told us that she could be saved if her pregnancy was terminated. We pleaded with the doctors to save her life but they refused to budge owing to the militant diktat. Both the unborn child and my daughter died,' revealed Marriam, Zenab's mother.[79] Some respondents recalled travelling to Jammu city for safeguarding their reproductive rights, which was both risky and costly. 'Only a few women could afford to travel to Jammu for operations (for sterilization or abortion). The cost factor was an obstacle. It was dangerous as well keeping in view the diktat of the militants,' said Haseena.[80] In the name of Islamic identity, attempts were made to impose cultural restrictions on women, particularly the veil. 'The popular character of the movement was overshadowed by a highly violent and extremist movement, forcing us to pull back. I did not understand how the *azadi* movement was linked to our veiling,' Ameena said.[81] Although the militant groups did not formally withdraw the veil decree, some factions gradually retracted from enforcing the edict. In 2001, extremist groups again attempted to force women to wear the veil at gun point but the campaign failed. In contrast to earlier times, some militant groups and the moderate faction of the Hurriyat Conference took a stand against coercing women to wear the veil perhaps in order to regain their support. But this move could not contain the damage already caused.

Endnotes

1. Prem Nath Bazaz, *Daughters of Vitasta: A History of Kashmiri Women from Early Times to the Present Day*, (Srinagar: Gulshan Publishers, 2003), 245.

2. *The Hindu*, (3 September 1990).
3. Personal Interview, 28 April 2011.
4. Personal Interview, 31 May 2011.
5. See, Seema Shekhawat, 'Engendering Armed Militancy in Kashmir: Women as Perpetrators of Violence', in *Understanding Collective Political Violence*, ed., Yvan Guichaoua, (Basingstoke: Palgrave Macmillan, 2012), 147–68. For an overview of women impacting conflict and vice versa in Kashmir see my following writings, 'Women in Kashmir Conflict: Victims, Survivors, Peace Builders or Perpetrators?', *ICFAI Journal of Governance and Public Policy*, 2, no. 4, (December 2007): 43–55 and 'Conflict and Women in Jammu and Kashmir', in *Conflict and Politics of Jammu & Kashmir*, eds, Avineet Prashar and Paawan Vivek, (Jammu: Saksham Books International, 2007), 124–42.
6. Personal Interview, 12 April 2011.
7. Personal Interview, 6 May 2011.
8. Personal Interview, 14 June 2011.
9. Personal Interview, 23 May 2011.
10. Personal Interview, 18 May 2011.
11. Personal Interview, 23 April 2011.
12. Personal Interview, 8 June 2011.
13. Personal Interview, 20 May 2012.
14. Personal Interview, 23 June 2011.
15. Personal Interview, 23 April 2011.
16. Kavita Suri, 'Veiled Women Show the Way to Terrorists in Kashmir', *The Statesman*, (20 October 2001).
17. Abhishek Behl, 'Terrorists Use Women against Indian Army in Kashmir', (31 July 2007). Available at http://www.merinews.com/article/terrorists-use-women-against-indian-army-in-kashmir/125810.shtml (accessed on 21 August 2011).
18. Pradeep Thakur, 'LeT Raises Women Jehadis in its Terror Network', *The Times of India*, (20 November 2006).
19. Personal Interview, 14 May 2011.
20. Personal Interview, 12 May 2011.
21. *The Tribune*, (16 December 2002).
22. *The Times of India*, (7 February 2003).
23. Personal Interview, 1 June 2011.
24. Personal Interview, 19 April 2011.
25. Manisha Sobhrajani, 'Women's Role in the post-1989 Insurgency', *Faultlines*, 19, (April 2008). Available at http://www.satp.org/satporgtp/publication/faultlines/volume19/Article3.htm (accessed on 23 November 2008).
26. Personal Interview, 24 May 2012.
27. Personal Interview, 29 May 2011.
28. Personal Interview, 30 April 2011.
29. Sudha Ramachandran, 'Helping Women Balance Family Life, Jihad', *Asia Times Online*, (15 September 2004). Available at http://www.atimes.com/atimes/Middle_East/FI15Ak02.html (accessed on 23 August 2011).

30. Swati Parashar, 'Gender, Jihad, and Jingoism: Women as Perpetrators, Planners, and Patrons of Militancy in Kashmir', *Studies in Conflict & Terrorism*, 34, no. 4, (2011): 308–09; and also see by the same author, 'Aatish-e-Chinar: In Kashmir Where Women Keep the Resistance Alive', in *Women, Gender, and Terrorism*, eds, Laura Sjoberg and Caron E. Gentry, (Athens: University of Georgia Press, 2011), 96–119.

31. Laura Sjoberg and Caron E. Gentry, *Mothers, Monsters, Whores: Women's Violence in Global Politics*, (London and New York: Zed Books, 2007), 13.

32. To cite a recent example, after the Amarnath Shrine Board agitation in 2008, Yasin Malik, a prominent leader of the JKLF, publicly honoured the mothers of men who had been killed. He conferred on them Shahid Maqbool Butt awards. Maqbool Butt was one of the first militants in the Kashmir valley. He was later captured by the Indian forces and eventually hanged.

33. Personal Interview, 13 May 2011.

34. Personal Interview, 9 June 2011.

35. Personal Interview, 29 May 2012.

36. Personal Interview, 20 April 2011.

37. Personal Interview, 23 April 2011.

38. Personal Interview, 26 May 2011.

39. Personal Interview, 3 June 2011.

40. Personal Interview, 8 June 2011.

41. Personal Interview, 22 May 2011.

42. Personal Interview, 26 May 2011.

43. Cynthia Enloe, *The Morning After: Sexual Politics at the End of the Cold War*, (Berkeley: University of California Press, 1993), 250.

44. Personal Interview, 1 June 2012.

45. Personal Interview, 23 February 2008.

46. Personal Interview, 4 May 2011.

47. Personal Interview, 23 February 2008.

48. Personal Interview, 5 June 2012.

49. Personal Interview, 24 February 2008.

50. Quoted in Sobhrajani, 'Women's Role in the post-1989 Insurgency'.

51. Mudassir Kuloo, 'Kashmir has 33,000 Conflict Widows', *The Kashmir Monitor*, (23 July 2012). For a detailed study of problems of these women see Afsana Rashid, *Widows and Half Widows: Saga of Extra-Judicial Arrests and Killings in Kashmir*, (Delhi: Pharos Media & Publishing, 2011).

52. See Kuloo, 'Kashmir has 33,000 Conflict Widows'.

53. Sukhmani Singh, 'Velvet Gloves, Iron Hands', *The Times of India*, (22 September 1990).

54. Personal Interview, 25 May 2012.

55. Personal Interview, 10 June 2011.

56. Personal Interview, 23 February 2008.

57. Personal Interview, 4 June 2011.

58. Personal Interview, 16 May 2011.

59. Personal Interview, 2 May 2011.
60. Personal Interview, 27 February 2008.
61. Personal Interview, 30 May 2011.
62. Personal Interview, 25 February 2008.
63. Personal Interview, 20 February 2008.
64. Personal Interview, 17 May 2011.
65. Personal Interview, 28 April 2011.
66. Personal Interview, 25 May 2012.
67. Personal Interview, 23 May 2012.
68. Personal Interview, 26 April 2011.
69. Personal Interview, 13 May 2011.
70. Personal Interview, 27 May 2011.
71. Personal Interview, 23 April 2011.
72. *The Asian Age*, (28 August 2004).
73. Personal Interview, 27 February 2008.
74. Personal Interview, 27 February 2008.
75. Rita Manchanda, 'Guns and Burqa: Women in the Kashmiri Conflict', in *Women, War and Peace in South Asia: Beyond Victimhood to Agency*, ed., Rita Manchanda, (New Delhi: Sage Publications, 2001), 80.
76. Abhishek Behl, 'Kashmir: Immorality and Drugs in the Garb of Jehad?'. Available at http://www.merinews.com/catFull.jsp?articleID=126033 (accessed on 23 October 2008).
77. Pamela Bhagat, 'Interviews', in *Speaking Peace: Women's Voices from Kashmir*, ed. Urvashi Butalia, (New Delhi: Kali for Women, 2002), 270.
78. Personal Interview, 22 April 2011.
79. Personal Interview, 17 June 2011.
80. Personal Interview, 20 June 2011.
81. Personal Interview, 19 May 2011.

Chapter 5

All-women Separatist Groups

In any discussion on the militant struggle in Kashmir, all-women groups acquire a key place not only in facilitating the struggle but also in widening its base in order to transform it into a mass movement. The members as well as leaders of these all-women groups did not resemble the stereotypical image of a combatant as they did not put on combat gear or carry weapons publicly. Most of them wore veils and did not participate in direct fights. The all-women organizations drew heavily from religion and tradition in justifying women's participation in violence. While these groups professed that they championed women's rights alongside fighting for *azadi*, the ground reality witnessed women's further suppression during conflict, which was aided by these very all-women organizations. In this sense Kashmir seems to be an apt example where women's organizations subjected women to a male-dominated order.

Dukhtaran-e-Millat

Under the leadership of Asiya Andrabi, Dukhtaran-e-Millat (DeM) was the most visible all-women militant and fundamentalist organization in J&K.[1] This organization, categorized by some analysts as a 'soft-terrorist outfit in the sense that it uses extra-legal means including threats to impose its doctrines, but has not taken up arms so far,'[2] was set-up by Andrabi in 1981 after she completed her graduation. The organizational structure of the group included a president, a general secretary, a committee comprising of two members from each district of the valley, a publicity secretary, district presidents and councils and cadres; the major public visibility however was that of Andrabi.[3] The exact numerical strength of DeM remains unclear but some of its members whom I met, claimed that their membership ran in thousands. This rough estimate can be contested in view of the difficulty in locating DeM members in most of the areas I visited.

The organization had a two-pronged strategy: to support militancy and thereby facilitate the merger of Kashmir with Pakistan and to reform society by prescribing and enforcing an extremist code of conduct among common people, especially women. The early objective was social and cultural 'reform' by convincing the Kashmiri women to lead lives in the Islamic way.[4] For nearly seven years Andrabi played the role of a 'social reformer' pressurizing the state government to make provisions for gender based segregation in public transport and other places through reservations for women. With the onset of militancy, Andrabi turned her energies towards sustaining the violent movement. Andrabi narrated her journey in detail to an interviewer:

> In 1981, I started a school. I gathered women – it was a door-to-door campaign. I wanted them to know the tenets of Islam and the status accorded to women. From one school, we went on to have units in six districts of the Valley. In 1987, we called upon women to come out and protest peacefully against the portrayal of women in the nude in advertising. But I also questioned the accession of Kashmir since I strongly believed that Kashmir is not a part of India. As a result, my office was raided and sealed. The police had an arrest warrant for me. I went underground for 21 days. When I resurfaced in 1988–89, the anti-India movement had started. We were among the first to join that movement, morally and politically. But as far as the militancy was concerned, we gave a call to our men that this was their job and not ours....We mobilised the people and told them of the problems faced by Kashmiris: how India has occupied it illegally and how we must treat India as an aggressor. This was something we had to educate the people about and this was the work our women were doing.[5]

Being born and brought up in an orthodox family, Andrabi was deeply ingrained in an extremist ideology. In an interview she revealed:

> The Holy Quran tells us that there is only one Lord. We believe in the oneness of Allah the Almighty. The whole universe has to be governed by the laws of Allah the Almighty. So, the strong belief of Dukhtaran-e-Millat is that we want the whole universe to be governed by the laws of Allah the Almighty. Based on Islamic teachings, we are fighting against India....I believe that there are just two nations – Muslims and non-Muslims....I believe in Islamic nationalism. So far as our ideology is concerned, Kashmir is not a part of India because united India was divided on the basis of religion. No one can deny this fact. We want our future too to be solved on the basis of religion.[6]

Andrabi's life simultaneously portrays the life of a feminist and that of a fundamentalist, which may appear contradictory. Andrabi retained her maiden name after her marriage to a militant, in contrast to the generally accepted tradition in Kashmir. A mother of two sons, she manages both her home and the organization almost single handedly. She believes in an individual identity for women and laments that 'only men go to the mosque, and women are told their only duty is to look after the children. In truth, Islam grants individuality to men and women. In heaven, before Allah, a woman too will be asked about her worldly deeds.'[7] At the same time she is always spotted in a veil that covers her from head to toe. She does not support the presence of women in the public space, but with a veil she is not hesitant to be photographed and interviewed. She is conversant in English and is in favour of education for women. However, the kind of education women may pursue is something that has been defined by DeM, which operates several religious educational institutions for women. The ideology followed by DeM is a strange mixture of progress and regression with malnutrition of the former and surfeit of the latter. The organization's endorsement of polygamy and its argument that the practice is for the benefit of women is an apt example in this context. Zaheena, a member of DeM, argued that

> If a man marries a raped or widowed woman he receives glory in this world and after death goes to heaven, where he is awarded the privilege of marrying beautiful virgin girls....Islam permits four marriages to a man...in Kashmir there are so many widows and orphans...in the name of Allah all men should marry as many times as possible to provide a better future to these women and their children.[8]

Andrabi publicly suggested to her husband that he should marry as many times as permitted by the religion, given the large number of widows in Kashmir.[9] Marriage is not forbidden for unmarried DeM members, but married members have to seek the 'permission' of their husbands to continue working for the organization.

Andrabi exemplifies a militant and extremist woman who perceives urgency of the movement not merely for independence from India but also for establishing an Islamic state of Kashmir within Pakistan. She contends, 'Kashmir rightly belongs to Pakistan. It has all the similarities: religion, culture, language....My mission is to drive India out of Kashmir, and then spread Islam throughout the state.'[10] Merger of Kashmir with Pakistan is DeM's immediate goal. In the long run, the organization believes that Muslims should not be divided into states and nations; rather they should all be a part of a united *Ummah.* Secularism does not form part of the DeM lexicon. A DeM member said:

> We believe that Kashmir rightly belongs to Muslims and therefore it should become part of Pakistan. In India Muslims will lose the purity of their religion

if they continue to live in a Hindu state. We share a common religion with our Muslim brethren in Pakistan. Religion should be the decisive factor for a state. In fact, we believe in a pan Islamic state where all Muslims can live together in a dignified Islamic way. Constructing a temple alongside a mosque or veiled Muslim women walking next to women of other religions wearing revealing clothes, all this is against Islam. Kashmiri pandits had to run from the valley because they were Hindus. They had a choice to convert to Islam but chose to flee. We will not change our ideology for any one. We just abide by the tenets of Islam. I am not authorized to speak on behalf of my organization, but members profess what I said.[11]

Andrabi spent most of the 1990s underground or in detention due to her visible role in violence. Her organization was banned in 1990 and she was incarcerated several times for her alleged links with Pakistan's intelligence agency, the Inter Services Intelligence (ISI), for disseminating anti-India propaganda and routing women to Pakistan for training in the handling of weapons and explosives.[12] On 28 August 2010, along with Masarat Alam Bhat, leader of the pro-Pakistan Muslim League, Andrabi was arrested on charges of spearheading violent anti-India protests that took place in Kashmir in mid-2010. There is no conclusive evidence to suggest that Andrabi or members of her organization were involved in direct fighting by taking up arms. Andrabi has been quoted as arguing that the Kashmiri women will resort to direct violence if men withdraw from the armed movement.[13] Most DeM members echo Andrabi's stand on the issue of women's involvement in combat operations. A DeM member argued, 'as long as men are fighting we have to be in support roles. Fighting is not a woman's primary role. It is for men to fight. But if all of them attain martyrdom or backtrack from the armed struggle, we will adorn ourselves in combat dresses.'[14] Some reports, however, suggest women's involvement in violent activities. In September 1995, DeM was held responsible for a bomb blast in Srinagar that killed Mushtaq Ali, a photographer from *Agence France Presse*, when he opened a letter bomb delivered by a veiled woman.[15] Notwithstanding claims and counter-claims about their direct involvement, Andrabi and her organization have no qualms about supporting militant violence. In an interview Andrabi was asked whether she supported the killing of Indian police and soldiers, and her response was, 'not only the police, but all the Indian politicians, too. We support that.' On being further questioned about her opinion on a call made by a Kashmiri militant group for the assassination of India's prime minister, she replied, 'we'd be very happy, *inshallah* (God willing).'[16] Similar violent sentiments were echoed by a DeM member who asserted that, 'violence against all Indian soldiers, administrators and politicians is justified. India is an obstacle in the way of the Islamization of Kashmir and whosoever represents India must be eliminated. They have caused so much pain to us. All of them deserve to be killed.'[17]

The organization played a crucial role in indoctrinating women into accepting rigours of the armed struggle. Mobilization was one of the major tasks that DeM performed aggressively with great success. Andrabi used her oratory skills at funerals of killed militants to instil courage and solidarity among those in attendance. Why and how women should support militancy were explained by the DeM members to women. Sameera recollected:

> A member of DeM advised us that we should raise a hue and cry during cordon and search operations by security personnel. We should attack them with household things. If the security forces respond with violence they will be criticized everywhere and we will gain the sympathy of the world. Even if they kill us, we will become martyrs. It will be a win-win situation for us. She also gave us other tips on how we can aid militancy.[18]

The organization planned scores of protest demonstrations against the atrocities and human rights violations by Indian security forces. There were all-women action squads known as *chapamaar* (raid) teams[19] to aid militant operations. One member of DeM claimed to have collected donations to support rebellious activities.[20]

The organization, which claimed to aid Kashmiri women to fight for their Islamic rights, used religion to push women to a more regressive order by vigorously campaigning for the implementation of various fundamentalist diktats such as the veil. DeM played a crucial role in the veiling drive initiated by some militant groups. Andrabi contended that the veil campaign was the 'beginning of a comprehensive social reform movement based on true Islamic thought.'[21] DeM members aggressively executed this diktat by using both ideological and coercive methods. Nazia, a DeM member, said:

> We just did our duty. Veil is an integral part of the Islamic dress code for women. It is mentioned in our holy book that the chastity of a woman is the most precious thing and it should be protected. If you put a precious thing in open, there is a possibility of theft. Similarly if sanctity of women is not kept under cover she may be targeted. Veil is to save women from prying eyes so what is wrong in remaining covered? Since many women do not know what is good and bad for them we had to guide them. Sometimes you have to punish the non-adherents to teach them a lesson and to set a precedent for others. Veil is for betterment of women. I do not understand why it has been opposed so much.[22]

Veil was unequivocally supported by all members and ex-members of DeM with whom I interacted. Raheema, an ex-member of DeM who had to leave the organization due to objections from her husband, questioned, 'who do you think will be more insecure in public, a woman wearing a veil or one wearing a skirt?'[23] Veil has been interpreted as an instrument of empowerment and not regression. Jenab explained, 'women had to conform to the Islamic dress code to be safe. Veiling does not mean a woman is being confined to home. It is a facilitator, not an obstructer.'[24] Was the veil merely for the 'facilitation' or did it have a utility beyond this proclaimed advantage?

Veil Unveiled

In conflict situations, women are forced to embrace markers of identity unique to the group. Women who do not conform to this ideology become vulnerable to attacks or threats from extremist elements in their own group. In Kashmir, veiling not only aimed at showcasing a distinct identity but also aiding militancy. It was a double-edged effective tool for strategic as well as socio-cultural purposes. Despite being an Islamic society, Kashmir had been liberal towards women. The Islam traditionally practiced in the region was liberal Sufi Islam, quite different from the radical variety. Veil was not an accepted custom of Kashmiri Muslim society. This practice came to Kashmir in the 14th century during Afghan rule. Even then, only upper class Muslim women wore the veil to disclose their high class status. The active participation of women from the lower strata of the society in economic activities might provide a plausible explanation for such a limited use of the veil. With the onset of militancy extremist armed groups projected the veil as an important marker of the identity of Kashmiri women. Various militant organizations repeatedly attempted to impose the veil and Kashmiri women were advised to adhere to completely covering their bodies and faces, except eyes, through advertisements such as posters on walls of buildings and distribution of pamphlets in schools, colleges and other public places. Door-to-door campaigns were launched by DeM to make women appreciate the importance of the veil. This persuasion was accompanied by intimidation as women were warned of dire consequences for defiance. On 13 June 1990 *Daily Aftab*, a Srinagar-based newspaper, carried a statement warning against a lax attitude on the veil. Most of the cases related to attacks by armed men to impose the veil or the Islamic dress code have gone unreported. Nevertheless, there are documented cases of splashing of coloured water and acid on the clothes and faces of women who refused to conform. Cases of firing on the leg and even killing were reported for non-compliance. For instance, on 22 March 1999 two young Kashmiri girls were shot in their legs for wearing trousers.

On 3 August 2001 armed men critically injured the daughter of Habib Dar of Nowgam accusing her of defying the diktat. Lashkar-e-Jabbar, an extremist militant group, in August 2001 claimed responsibility for throwing acid on two women who were not wearing the veil.[25] Women did not accept the veil as a symbol of Kashmiri identity. They raised their voices against this diktat by writing emotive letters to the militants. For instance, an open letter by one Sara Bano was published in a local newspaper, *Daily Alsafa*, on 9 June 1990. The following is the translated extract of the letter:

> It is unfortunate that this movement has gone beyond its legitimate purpose.... Burqa is a symbol which makes the woman feel inferior. How can a religion which gives equal status to men and women compel the woman to feel inferior?...This move to impose burqa is madness....My brothers, you are compelling me to wear the burqa on the threat of death, you want me to become faceless, you are proving that Islam has spread on the strength of the sword. If I am actually murdered then I will name these Islamic fanatics as my murderers. If I am made a target of acid and poisonous colour in the name of Islam I will give up this kind of Islam and become a Christian but I will never accept to become a black demon...and live with sense of inferiority.[26]

Such efforts notwithstanding, women were forced to follow this extremist ideology which, in the words of Fareeda Sayeed, 'had nothing to do with the *azadi* struggle'.[27]

The purpose of imposing the veil might not be concluded as purely a 'social reform' agenda. It had logistic considerations in aiding militancy. Veiling could be best described as a two-pronged strategy whereby the militia could carry out guerrilla warfare with ease and impose extremism in Kashmir. As developments during the separatist movement unfolded, the veil became a facilitator for militant activities since it provided a cover to hide weapons and to carry out clandestine operations.[28] It provided anonymity to veiled persons (women and men) to execute the assigned tasks successfully. Due to the conservative patriarchal nature of Kashmiri society, Indian security forces largely shied away from frisking veiled women as this action might be construed as an assault against the tradition of Kashmiri society, thus further protracting the conflict. An Indian army official said:

> Being less suspicious and less searched, women were ideal messengers, couriers and smugglers for militants. They were used by militants to transport their weapons and money, as women were not searched thoroughly or sometimes they were not frisked at all. We did not even thoroughly search the vehicles carrying women. On many occasions, lack of female security personnel helped the veiled women to sneak out militants.[29]

A retired army officer who served in J&K for nearly six years in the early 1990s claimed that militants extensively and effectively used the veil to facilitate their activities:

> The veil provided anonymity to the militants to move from one place to another, to transport weapons, money, etc. This tactic was used effectively and frequently. It was a nightmare to deal with veiled persons. We used to watch helplessly when a group of veiled persons would pass from our checking post and there was no lady officer to frisk them. Without lifting the veil it was not possible to identify the person or know what she/he was carrying. Sometimes we knew that out of five veiled individuals crossing our post at least one was a male militant but we could not verify this since we did not have the orders. There could have been a backlash in an already volatile situation. At times officers lifted the veil and we did catch some armed men but the mass protests that followed were intimidating.[30]

The veil provided anonymity to women actors as it made it difficult for security forces to identify active women supporters of the movement. Carla J. Cunningham points out that in Kashmir 'women's roles as couriers have been improved by a "requirement" to wear a burqa'.[31] Yasmeen gave details of her 'veiled' activities:

> Veil is important in Islam but in Kashmir it was not an integral part of the culture till the movement for independence started. Veil was more a part of the strategy for spearheading the movement. We carried arms and ammunition, money and all other required items for our brothers in their hideouts. I facilitated the movement of two brothers from one place to another in the garb of *burqas*. There were seven women and two men and we all had to pass two checkposts before reaching the destination. We were all carrying guns hidden in our *burqas*. Both the checkposts had no lady security personnel. While passing the first checkpost a security official all of a sudden lifted my veil. Probably he had become suspicious. But we were prepared. We all started shouting at the supposed attempt by a security person to outrage the modesty of a Kashmiri woman. The strategy worked and we crossed the post without any further checking. On the second post the security official asked where we were going. His question was directed to a veiled militant. I immediately intervened telling the officer that the woman was deaf. I then informed the officer that we were visiting the house of an acquaintance whose husband had died of a sudden illness. The veil also helped women to remain faceless so most of the active supporters of militancy could never be detected.[32]

The veil aided the process of imparting religious extremism to Kashmiris who had espoused liberal Islam. In this pursuit entertainment and beautification were pronounced un-Islamic. Extremist groups such as DeM were involved in targeting and ransacking internet cafes, restaurants and hotels for ostensibly corrupting young Muslim minds. Moral policing, under the leadership of Andrabi, involved targeting gift shops particularly on Valentine's Day. A news report summed up these activities of this extremist woman, 'one has heard stories about her (Andrabi) spraying paint on women who do not wear the burkha (veil). She is known to have sent burkha-clad activists to burn Valentine's Day cards and posters, raid liquor shops, and restaurants boasting special seating arrangement for couples'.[33] In fact this ban on forms of entertainment was cited as a major reason by a Kashmir university professor for the unprecedented visibility of young boys in the 2010 anti-government agitation.[34] On condition of anonymity, he said:

> In Kashmir our young boys have very few means of entertainment. If there are no theatres to watch recent movies, no alcohol to consume, no internet to connect with the outside world, no place to dine with a person of the opposite sex, then what can be expected? Many of the stone pelters were paid but there were many others who pelted stones for fun. This way they wanted to vent their frustration of leading an abnormal life in a violent place. Militants do not want young Kashmiris to get involved in the activities that may divert their attention from the anti-India struggle. That is why scores of dos and dont's exist. Interestingly the militants have a different code of conduct for themselves. How else do you explain that militants enjoy all comforts and luxuries in remote forests but issue diktats prohibiting common Kashmiris to even lead an ordinary, relaxed life?[35]

Though most of the extremists' diktats had been opposed, the adverse impact was noticeable all over the valley. A shift from the traditional liberal values of Sufi Islam towards a radical ideology was starkly evident. Most women wore the veil or at least covered their heads. Many did not venture out of their homes unaccompanied. The draconian diktats were categorized as 'attempts to Talibanize Kashmir'[36] by a young respondent who was quite eager to find out the fashion trends followed by college girls in Mumbai, the city where I resided then. The blame for this Talibanization drive has to be shared by DeM for it 'locates women's identity within a fundamentalist, Islamist discourse in which women are relegated to the private sphere'.[37]

Muslim Khawateen Markaz

The Muslim Khawateen Markaz (MKM) which was set-up in 1989 attracted scores of Muslim women including professionals such as doctors and lawyers. This group, initially involved in charity work, later started working in tandem with militants. It advocated independence of Kashmir from both India and Pakistan. Nazia, a MKM member said, 'we are in favour of an independent Kashmir. Our Kashmir has been occupied by both India and Pakistan. We have to fight both these countries.'[38] Despite being a religious organization, MKM was comparatively less fundamentalist than DeM. It largely abstained from moral policing, particularly in terms of imposition of the veil. For MKM, the veil implies, *jism pe libas is purdah* (clothing which does not reveal the contours of the body and a cloth which will cover the hair [is a veil]).[39]

Though DeM and MKM had ideological differences, both played a crucial role in the continuation of militant violence and enlisting women's support. MKM members covertly carried out an array of auxiliary tasks akin to their DeM counterparts. The group organized many anti-India demonstrations. In the initial days of the militancy it was a common sight to see veiled MKM members acting as guards, alerting militants about the movements of security forces and helping them escape by blocking the paths of security forces.[40] The members took care of injured militants as well. A member of MKM revealed that, Shaikh Hamid, a JKLF leader, sustained injuries during a militant operation and was rushed to hospital by women from her organization. On being discharged he was looked after discreetly in the home of a MKM affiliate.[41] One of the MKM members, Anjum Zamrooda Habib, was detained and imprisoned by Indian security forces on the charge of acting as a courier for transferring money to armed groups. MKM activist Yasmeen Raja was dismissed from her government job following her anti-India activities and was also detained on several occasions. At present, MKM is a member of the APHC and its activities are largely restricted to occasionally raising the issue of human rights violations by Indian security forces.

Another separatist group in Kashmir headed by a woman named Farida Dar, commonly known as Farida *bahenji* (sister), is the Jammu and Kashmir Mass Movement. Unlike DeM and MKM, this organization's membership is not restricted only to women. Dar has been vocal in advocating for Kashmir's independence from India and acknowledges the 'support' of Pakistan in this context. She has been involved in coordinating activities between various militant groups and in the transfer of funds for militant operations. Dar has denied her role in violence and has claimed that she was innocent,[42] but her involvement in militant violence was established when she was accused of being involved in a series of bomb blasts in Delhi in 1996 which killed 13 people and injured 38.[43] In 2010 the court convicted and awarded her four years imprisonment.

All-women Wings

The HM's women wing, following in the footsteps of its parent organization, has professed a conservative attitude towards women. The group opposed political activism by women though it approved 'social activism' to aid militancy. It held the view that women should generally refrain from actively getting involved in public life and that a leadership role for them was unacceptable. The group was projected as a humanitarian wing with the assigned task of aiding the families of slain militants. Evidently the faction had been set-up primarily to provide logistic support as and when required by the HM's male leadership.[44] In January 2011, three persons, including two women, were arrested for being ground workers for HM. In a raid on a hideout, Shamina Begum, the 30-year-old wife of a top HM militant Gulam Qadir Malik, was arrested in Ramban district for acting as a 'courier, guide and informant' for militants.[45] In another incident, a HM module was busted in Doda district leading to the arrest of one man and one woman.[46]

The LeT too set-up its own women wing called the Dukhtaran-e-Toiba. Reports suggest that nearly 20 girls were trained by LeT in Pakistan controlled Kashmir to launch this division. Intercepts by Indian intelligence agencies revealed that the new front was primarily involved in mobilizing women.[47] Earlier in 2007, an Indian intelligence report revealed that LeT had a full-fledged training camp for women, situated 6 km from Muridke between Lahore and Rawalpindi in Pakistan. The camp, headed by a female Pakistani citizen, was equipped with the required infrastructure to provide rigorous training to cadres. As per the report, women were imparted 21-day training in handling arms and ammunition, in addition to extremist indoctrination.[48] The presence of women in LeT came to the public domain in September 2006 when 20-year-old Khalida Akhtar was arrested in Srinagar. This young woman reportedly developed links with militants in 2002 and was arrested under the Public Safety Act. She was released a few months later and was again detained in 2004. Following her release in 2005, Akhtar went to Pakistan controlled Kashmir in April 2006 for arms training. She was trained in the use of sophisticated weapons including pen pistols, cyanide pistols and toy grenades. Her interrogation revealed that besides arms training, women were taught to 'honey trap' officials from Indian security forces to monitor troop movement so that LeT could gain vantage positions during encounters.[49] Akhtar's assignment was to befriend officials of the Indian security forces and kill them. She was arrested while attempting to accomplish this task. Akhtar befriended an Indian army officer, of colonel rank. Following a series of interactions with him Akhtar called him at Iqbal Park in Srinagar reportedly to kill him with the help of her male accomplices Zahir Mansoor and Rizwan, LeT's area commanders. Since the security forces kept a close watch on the activities of the colonel, they managed to arrest Akhtar before the plan could be executed, though her associates escaped.[50]

During the interrogation of 23-year-old Asiya Malik, arrested by Indian security personnel in the Sunderbani sector of Rajouri district when she entered J&K by crossing the LoC in 2008, it was revealed that several militant groups operating from Pakistan controlled Kashmir were training women to aid combat operations. She disclosed that women, besides other things, were trained to infiltrate into J&K by dodging the Indian security forces guarding the border. During this infiltration they smuggled secret documents and small arms. Women were prepared to act as spies and messengers. They were skilled to provide logistical support to armed male cadres and even execute violent activities.[51] In a video footage shown on Indian news channels in January 2009 Malik revealed that hundreds of women were trained in camps in Bhimber and Kotli areas in Pakistan controlled Kashmir. 'I have seen the Mujahideen training camps. Women are also being trained there. Right now, there are about 700 women receiving arms training in different militant camps run by Pakistani Intelligence Agency ISI. These women are also provided with terror literature and taught how to use small arms like guns and grenades,' she said.[52]

I interacted with three women who claimed that they had received arms training in Pakistan but insisted that it was for self-defence. All the respondents took the stand that women had not been involved in direct combat operations though some, such as Hameeda, argued that though women did not take up arms to fight with Indian security personnel it did not imply that they were not trained in handling arms.

> We received training in handling guns and grenades. This was essential for responding in an emergency situation. There were groups of women in every locality who had guns at their disposal to confront any eventuality. I was part of one such group and we would have used guns if a need had arisen, Hameeda said.[53]

In her work Swati Parashar cites a Kashmiri woman, who echoed Hameeda:

> I do not want to glorify the women by saying that we held guns and all that because this will create trouble for the women folk, for this reason only I do not want to say anything about women holding guns. Otherwise, I used to have a gun under my bed; there is nothing great about it. At that time every locality used to have 2 to 3 militant (women), they used to have guns, and everyone used to know that so, it is an open secret.[54]

Rita Manchanda in her work on women in Kashmir points out how many women were implicated in such cases due to familial associations such as being the wife or sister of a militant. She cites the case of Mehbooba who was arrested in 1992 from Hyderpora in Srinagar for crossing over to Pakistan in November 1989 for arms training. Mehbooba was later released, but her husband, a prominent militant leader claimed that her arrest was aimed at pressuring him to surrender.[55] This claim might have grains of truth, but the increasing number of reports of women receiving arms training cannot be dismissed.

Till the October 2005 Avantipura explosion on the Srinagar–Jammu National Highway, there was no documented case of the direct involvement of women in militant activities as suicide bombers. It has been contended that the 22-year-old Yasmeena Akhtar killed in the explosion was a JeM suicide bomber. JeM claimed that she was the wife of one of its cadres and a member of the Banaat-e-Ayesha, its women wing. Though investigations have not conclusively established whether Akhtar was a suicide bomber or was transporting explosives that exploded on the way, Basharat Peer in his article argues that her involvement could be beyond the role of being a mere carrier:

> I walked to the police and paramilitary HQ (head quarter), ringed with razor wire and heavily guarded. Some officers believe their camp was Yasmeena's target and the explosives went off accidentally. At the blast site they had found three live hand grenades and pieces of a torn combat pouch – a belt with big pockets, that's tied around the chest. 'A person wearing a body belt tends to itch and adjust it frequently,' said Mumtaz Ahmad, a police superintendent, by way of explanation.... At the district court in Pulwama, 20 miles away, a clerk showed me the records of the investigation and pictures of the explosion. The file describes Yasmeena as a girl who 'wore explosives on her body for the purpose of a terrorist suicide attack aimed at hurting the security forces and the police. She killed herself when the explosives went off accidentally near the Avantipura police headquarters.'[56]

Most respondents argued that Akhtar was not a suicide bomber but merely a courier of the explosives that detonated accidentally. There is strong reason to accept this widely held view. Unlike in Sri Lanka, Chechnya and Palestine the militia in Kashmir did not generally resort to suicide bombing as an optimal strategy against security personnel. Incidents of suicide bombers walking to a camp or a crowded place with bombs strapped on their bodies and then exploding themselves are not common in Kashmir. Armed groups more frequently followed the strategy of *fidayeen* (those willing to sacrifice themselves in the name of god) attacks whereby a group or a single militant challenged state security personnel by engaging with them in a fight with guns, explosives and grenades from hideouts. The fight could go on for few hours to even a few days. The *fidayeen* arrived fully equipped with their backpacks and pockets loaded with arms, ammunition, dry fruits and water. If there was a possibility of escape after causing the intended damage, they had prior instructions to flee. Most of the times *fidayeen* did not kill themselves, they were shot and killed by state forces. Keeping in view this widely practised strategy of the militia in Kashmir, it is unlikely that Akhtar was a suicide bomber. Scores of *fidayeen* attacks have taken place in J&K, but not even once has the participation of women been established. One reason behind the non-participation of women in *fidayeen* attacks can be attributed to a particular strategy wherein male militants usually disguised themselves as security personnel by wearing police uniforms to access the target without difficulty. Nonetheless, concluding that armed groups in Kashmir will not resort to suicide bombing may amount to conceptual dogmatism.

Absence of Female Mujahideen

Training in handling arms may not necessarily transform women into active actors in direct combat. Though women's direct participation in violence has assumed global proportions with women being seen in combat uniforms, Kashmir's case does not fully subscribe to this emerging global trend. In Kashmir, the presence of women and their contribution to the militant cause have of late been recognized by scholars and have also been covered by the media. There may have been reports of women's involvement in activities such as planting bombs and transporting funds and arms, but these sparse reports do not lead to any generalization about women's role in direct combat. While in conflict situations as in Sri Lanka and Nepal women played a direct role, the story of Kashmiri women may not reveal much in this context. The Kashmir conflict has not produced a female *mujahid.* Why did Kashmiri women remain confined to support activities? Many of the respondents like Tahmina found the question perplexing, who said,

> I do not know how to answer this question. I have never thought about it. Most of the questions that you asked until now I could respond to as they pertained to the details of my activities but this question is about an activity I did not do. Let me think about it for a while.[57]

A few minutes later she responded, 'I do not know.'[58] Those who responded offered interesting answers to women's non-involvement in direct action. Some argued that the absence of women fighters was a well-drawn out strategy for facilitating the continuation of the armed movement. They asserted that if a situation arises where all Kashmiri men are dead fighting for independence, women would take up arms to continue the struggle; reinforcing the all-pervasive patriarchal approach of 'first men and then women' wherein women had to remain passive till men's power wore thin. Jaheen contended:

> Challenging a mighty state like India is not an easy task. A well-calculated strategy had to be drawn so that we Kashmiris could achieve our objective. Taking up arms means we could be killed anytime. Men took the charge. They fought and we helped. I think our leaders had planned that if there was a need in view of the death of a majority of the men, women would join the fight. After that it would have become a do or die situation. Until that time women had to wait and watch and perform auxiliary tasks.[59]

Safeena added:

> There has been no dearth of male militants since the onset of militancy till date. Our movement was initially indigenous and we had thought that a time will soon come when all men will be killed and we will have to take up arms. We were prepared for this. With the arrival of foreign militants the whole scenario changed. I think now we have more militants than required. There is a mushroom growth of training camps in Pakistan which are producing militants *en masse*, just like Chinese products.[60]

More convincing are two inter-related arguments focusing on the socio-religious aspect. Radical female leaders of Kashmir such as Andrabi believe that Islam does not allow women to be combatants, especially suicide bombers. 'It is against the dignity of a Muslim woman that the parts of her body be strewn in a public place. If a combatant or a suicide bomber is a woman, her dead body is bound to fall or be scattered in a place full of men,' said Andrabi in an interview where she supported suicide bombing by men[61] thus exemplifying a gender based distinction in the name of religion. Khalida reiterated Andrabi's opinion, 'for women *jihad* (holy war) does not mean fighting directly with men or getting killed. A woman can be called *jihadi* (holy warrior) when she performs all possible tasks to help *jihadi* men to fight against *kafirs* (non-believers) and *zalims* (dictators) and at the same time look after her family.'[62] This religion based justification is made more credible by emphasizing on socio-cultural imperatives. Universally in all patriarchal societies women's primary role is to look after their families and run the households. These societal values that women should confine themselves to boundaries of the home nurturing children and managing the family, may limit their involvement in conflicts. Razia, whose husband was in detention for nearly seven years and later went missing with no trace in 2001, argued:

> Taking up arms is not the only way to uphold a cause. If everyone in a community takes up arms, the socio-cultural set-up may collapse. I stood with my militant husband but behind me were my five children, all below the age of twelve. I had to take care of them. In all situations a woman has certain prescribed roles the foremost being that of a mother. No woman can shun family responsibilities howsoever she may be devoted to a cause.[63]

The killing of men-folk, unlike in Sri Lanka and Nepal, instead of spurring direct participation worked as a discouragement for many women. Loss of family earners meant an additional burden to cater to the needs of the family. Rabina, widow of a JKLF cadre, argued,

> We stretched our roles as mothers, sisters and daughters for the struggle but we did not want to become fighters. We had to take care of our families in the absence of men who were either hiding or who got killed. How could I pick up a gun when I know nobody is there to look after my three children?'[64]

In masculinized violent struggles women may be deemed less competent to fight. This assumption reverberated during scores of informal interactions with male ex-militants in Kashmir. The primary reason according to them which led to the absence of women fighters was because the biological build up of women made them 'unfit to face the austere life of a combatant'. According to a male ex-militant,

> Fighters have to live in mountain terrains and under difficult conditions, at times without food and shelter. It is not easy for a woman to lead such a life. In fact, women's presence would have made our tasks difficult. They are good in support activities but fighting is the job of men, not women.[65]

Many of the female respondents conceded this viewpoint. Shazia reasoned:

> It is a fact that women are not physically fit to fight. Combatants do not have a definite lifestyle and daily routine. Their life is very uncertain. They have to perform difficult tasks. They may have to jump from one roof to another while escaping from security personnel. They have to live in caves and hide in bushes for days together. All these hardships a woman cannot endure. God has made women physically weak and nobody can deny this. Keeping in view this weakness we have to think what we can do and what we cannot and should not do.[66]

The religioarchy (mixture of religion and patriarchy), thus, largely discouraged or prevented Kashmiri women to come out in the open and join their men-folk in a direct fight against the Indian state.

Women played an indirect, albeit, crucial role in the conflict in Kashmir and all-women groups facilitated categorical support to militia activities. Beyond this, these groups have failed to leave an indelible mark on Kashmiri society. These groups did not have gender as their core concern as they were governed by a patriarchal order and extremist ideology. They either supported extremist edicts such as the veil or remained silent. None of the groups emerged as true representatives of Kashmiri women, and none of them championed women's rights. In fact, they did not operate independently in a real sense. While DeM and MKM have been co-opted by male dominated separatist politics, others operate under the shadow of their parent militant groups. In the absence of an organized voice for gender equality a dismal scenario has emerged wherein women who had been the face of militancy have been denied the opportunity to become the face of peace. Women's groups succeeded to a large extent in bringing women to the fold of militancy but failed abysmally to negotiate their due space in the peace process.

Endnotes

1. Shiraz Sidhva, 'Dukhtaran-e-Millat: Profile of a Militant Fundamentalist Women's Organisation', in *Against All Odds: Essays on Women, Religion and Development from India and Pakistan*, eds, Kamla Bhasin, Ritu Menon and Nigat Said Khan, (New Delhi: Kali for Women, 1994), 123–31.
2. 'Profile: Dukhtaran-i-Millat,' South Asia Terrorism Portal. Available at http://www.satp.org/satporgtp/countries/india/states/jandk/terrorist_outfits/dukhtaran.htm (accessed on 23 November 2011).
3. Personal Interview, 11 May 2011.
4. Barry Bearak, 'Behind the Veil, a Muslim Feminist', *The New York Times*, (26 August 2000).
5. Aditi Bhaduri, 'Inshallah, Kashmir Will Become Part of Pakistan: Interview, Asiya Andrabi', *Outlook*, (14 August 2006). Available at http://www.outlookindia.com/article.aspx?232194 (accessed on 17 March 2012).
6. Bhaduri, 'Inshallah, Kashmir Will Become Part of Pakistan'.
7. Quoted in Bearak, 'Behind the Veil, a Muslim Feminist'.
8. Personal Interview, 5 June 2011.
9. M. Mazharul Haque, 'Asiya Andrabi: Warrior in Veil', *The Milli Gazette*. Available at http://www.milligazette.com/Archives/01092002/0109200264.htm (accessed on 12 October 2011).
10. Quoted in Manisha Sobhrajani, 'Women's Role in the post-1989 Insurgency', *Faultlines*, 19, (April 2008). Available at http://www.satp.org/satporgtp/publication/faultlines/volume19/Article3.htm (accessed on 23 November 2008).

11. Personal Interview, 29 May 2012.

12. *The Times of India,* (15 February 1993). See, Mohan Lal Koul, *Kashmir: Wail of a Valley,* (New Delhi: Gyan Sagar Publications, 1999).

13. 'Women's Testimonies from Kashmir: "The Green of the Valley is Khaki", Women's Initiative 1994', Urvashi Butalia, *Speaking Peace: Women's Voices From Kashmir,* (New Delhi: Kali for Women, 2000), 87.

14. Personal Interview, 12 May 2011.

15. 'Profile: Dukhtaran-e-Millat'.

16. Quoted in Andrew Whitehead, 'Daughter of Faith Who Will Fight the Holy War for Ever', *The Guardian,* (23 April 2001).

17. Personal Interview, 25 April 2011.

18. Personal Interview, 6 June 2011.

19. 'Women's Testimonies from Kashmir', 86.

20. Personal Interview, 26 May 2011.

21. Haque, 'Asiya Andrabi: Warrior in Veil'.

22. Personal Interview, 29 April 2011.

23. Personal Interview, 23 April 2011.

24. Personal Interview, 31 May 2011.

25. On 7 August 2001 Lashkar-e-Jabbar militants threw acid on the faces of two female teachers of Nagbal Government High School, Srinagar, while they were returning from a school picnic. The women, who were accused of not adhering to the Islamic dress code issued by this extremist militant group, suffered injuries on their faces and necks.

26. Quoted in Urvashi Butalia, ed. *Speaking Peace: Women's Voices from Kashmir,* (New Delhi: Kali for Women, 2002), 80.

27. Personal Interview, 30 April 2011.

28. Sidhva, 'Dukhtaran-e-Millat: Profile of a Militant Fundamentalist Women's Organisation', 128. Also see Ashima Kaul Bhatia, 'Behind the Veil', *The Times of India,* (28 August 2001).

29. Personal Interview, 28 August 2007.

30. Personal Interview, 19 May 2011.

31. Carla J. Cunningham, 'Cross-Regional Trends in Female Terrorism', *Studies in Conflict and Terrorism,* 26, no. 3, (May 2003): 181.

32. Personal Interview, 30 April 2011.

33. Bhaduri, 'Inshallah, Kashmir Will Become Part of Pakistan'.

34. The protest reminded of the early days of militancy with thousands of people on the streets. It was mainly to oppose the state government's decision to allot land in the Kashmir valley for constructing shelters for the annual Amaranth pilgrimage that is carried out by Hindus. I heard slogans not only against the Shrine Board and the J&K government but also against the Indian state from my hotel located in the heart of Srinagar. Separatist leaders proclaimed that the decision was part of a conspiracy to alter the demography by settling Hindus in Muslim dominated Kashmir valley region.

35. Personal Interview, 23 June 2011.

36. Personal Interview, 18 May 2011.

37. Swati Parashar, 'Feminist International Relations and Women Militants: Case Studies from Sri Lanka and Kashmir', *Cambridge Review of International Affairs*, 22, no. 2, (2009): 247.

38. Personal Interview, 12 June 2011.

39. 'Women's Testimonies from Kashmir', 86.

40. Harinder Baweja, 'Challenge of the Veil', *India Today*, 15 September 1991.

41. Personal Interview, 18 May 2011.

42. Sudha Ramachandran, 'Arms and the Women', *Deccan Herald*, (25 February 2001).

43. *The Hindu*, (13 April 2001).

44. Muzamil Jaleel, 'Spawning Militancy: The Rise of Hizbul', *Indian Express*, (22 May 2003).

45. *Daily News and Analysis*, (23 January 2011).

46. *Daily News and Analysis*.

47. *The Hindu*, (4 January 2012).

48. Pradeep Thakur, 'LET Training Women Militants', *The Times of India*, (6 April 2007).

49. *The Times of India*, (20 November 2006). Also see Mohd. Sadiq, 'Militants Misusing Kashmiri Women', (22 September 2006). Available at www.jammu-kashmir.com/insights/insight20060922a.html (accessed on 4 October 2011).

50. *The Times of India*, (20 November 2006).

51. 'Militant Training Camps in PoK Recruit Women to Infiltrate J&K: "Spy"'. Available at http://news.webindia123.com/news/Articles/India/20081114/1104857.html (accessed on 24 December 2008).

52. *The Times of India*, (14 January 2009).

53. Personal Interview, 18 June 2011.

54. Swati Parashar, 'Gender, Jihad, and Jingoism: Women as Perpetrators, Planners, and Patrons of Militancy in Kashmir', *Studies in Conflict & Terrorism*, 34, no. 4, (2011): 298.

55. Rita Manchanda, 'Guns and Burqa: Women in the Kashmiri Conflict', in *Women, War and Peace in South Asia: Beyond Victimhood to Agency*, ed., Rita Manchanda, (New Delhi: Sage Publications, 2001), 78.

56. Basharat Peer, 'The bride with a bomb', *The Guardian*, (5 August 2006) and *The Indian Express*, (14 October 2005).

57. Personal Interview, 14 June 2011.

58. Ibid.

59. Personal Interview, 20 June 2011.

60. Ibid.

61. Peer, 'The Bride with a Bomb'.

62. Personal Interview, 21 May 2011.

63. Personal Interview, 14 May 2011.

64. Personal Interview, 29 April 2011.

65. Personal Interview, 27 May 2011.

66. Personal Interview, 25 May 2012.

Chapter 6

Making Peace Sans Gender

In the 1990s, geo-political changes brought about by the end of the Cold War altered the dynamics of international relations with implications for conflicts around the world. The rising profile of globalization brought a new perspective on transition in violence infested regions. Many conventional armed disputes became manageable due to globalization and increasing acceptance of peaceful means for conflict resolution.[1] The major players involved in the complex Kashmir conflict, India and Pakistan, were influenced by these developments. The peace process gathered momentum with the National Democratic Alliance (NDA) coming to power in New Delhi in 1998. The NDA government furthered peace efforts, with the bus journey from New Delhi to Lahore in 1999 with Indian Prime Minister Atal Bihari Vajpayee on board. The process of negotiations halted due to the Kargil war in 1999. After a gap of about four years, in October 2003, India proposed a series of confidence building measures aimed at improving communications by road, rail and sea with Pakistan. On 26 November in the same year, it announced a ceasefire on the Indo-Pak dividing line in Kashmir. Since its creation in 1949, the area around this line had remained tense, experiencing shelling and firing during times of active conflict and even during periods of peace.[2] This ceasefire is significant as being the first formal ceasefire agreement between India and Pakistan since the outbreak of militancy in J&K.[3] Despite reports of occasional violations, the ceasefire has continued for about a decade with noticeable normalcy in border areas on both sides of Kashmir and eventually, as a respondent claimed, bringing 'historic relief'[4] to borderlanders who have borne the brunt of Indo-Pak hostility.[5] On the sidelines of the 2004 South Asian Association for Regional Cooperation (SAARC) summit meeting, India and Pakistan expressed their willingness to engage in a composite dialogue aimed at the peaceful settlement of all bilateral issues, including Kashmir. Since then, officials and ministers of both countries have met a number of times to deliberate on issues of common concern, and have agreed to cooperate in many areas.[6] In October 2009, during a visit to J&K, Indian Prime Minister, Manmohan Singh, said, 'we had the most fruitful and productive discussions ever with the government of Pakistan during the period 2004–07 when militancy and violence [in J&K] began to decline. Intensive discussions were held on all issues including on a permanent resolution of the issue of Jammu and Kashmir.'[7] The dialogue process was adversely affected in the aftermath of the 2008 Mumbai terror attacks when India accused Pakistan of not initiating stern action against the Pak-based masterminds behind these attacks.[8] The development was a setback to the peace process, but there was an overall perception that the process towards peace should continue. After a gap of about 14 months, the dialogue process resumed as the foreign secretaries of both the countries met in New Delhi in February 2010. The prime ministers of the two countries met on the sidelines of the 16th SAARC summit in the Bhutanese capital, Thimpu on 29 April 2010 with the main objective of consolidating the composite dialogue process. Thereafter negotiations have sustained giving rise to a widely held assumption that the major parties to the Kashmir conflict have realized the importance of dialogue for peace and development in the region.

A two-pronged dialogue process can be deciphered in India's policymaking particularly during 2000s and afterwards. First, Indian policymakers aimed at strengthening relations with Pakistan by expanding the scope of relations to areas such as trade and commerce, and people to people interactions. This approach particularly veered around the argument that those issues which are least contentious need to be cultivated in bilateral relations, keeping controversial subjects aside with the belief that the increasing bonhomie between the two countries will gradually help address complex issues such as Kashmir. Second, Indian leaders strove to gear policy mechanisms to address the issue of alienation within J&K. Such an approach was guided by the perception that unless the people's hearts and minds are won, it will be difficult to bring peace to the state. Though the presence of the security forces could establish a semblance of peace and tranquillity, at least from an Indian perspective, the continuation in violence and alienation indicated that the coercive policy has to be replaced by a persuasive one.[9] India launched a major peace mission to involve civilians as well as separatist groups in the peace process in J&K. Another factor that guided the peace venture is the tangible and intangible costs of militant violence that included far-reaching physical, psychological, socio-cultural, economic and infrastructural devastation.[10] Even by conservative estimates, thousands of civilians lost their lives due to the violence. The number of missing people ran into hundreds. Civilians suffered from pervasive violence, fear and coercion and became indirect victims through arrests, torture, disappearance and loss of their loved ones. The conflict created an atmosphere in which violence became an integral part of day-to-day life, inducing a sense of resignation and frustration among the people and negatively affecting their physical and mental health. The conflict led to large-scale population displacement among several demographics.[11] Important sources of livelihood including tourism, agriculture, horticulture and handicraft industries were adversely impacted. Essential infrastructure including roads and communications remained underdeveloped. The all-pervasive atmosphere of violence discouraged private industries to invest in the region.

The perceptible decline in militant violence since late 1990s provided requisite atmosphere for initiating measures towards peace and for avoiding further devastation caused by violence. Since the decline in violence in the region, a series of steps have been initiated by India to address the militancy and foster mechanisms for peace. These initiatives have neither been declared as being a part of a single process nor have they been documented in a single framework though they are all aimed at addressing alienation and separatism in J&K. In 1996, after nearly six years of President's rule, elections were held to the J&K State Assembly and the NC, that had governed J&K singlehanded, or in coalition with INC, since the start of the electoral process in Kashmir, regained power. Elections held in 2002 brought about a perceptible change to the State Assembly's composition by bringing a coalition of the People's Democratic Party (PDP) and INC to power. For the first time in the electoral history of J&K another political formation except the NC had risen to power. Elections were again held in 2008 and the results ensured the return of NC-INC coalition to power. The seven-phase elections to the 87-seated J&K Assembly starting on 17 November 2008 and ending on 24 December 2008 marked a shift owing primarily to three factors. First, despite calls from separatist groups such as APHC and militant groups such as the LeT to boycott the polls, an overwhelming number of the electorate exercised right to vote. The separatists lost much of their influence as the voter turnout at 63 per cent surpassed voting records of the last two decades. Second, the voters seemed to be concerned with the issues of common concern such as roads, electricity and water rather than calls for *azadi*. Third, the elections were held amidst heightened Indo-Pak tensions due to the Mumbai terror attack in November 2008. The uncertain atmosphere did not deter the people from taking part in the elections in significant numbers.[12] The democratic exercises in terms of periodic fair and free elections and change of government are significant for the reason that lack of democracy is considered a major reason for the onset of militancy in the state. The Indian government has initiated a series of other people centric initiatives to reintegrate the state's discontented people to the mainstream. Keeping in view the focus of the book, I evaluate some of these initiatives, including the much hyped rehabilitation policy, to provide an overview of the position of women in these peace making attempts. I do not aspire to be exhaustive or definitive about the peace process but during the course of analysis I attempt to draw some tentative conclusions both to the extent to which peace and reintegration have been attempted and how far they reflect gender.

Negotiating Peace

On 19 November 2000, India announced unilateral ceasefire in J&K aimed at persuading militants to renounce violence and join the peace process. This ceasefire initiative was extended twice, and lasted until 26 February 2001. Thereafter New Delhi adopted a position that it will negotiate with only those groups which shun violence and espouse peace. In 2004, New Delhi initiated a dialogue with the moderate faction of APHC with two rounds of talks between its leaders and the Deputy Prime Minister of India, Lal Krishna Advani. For the first time since the onset of militancy, New Delhi started direct talks with the separatist groups. These talks continued even after the INC-led United Progressive Alliance (UPA) came to power in 2004. Thereafter talks were elevated to the highest level, with Prime Minister Manmohan Singh participating in the next two rounds of talks. During the second round of these talks, which took place on 5 September 2005, the Prime Minister assured APHC leaders of the Indian government's commitment to provide 'a life of peace, self respect, and dignity'[13] to the people of J&K. In 2009, New Delhi and APHC reaffirmed their commitment to the dialogue process on various occasions. These initiatives continued despite an assault by opponents of the dialogue process on senior Hurriyat leader Fazal Haq Qureshi who supported a negotiated settlement of the Kashmir problem and the continuation of dialogue with New Delhi. Prime Minister Singh stated in October 2009, 'we would be happy to engage in dialogue with any group which is interested in talking. That option remains. We will welcome even those who are not in the political mainstream. If they have any views, they are welcome to give.'[14] He reiterated India's offer of dialogue with the separatists, 'we are willing to engage in serious discussions with every group, provided they shun the path of violence…I made an appeal yesterday [28 October 2009] for dialogue, and I hope it will be reciprocated in the spirit in which it was made.'[15] The last months of 2009 witnessed a noticeable change in New Delhi's strategy as it engaged in 'quiet diplomacy' with the Hurriyat, away from public glare. On 2 December 2009, when questioned in the Indian Parliament's Lower House, then Home Minister, P. Chidambaram, explained his strategy of dialogue and negotiation, 'I am in favour of quiet talks, and quiet diplomacy far off from the glare of the media.'[16] A sustained dialogue process with the moderate faction of APHC, along with attempts towards bringing other separatist groups to the negotiating table, can be considered a significant step towards realising peace in the region. India took another far-reaching step by not restricting the dialogue merely between the Srinagar based separatist factions and New Delhi. Hurriyat leaders and leaders of mainstream political parties in J&K were allowed to visit Pakistan and Pakistan controlled Kashmir in order to interact with their counterparts as well as other groups, thus allowing a broadening of the peace discourse. The Indian government's acquiescence to Hurriyat leaders' plan to visit Kashmir across the LoC has been hailed as a step in the right direction towards an 'honourable and durable solution' to the Kashmir issue.

But where are women in this process of engaging the separatist groups through dialogue? The male leadership of the Hurriyat Conference dominates separatist politics. This umbrella organization consists of more than 20 separatist groups but, except the two all-women organizations, no other groups have women on their executive bodies. New Delhi and Hurriyat have come together on several occasions to negotiate peace but Kashmiri women have not been part of official delegations of separatist groups. Hurriyat members have visited Pakistan and parts of Kashmir controlled by it several times but the gender component has remained missing in almost all these visits.

Addressing the Alienation

Kashmir is highly diverse in terms of history, geography, ethnicity, religion, culture and society. The three regions of the state – Jammu, Kashmir valley and Ladakh – have different regional aspirations. While the people of Jammu are largely in favour of the full integration of the state with India, Ladakh seeks Union Territory status within India. Kashmir valley comprises divergent aspirations in political terms: those who want to be independent from both India and Pakistan; those who want Kashmir to join Pakistan; and those who favour the status quo, that is, remaining with India with a measure of autonomy. The varying aspirations do not end here; there are intra-regional demands revolving around issues of culture, ethnicity and language. The divergent demands, at times contradictory, have added layers of complexity to the conflict resolution process. In order to address the diverse voices and concerns, New Delhi initiated a series of round table conferences to which representatives of diverse groups such as political parties, ethnic groups and civil society activists from within J&K were invited to express themselves and interact with each other and with New Delhi on a single platform. Three round table conferences, presided by the Prime Minister of India, were held (the first in February 2006 in New Delhi, the second in May 2006 in Srinagar and the third in April 2007 in New Delhi). In a statement adopted at the third round table conference, the participants acknowledged that the three meetings of representatives from diverse sections of J&K who had stakes in a peaceful Kashmir had helped

> Evolve a better understanding of the issues and problems that affect the lives of the people of Jammu and Kashmir. It had produced an environment in which the citizens of all parts of the State could hope to lead a life of dignity, self-respect and fulfilment without fear of war, and want or exploitation and discrimination.[17]

Though the round tables could be considered significant, at least in terms of bringing diverse groups on a single platform, the absence of many groups such as the displaced other than Kashmiri pandits and women made the meetings an exclusive exercise. Restriction of participation only to invited groups diluted the basic goal of the meetings – listening to varied voices. With discussions being largely monopolized by mainstream political parties, it became difficult even for the invited groups to put forward their voices effectively. It was expected that over time the meetings will become more inclusive and accommodate marginalized groups, which in turn will provide a fair chance to all groups with a stake in peace in the region to raise their concerns. This did not happen. The meagre results achieved by these dialogues have suffered setbacks as there have been no further round tables since 2007 despite the Prime Minister's assurance that the dialogue process will continue.[18] This peace initiative was an almost all-men affair with nearly all chairs around the table being occupied by male leaders. Women's voices remained absent. There were no significant discussions on or by women in these round tables. A major outcome of these gender insensitive round tables was near absence of women's concerns as well as their due representation in the working groups set-up to foster conflict transformation.

Seeking Expert Advice

During the second round table conference in Srinagar in May 2006 the Indian Prime Minister announced the establishment of five working groups entrusted with the task of looking into various contentious issues related to Kashmir. The first working group focused on confidence building across segments of society in the state, the second on strengthening relations with Pakistan controlled Kashmir, the third dealt with economic development of the state, the fourth aimed at providing good governance to the people of J&K, and the fifth looked at strengthening relations between New Delhi and Srinagar. The first four working groups submitted their reports before the third round table held in April 2007, while the fifth working group submitted its report in December 2009. In its report, the second working group recommended people-to-people contact, facilitating and increasing trade and commerce and opening new routes between the two parts of Kashmir.[19] The third working group, which aimed at promoting inclusive growth and balanced economic development of all the three regions of J&K, recommended, among other things, reconstruction and maintenance of existing physical assets, investment in physical infrastructure, particularly power and roads, investment in social infrastructure and the creation of a favourable atmosphere for private investment.[20] The fourth working group recommended effective implementation of the Right to Information Act, introduction of e-governance, setting up committees for time-bound performance appraisal of key government departments such as the Revenue Department and simplification of procedures in departments with which the public frequently interacted. It favoured greater transparency, efficiency and accountability in the process of governance.[21] The fifth working group suggested measures to ensure the autonomous status of the state.

From a gender perspective the first working group was crucial; hence, it needs a detailed assessment. This group dealt with 'Confidence Building Measures across Segments of Society in the State' and was chaired by Mohammad Hamid Ansari, currently the Vice President of India. The principal agenda of the working group was improving the conditions of the people affected by militancy-related violence.[22] The mandate of this group included six major issues: measures to improve the condition of the people adversely impacted by militancy; schemes to rehabilitate all orphans and widows affected by violence; issues relating to the relaxation of conditions for persons who have foresworn militancy; an effective rehabilitation policy, including employment, for displaced Kashmiri pandits; an approach considering issues relating to return of Kashmiri youth from areas controlled by Pakistan; and measures to preserve the unique cultural and religious heritage of J&K. In the context of women, the group had the mandate to merely recommend provisions for 'orphans and widows affected by militancy'. Hence, the group restricted its recommendations for this particular section of society. It put forward three recommendations in this context. Complete data of widows and orphans should be collected for making effective schemes for their rehabilitation. All widows should be provided relief and for those already receiving financial assistance of ₹ 500 the amount should be raised to a realistic level. Lastly, administrative delays and malpractices in the distribution of relief to the concerned should be curbed. A designated officer at the district level should have the power to ensure that the relief measures were monitored regularly.[23]

The composition of working groups and their functioning displayed the gender insensitive nature of this peace initiative. None of the five working group was headed by a woman. The fifth working group, also called the Saghir Ahmed Panel, which remained controversial in its deliberations and recommendations on centre-state relations between New Delhi and Srinagar, had one woman member, Mehbooba Mufti, leader of the PDP.[24] This group did not have the mandate to review issues related to women. None of the political parties or civil society organizations raised this gender insensitive formation of the committees. Core gender issues did not figure in the deliberations of any of the working groups including the one specifically formed to recommend confidence building measures for the people of J&K. There was not a single woman member in working group, which was assigned the task of studying the problems of widows and providing recommendations. As mentioned earlier, the only women specific recommendation was that widow victims of militancy should be properly rehabilitated. What does this imply? That the rehabilitation of widows is restricted to collecting data and providing meagre financial aid for survival? Even this recommendation has not been implemented so far.[25] This overall dismal scenario implies that women are not active stakeholders in the peace process, and if at all they have a place in the conflict and peace discourse, it is limited to victimization. The restricted mandate of the first working group testifies to the gender insensitive nature of the peace process and perpetuates the patriarchal belief that beyond victimization women do not count in the conflict and peace discourse. Such an asymmetric discourse further implies that women are not capable of even detailing their victimization and suggesting remedies. This burden too has to be borne by benevolent men who have to plan for their rehabilitation. The question that remains unaddressed is: who is responsible for the victimization of women during conflict and peace? I am reminded of the Hindi saying *dard bhi ham dava bhi ham* (I am the pain and I am also the pain reliever) that summarizes this concern.

Upholding Human Rights

Addressing human rights violations by bringing the perpetrators to justice is crucial in ensuring sustainable peace. In the case of Kashmir, both the militants and the security forces violated the human rights of civilians; while violations committed by militants only occasionally come to light, those committed by security forces are frequently highlighted by the media and non-governmental human rights organizations. Allegations of custodial killings, arbitrary detentions, fake encounters, crackdowns and rape by security forces have repeatedly been reported. Human rights violations by militants can only be dealt with if the militants are apprehended and prosecuted but what about the violations by security forces?

Indian security forces in J&K are accorded unbridled powers that have been misused on several occasions. New Delhi initially refused to acknowledge human rights violations by security forces. There has been a significant shift in its approach towards the issue in recent years. During the third round table the Indian Prime Minister expressed concern over human rights violations by armed forces personnel and promised to take steps to minimize such abuses. The Prime Minister's promise was echoed by other Indian leaders who reiterated the newly crafted approach that New Delhi has zero tolerance against human rights violations and effective action will be taken in all reported cases of atrocities. J&K Chief Minister Omar Abdullah, while addressing his first meeting of the Unified Command on 14 January 2009 to review the security situation in the state, repeated the principle of zero tolerance. He pointed out that the authorities must investigate any violation in a transparent manner and should prosecute the guilty. He further urged troops not to cordon off residential areas gratuitously and to avoid making needless arrests.[26] In June 2009, in a speech in J&K, then Home Minister of India, P. Chidambaram, called upon security personnel to respect the human rights of Kashmiri people. The Defence Minister of India, A. K. Antony, reiterated the government's policy of zero tolerance in 2010 stating,

> Our Armed Forces personnel must be conscious of the respect for human rights all the time. They must follow the twin ethics of "minimum use of force" and "good faith" during operations. Though the constraints of the security forces are understandable, the security forces too must bear in mind that the process of winning the hearts and minds of people is never an easy one.[27]

The first working group had the mandate to recommend measures to check human rights violations. The members stressed,

> The necessity of curbing human rights violations was stressed....Emphasis was placed on Prime Minister's assurance of "zero tolerance" for human rights violations, as on India's international commitments and international image. It was considered imperative to develop a mechanism in which responsibility for specific human rights violations can be fixed and derelict officials identified and proceeded against.'[28]

The group recommended that,

> Human rights awareness should be inculcated in all civil and military government functionaries, and in the public. The State Human Rights Commission (SHRC) should be strengthened, along the lines of the NHRC (National Human Rights Commission), to enable it to ensure that innocent persons do not become victims of counter-insurgency measures.'[29]

The report put forward some specific measures: an investigative machinery, independent of the regular police, be provided to SHRC, implementation of the recommendations of the commission be made obligatory and an empowered committee be appointed to report regularly on the action taken by the state government on SHRC's recommendations. Although J&K has a Human Rights Commission that investigates human rights violations, it is perhaps best described as a 'toothless tiger'[30] lacking substantial powers and resources such as staff and funding. Justice Abdul Qadir Parray, the former chairperson of SHRC, observed in 2002 that,

> Cases of human rights violations in Kashmir at the hands of security forces are gathering dust in the official chambers of L. K. Advani (then Home Minister of India). Our commission is only a recommendatory body and has not been provided with enough powers to force implementation.[31]

Concerns related to the watchdog of human rights need to be addressed by the government. Strengthening institutions such as SHRC should be urgently considered a vital step in providing justice to victims of abuses. Further, debates regarding the withdrawal of special powers accorded to security personnel in order to minimize human rights violations are important. Gradual withdrawal of the Armed Forces Special Powers Act that allows security forces to carry out searches without warrants and to detain people could be a key step in restoring people's faith in government institutions.

Although a court of inquiry found three army personnel guilty of killing civilians in Kashmir in March 2009, and court martial proceedings were initiated against them later, this could be counted as a rare instance. There are no reports from the ground indicating a substantial decline in human rights violations following the proclaimed policy of zero tolerance. Full implementation of this policy could be a significant step in assuring people caught in the conflict situation that New Delhi is earnest in facilitating a transition process in the region. The state should be accountable for the misconduct and criminal activities of its security forces:

> Claiming to be a democracy, a land of Mahatma Gandhi, a sovereign country that does not need a certificate on human rights from other countries that

indulge in the human rights violations and the militants that commit the atrocities, all this can in no way justify the abuses by the state against its own people. There is a need to deal with the conflict situation by a two-pronged strategy: being harsh with militants and humane with the common people.[32]

Elimination of impunity is critical for preventing violations of people's basic rights. Addressing impunity and healing personal wounds can restore the confidence of the people in state authorities to a great extent.[33] There is further need to chart out specific strategies to deal with women specific human rights violations. The oft repeated zero tolerance policy does not specifically mention women's concerns. It is essential to discuss the issue and chart out specific strategies to deal with gender specific rights violations since 'the confidence and security perceptions of people...depend to an extent on how past and ongoing human rights violations...are being handled.'[34] Hundreds of cases of gender specific violence against women have been documented by the media and various national and international organizations. All of them cannot be dismissed as propaganda by the militants. I cite one instance. In mid-2009 Kashmir valley witnessed violent protests and demonstrations for several days over the rape and murder of two girls in Shopian by security personnel. There were fierce anti-India protests across the Kashmir valley when the bodies of the women were found in a stream. Indian officials initially insisted that the two had drowned, but the families of the victims accused the security forces of abducting, raping and killing them. The initial refusal on the part of the police to register a first information report to initiate proceedings against the culprits brought into the picture the insensitivity on the part of the state administration and made a sham of the government's commitment to zero tolerance of human rights violations. Popular pressure led to a criminal investigation of the incident. Forensic tests proved that both the women had been raped before being killed. Later investigations by Central Bureau of Investigation revealed that it was a case of death by drowning. The family of the women did not deem this investigation as trustworthy and approached the court. The point is that the government of J&K failed to initiate a prompt investigation to bring out the truth, arousing public suspicions about the transparency of the enquiry process. In such a sensitive region, the government is expected to be highly responsive and take immediate measures to control the situation. The government with a slew of damage control measures cannot win the hearts and minds of the people as the alienated people will not be content with ad-hoc measures.[35] There is a need for a proactive approach in which justice should be seen to be done and reflected in the very acts of the government in terms of swift investigations against alleged human rights violations. A strong mechanism to deal with cases of violations to bring the perpetrators to justice is crucial. There are other crucial issues including the one of missing people that need to be addressed effectively. During the days of heightened militancy hundreds of Kashmiri people, particularly men, 'disappeared'. Recently mass unidentified graves have been discovered, which has led to allegations that many missing men had been buried in these graves after being killed by security forces. Parveena Ahangar formed the Association of the Parents of Disappeared Persons in 1994 to trace missing Kashmiri people. Her son has been missing since 1990. Relatives of missing people have a right to know about their whereabouts but they continue to lead a life of uncertainty. A respondent, Naseema, whose husband was taken away by security personnel in 1991 'for some investigation' did not come back. Following years of this trauma, Naseema merely desires official confirmation of the death of her husband to put an end to persisting uncertainty.

> I am sure that he has been killed and buried somewhere by Indian security personnel. Earlier I was constantly cursing them for making my life hell. I wanted to know his whereabouts. But now I do not have any grudge against anyone, just a request. Please inform me officially that my husband is dead, she pleaded.[36]

Is this too much to ask for? How can human rights be upheld when people are not even able to perform the last rites of their loved ones? How can peace be attained if the trauma of women like Naseema is not talked about and addressed in right earnest?

One of the earlier attempts by India to address the alienation of the people and foster the process of reintegration included Operation Sadbhavana (good will), which was initiated in the 1990s. Its aim was two-fold: to win over the common people from the influence of the militants and to reintegrate them in the national mainstream. It was envisaged that the 'goodwill' activities will provide a healing touch, redress the grievances of the people and restore their trust in the Indian Army and the Indian state. Under this programme Indian security forces, deployed in J&K, were to take part in the areas of healthcare, education, community development and infrastructure. Sadbhavana schools, adult education centres and hospitals were set-up in militancy infested parts of J&K. There are centres which offer employment skills to women such as weaving of shawls and carpets and computer training. Nonetheless, until the basic human rights of the people, including that of women, are upheld these attempts to 'win hearts and minds' will not be effective.

Towards Reintegration

Two different policies have been drafted by the Government of India for the rehabilitation and reintegration of ex-militants in Kashmir. The first one is for local militia who gave up violence and surrendered before Indian security personnel. The second policy is a recent one and is meant to facilitate the return of Kashmiri militants who had crossed the LoC to Pakistan controlled Kashmir and after the decline of violence in J&K intended to return to their native place and lead a normal life. Since the mid-1990s the number of ex-militants, who have surrendered before the authorities, has witnessed a steady increase.[37] The scheme in its current form was titled 'Policy for Surrender of Militants and Rehabilitation of Surrenderees'.[38] It offered rehabilitation and monetary incentives and included provisions for vocational training. The other salient features of the policy included a monthly stipend of ₹ 2,000 for a period of three years after surrender and a grant of ₹ 1,50,000 in the form of a fixed deposit that could be drawn after three years. The surrendered militants received monetary incentives for surrendering weapons.[39] It has been reported that the policy had benefitted as many as 2,876 ex-militants until November 2011.[40]

The issue of return of ex-militants from across the LoC emerged in policy circles in 2006 when a delegation of leaders from J&K visited Pak controlled Kashmir. The delegation met several ex-militants who were keen to come back to J&K. The second round table conference of 2006 too deliberated on this issue. The first working group had recommended that the Indian government should initiate measures to facilitate the return of these people. In early 2010 the Indian government approved the policy to allow ex-militants, who had shunned violence, to return to J&K. In February 2010, the then Indian Home Minister, P. Chidambaram announced that, 'the idea of granting amnesty to Kashmiri youth in PoK (Pakistan-occupied Kashmir) has been accepted. The idea must be translated into action now.'[41] The document titled 'Policy and Procedure for return of Ex-Militants to Jammu and Kashmir State', generally referred to as the amnesty policy outlined an elaborate process that included 'identification, monitoring, debriefing, rehabilitation and reintegration' of former militants and their dependents.[42] The policy aimed at facilitating the return of local ex-militants, who had crossed the LoC for arms training between 1 January 1989 and 31 December 2009 but who had shunned violence later. There was no provision for general amnesty as each individual case had to be decided on its own merit. All those permitted to return after a thorough scrutiny of their application could enter India only through specific points of entry – Wagah border in Punjab, through Salamabad (Uri in J&K), Chakan-da-bagh (Poonch in J&K) or through the Indira Gandhi International Airport, New Delhi. The returnees' along with their dependents had to register their arrival in the office of the district (of their native place in J&K) superintendent of police. Cases pending against the applicants were to be reopened, and if found guilty the ex-militants would serve prison terms at special counselling camps. There was also provision for financial assistance and skill training for these former militants in the policy document.[43] Until early August 2012, the government had received 1,054 applications, out of which 291 cases had been approved for return while the others were being scrutinized.[44]

On conditions of anonymity a senior J&K police official revealed that there were about 4,000 'inactive' militants residing in Kashmir across the LoC. 'They are no longer involved in violence because of their growing age or a change of heart. Most of them crossed in the early 1980s and have not returned since then. Now they want to come back and join the mainstream and lead a normal life in their own homeland. They are very homesick,' the official said.[45] He further added that since early 2011 about 300 ex-militants had returned to J&K individually as well as in small groups.[46] An ex-militant who returned to J&K after a long spell of 18 years said, 'I had crossed the LoC to get trained in handling arms. After a month of training I lost interest and left the training camp to start life afresh in Azad Kashmir. I married and settled there but I always remained an outsider. I wanted to return but feared being imprisoned for life or even killed. With the announcement of the amnesty policy by J&K government I decided to take the risk of returning. It is better to die in one's own place amidst one's own people.'[47]

The Indian government's decision of wooing ex-combatants sent positive feelers on both sides of Kashmir. It motivated ex-militants stranded in Kashmir across the LoC to consider homecoming. The procedure is, however, slow, cumbersome and even complicated as is revealed from the fact that from the time that the policy was approved till August 2012 not even a single ex-militant could return through proper channels. Procedural difficulties prompted many to take the unauthorized route through Nepal by crossing the porous India-Nepal border illegally. A returnee said,

> I was contemplating homecoming since late 2010. On my behalf, my father had filed the amnesty application as soon as the policy was initiated. For all these years I had somehow managed to console myself at being away from my homeland and my family. But after filing the application and knowing that I can return it was very difficult to wait. I became impatient with no response on my application for more than a year. Hence I decided to return via Nepal. Some of my friends had returned from that route earlier and I too came back through this route.[48]

According to a BBC report the Nepal route is frequently used by former militants because, 'the Kathmandu route has two advantages; it is familiar to former militants and their "handlers" who have used it in the past to smuggle militants into India, and it is away from the public glare and therefore suitable to keep this exodus under wraps.'[49] The route came to the notice of the authorities when a large group of 40 ex-militants along with their family members used it to return in May 2012. 'This was the first time when such a large group of ex-militants entered India illegally to return to J&K under the new amnesty policy. Earlier the comeback was individual or in very small groups only,' said a senior police official in J&K.[50] The returnees travelled on Pakistani passports to Nepal and then destroyed their passports. Thereafter they crossed over to India near Gorakhpur in Uttar Pradesh claiming to be Indian citizens. From there they reached J&K and surrendered before the J&K police claiming rehabilitation under the amnesty policy.

Return through this alternate route was both expensive and troublesome. 'Our expenditure included, but not was limited to, paying the agents who facilitated the passport and visa issuance for travelling to Nepal, flight tickets to Nepal, accommodation in Nepal and travel from Uttar Pradesh to J&K,' a returnee said.[51] The cost factor has prevented many aspiring returnees to take this route. They have no option but to wait for government approval for their return. 'Some of my neighbours too wanted to return but did not have enough money. My father-in-law arranged money for the homecoming of my family of five people. He arranged for about US $ 3,500 by selling part of his fertile land. I will repay him once I have enough money,' said one respondent.[52] A BBC report detailed the expenses involved in this journey,

> Ejaz Ahmad (a returnee) exhausted almost all his savings on his return journey – he had to pay close to 300,000 Pakistani rupees ($3,184; £2,039) to arrange travel documents and tickets for his family….And because they had entered India illegally, they had to seek bail from a court which cost him 210,000 Indian rupees ($3,801; £2,430).[53]

To check this trickle from an unauthorized route the Indian government decided to rope in former militants who would serve as 'spotters' at 15 crossing points on the Indo-Nepal border to identify these returnees.[54] It does not seem feasible to check this illegal comeback until legal return is simplified.

Lack of coordination between the establishments of the two parts of Kashmir, and also between India and Pakistan, has contributed to the cumbersome process of direct return. The process involves another complex layer of threats from extremist militant groups. Syed Salahuddin (himself a native of J&K but residing in Kashmir across the LoC), the Chief of HM and leader of the radical organizations conglomerate United Jihad Council has been quoted as saying, 'the most precious thing for a human being is honour and dignity. I put a thousand curses on those who return to Kashmir in a way that they have to surrender before and seek forgiveness from the enemy and go behind bars.'[55] The return procedure with layers of provisions to ensure that ex-militants do not take up the 'old profession' has added to the intricacies. Suspicions prevail, as the authorities believe that the policy might backfire, leading to renewed violence and taking away the hard earned modicum of relative peace and stability in the region. There are administrative difficulties as well. The legalization of family members, including of the wife and children is a core concern for most returnees. The issue of citizenship of an ex-militant's dependents (who might be a citizen of India, but his wife and children may be citizens of Pakistan) has made implementing the policy difficult. A returnee asserted:

> I was born in J&K and carry a domicile certificate but my wife is a Pakistani citizen. My children were born in Kashmir across the LoC and had Pakistani passports. Before entering India via Nepal we destroyed all the passports and now my wife and children have no identity of their own. I am sure they will not be sent back to Pakistan but till the time the issue of their citizenship is sorted out we will continue to lead a life of uncertainty.[56]

There are a number of other issues that afflicted the returnees. Mukeet Akmali gives details of some of these issues in the words of the returnees:

> We used to yearn for our return to Kashmir. But now we feel disappointed despite having left all our belongings and valuable things there. We are facing a worst situation. We have no jobs. Our children cannot join schools and we cannot even have ration cards....Our children are even denied their Right to Education which is a basic need of all individuals. Our children want to study but the government is not allowing them to get admitted in schools. Even our qualification certificates from Pakistan are not being entertained....We are being denied basic rights. We decided to return only after the state government issued statements regarding our settlement. We had never thought that our lives here will be miserable.[57]

The government initiated the process of return for the first batch of ex-militants via the direct route but did not put in place a clear and proper mechanism for their proper resettlement. Since independence New Delhi's strategy towards J&K has remained ad hoc and this new policy for returnees reaffirms this. Even the earlier policy of rehabilitating local militants has not been implemented effectively. One of the respondents who had returned to J&K via the Nepal route posed this question: 'Local militants who surrendered years before have not been rehabilitated so far. Do you think we will reap the benefits of this policy so early?'[58] Many of the local ex-militants whom I interviewed lamented that they were still waiting for proper resettlement.

'There are thousands of surrendered local militants but most of us are suffering on all fronts – economically, socially and psychologically. Framing a policy and implementing it in letter and spirit are two different things,' argued an ex-militant.[59] Many ex-militants alleged that they continue to be harassed by the authorities as they have to frequently visit police stations for investigations. Many of the former militants did not have steady incomes or secure jobs. They claimed that even their relatives were denied government jobs or even passports to travel abroad for work or for visiting religious places. Abdul Qadeer, Chairman of the People's Rights Movement, a group of released militants has been quoted as saying, 'the scenario is when our children get government jobs or work outside, police releases adverse reports. Our relatives can't go for Haj; we can't travel out of the state for work. Getting a passport is a herculean task.'[60] Farookh Ahmad, Chairman of the Jammu-Kashmir Ex-Militants Welfare Association argued,

> The government assured of rehabilitating us respectfully and to give employment opportunities and security of our families...sadly, we have not received what we were promised. Instead we are harassed in police stations and have to go to the nearby camp to mark our attendance.[61]

The suspicion of authorities partly contributed to the negative atmosphere and affected the process of social assimilation of former militants, most of whom had crossed their prime age. Many of them remained single with least prospects of marriage and jobs, adding to the wretchedness of their life. A former militant lamented, 'I am now of 45 years and I am still unmarried and unemployed. I do not know why I am living. It would have been better if I had died like a brave militant.'[62] In her study on Kashmir Shobha Sonapur argues that ex-militants are:

> in an ambiguous position since they were in neither of the idealized roles of active militant, nor martyr. Feelings of inadequacy, betrayal, frustration, depression and anxiety were common....A significant source of tension is continuing humiliation, intimidation and harassment at the hands of the security forces....Those who surrender...experience grave physical danger from active militants and have to endure social stigma and suspicion....Another important source of distress is the harm and anguish suffered by their families during the time they were active militants. Their current circumstances add to stress because of the difficulties in fulfilling civilian gender roles as providers and caretakers of their families.[63]

The narrative of an ex-militant sums up the trauma of all those who continue to long for a normal life, 'we have been ostracized by both the government as well as society. For the former we are subjects of suspicion and for the latter we are pariahs.'[64] The overall apathy of the state towards their demands prompted some former militants to use the Gandhian method of non-violent protests and some others to again take up arms. There are reports that a fresh initiative has been launched by militant groups operating in J&K to enlist ex-militants.[65] According to a newspaper report of 17 April 2012 out of about 65 ex-militants in Sopore who returned using the Nepal route, at least five had re-joined militancy.[66] Keeping this in view, any lax attitude towards the proper settlement of former militants can prove to be hazardous. Unless expeditious measures are adopted to arrest this declining trust of ex-militants in government policies, the situation may worsen.

There are indications that of late the authorities have tried to address the alienation of ex-militants. Within a span of three months, claimed Inspector General of Police of J&K, S. M. Sahai on 25 February 2012, while interacting with about 1,500 ex-militants in Srinagar, the state police had cleared 52,000 passport verifications of relatives of ex-militants. In a move to boost the trust of ex-militants, Sahai assured that, 'now the police department will not create any hurdle,' rather it will provide 'a platform for the released militants to coordinate with the state government and the police for their rehabilitation.'[67] In early February 2012, Sahai had advised senior police officers to help ex-militants manage their livelihoods through all possible ways including private employment and contractual jobs in government departments.[68] He advocated formation of non-governmental organizations by ex-militants and channelizing their energies for constructive purposes. Sahai argued that, 'forming NGOs is one method to rehabilitate former militants,' as the idea revolves around two major objectives: 'one is the idea of restoration of respect of former militants. They are being ostracized by the society;' and the other being 'the removal of impediments coming in the way of their progress'.[69]

On ground the situation remains precarious with palpable frustration evident among many former militants. The people of J&K have suffered immensely and any half-hearted attempts to tackle the situation or making policies just for receiving media attention can prove perilous. Though the amnesty policy was announced in 2010, no exact package had been announced until late 2012. In June 2011, the J&K Chief Minister, Omar Abdullah argued for an urgent need to rehabilitate surrendered and released militants, but he did not elaborate what measures were being pursued to achieve this objective. He stated that the authorities were trying 'to ascertain how educated they (surrendered militants) are, and what sort of skills they possess. Once we establish that, we will see what sort of avenues they can be employed in', further adding 'once complete information about them (surrendered militants) is obtained by the state government we will then work out a package with government of India'.[70]

No progress on these aspects is perceptible so far. Perhaps the government does not intend to prioritize the rehabilitation policy. Seemingly it considers this policy as incidental to the larger objective of establishing peace and stability in the region. Even senior state officials concede off the record that not only is this amnesty policy but even the earlier one for local militants was flawed.

The long-term consequences of militants laying down their arms and joining the mainstream can prove to be opportunity for the peace process. In its own interest the Indian government should initiate effective steps for ensuring the proper rehabilitation of former militants, which in turn could foster a return of normalcy. It may further lead to decline in violence by prompting active militants to re-join the mainstream. A report on the amnesty policy suggests:

> The state government's rehabilitation policy for youth, who had crossed to other side of border, most of them in early 1990s may augur well for the government if it is implemented properly. The policy first of its kind could act as a Confidence Building Measure (CBM) and may contribute towards building the atmosphere of peace, provided the youth, whose return to their homeland is facilitated are not harassed unduly by different intelligence agencies but encouraged to settle down. Even if the intelligence agencies scrutinize their activities, they should be at the same time encouraged and not caged to ensure that they join the mainstream. By doing so, government would certainly motivate more Kashmiri youth based in PoK (Pakistan occupied Kashmir) to return to their homeland with the hope that they would live a normal life.[71]

Violence cannot be condoned but those who have renounced it should be allowed to resume life with dignity and honour. Strategies should be charted out to check undue harassment and suspicion of ex-militants and at the same time to facilitate their socio-economic rehabilitation. The conflict cannot be resolved by merely implementing such policies but they can go a long way in strengthening the constituency of peace. Where is the gender component in this rehabilitation and reintegration policy? Gender insensitivity in this peace attempt is starkly visible. In Kashmir, women did not take up arms and hence did not possess the weapons to surrender and claim rehabilitation and reintegration. Does non-wielding of weapons mean abstention from conflict making? Women who performed support activities during the militancy did not have weapons to trade in but their lives had been affected by their participation in the armed struggle. How could any dispassionate observer of the Kashmir conflict ignore the role of women in the overall movement? Without women's support militancy in Kashmir could neither have been a mass movement nor sustained for such a long time. It is difficult to comprehend the *azadi* movement in Kashmir without its gender component. Who would have transported arms and armaments by hiding them in veils, facilitated the movement of male militants, sheltered them and cooked meals for them and led mass protests when a majority of the men had either crossed the LoC for training or were hiding? Isn't the undermining of the exceptional courage of raped women who, despite being born and brought up in traditional Kashmiri society, testified the rape in public glare, deplorable? The lack of gender sensitivity on the part of the authorities as well as separatist leaders exhibits a stark reality of a majority of conflict situations, in which women despite their contributions are relegated to the background during peace making. Women should not have been ignored in the overall process towards peace making, but this is exactly what has happened. None of the peace attempts including meetings, round tables and negotiations have accorded due representation to women or due space to their concerns. Women are neither at the formal peace table to negotiate nor are they major beneficiaries of any of the peace attempts.

Endnotes

1. Debidatta Aurobinda Mahapatra, 'A Perspective on Peace in Kashmir', *ICFAI Journal of Governance and Public Policy*, 2, no. 4, (2007): 31–2 and by the same author 'Conflict Management in Northern Ireland: Lessons for Kashmir', Public lecture, Nehru Centre, Mumbai, (21 August 2010).

2. The border dividing Kashmir between India and Pakistan is disputed and remains tense. For details on this issue see Seema Shekhawat and Debidatta Aurobinda Mahapatra, *Contested Border and Division of Families in Kashmir: Contextualizing the Ordeal of the Kargil Women*, (New Delhi: WISCOMP, 2009), 17–27.

3. The onset of militancy and cross-border infiltration from Pakistan controlled Kashmir made the border more tense and rigid.

4. Personal Interview, 28 September 2012.

5. For details on problems of the borderlanders in Kashmir see, Debidatta Aurobinda Mahapatra, 'Positioning the People in the Contested Borders of Kashmir', Working paper, Centre for International Border Studies Research, Queen's University, Belfast, 2011. Also see, by the same author, 'Conflict and Contested Borders in Kashmir: Contextualizing the Ordeal of the Divided Families', Public lecture, Queen's University, Belfast, (22 March 2010) and 'The Border Displaced aftermath of the 1999 Kargil War: Enduring Ordeal and the Challenges Ahead', Paper presented at an international conference on Peace and Reconciliation, University of California Los Angeles, (7–10 July 2009). Seema Shekhawat, 'Ordeal of Kargil Displaced,' *Kashmir Images*, (2 August 2006) and by both Shekhawat and Mahapatra, 'Kargil Displaced of Akhnoor in Jammu and Kashmir', Report, Internal Displacement Monitoring Centre, (Geneva, 2006).

6. For a chronological description of India-Pakistan peace process see http://www.rediff.com/news/peacetalk.html (accessed on 11 June 2012).

7. *The Hindu*, (29 October 2009).

8. Debidatta Aurobinda Mahapatra, 'Ugly Face of Terror', *Journal of Alternative Perspectives in the Social Sciences*, 1, no. 2, (2009): 459–62.

9. See Debidatta Aurobinda Mahapatra, 'Mapping Transitional Justice in Kashmir: Drivers, Initiatives and Challenges', Working paper, Centre for Socio-Legal Studies, University of Oxford, (Oxford, 2010).

10. For a detailed study on the costs of the Kashmir conflict see, Debidatta Aurobinda Mahapatra and Seema Shekhawat, 'The Peace Process and Prospects for Economic Reconstruction in Kashmir', *Peace & Conflict Review*, 3, no. 1, (2008): 1–17; Seema Shekhawat, 'Linking Peace and Development: An Imperative for Conflict Transformation in Kashmir', in *Conflict and Peace in Eurasia*, ed. Debidatta Aurobinda Mahapatra, (New York: Routledge, 2013), 194–209 and by the same author, 'Fragile Kashmir, Costs and Hopes for Peace', *Journal of Alternative Perspectives in the Social Sciences*, 1, no. 3, (2009): 976–81; Debidatta Aurobinda Mahapatra, 'Symbiosis of Peace and Development in Kashmir: An imperative for Conflict Transformation', *Conflict Trends*, Issue 4, (2009): 23–30 and by the same author, 'Conflict and Development in Kashmir: Challenges and Opportunities', in *Sustainable Development in Conflict Environments: Challenges and Opportunities*, eds, Hari Dhungana and Marty Logan, (Kathmandu: Centre for International Studies and Cooperation, 2007), 68–77.

11. Seema Shekhawat, *Conflict and Displacement in Jammu and Kashmir: The Gender Dimension*, (Jammu: Saksham Books International, 2006) and by the same author, 'Displacement in Jammu and Kashmir', *Kashmir Images* (19 June 2006).

12. Debidatta Aurobinda Mahapatra, 'Elections in Trouble-torn Kashmir and Regional Dynamics for Peace in South Asia', *Strategic Culture Foundation*, (29 December 2008). Available at http://en.fondsk.ru/article.php?id=1833 (accessed on 23 July 2011).

13. *The Hindu*, (6 September 2005).

14. *Indian Express*, (17 June 2009).

15. *The Hindu*, (29 October 2009).

16. *The Hindu*, (2 December 2009).

17. Statement adopted at the third Round Table Conference on Jammu and Kashmir, (25 April 2007). Available at: http://www.satp.org/satporgtp/countries/india/document/papers/thirdgol.htm (accessed on 14 August 2011).

18. In his closing remarks at the third round table conference on Jammu and Kashmir, 24 April 2007 Prime Minister Singh said,

The purpose of this Roundtable process is to tap into a wide range of opinion and views that exist across the political spectrum and I believe that purpose is certainly being achieved….The Roundtable process has moved substantially forward in delivering on the vision of a Jammu & Kashmir…. A vision of a Naya (new) Jammu, Kashmir and Ladakh which is symbolised by peace, prosperity and people's power. I am sure that this dialogue process is the best way forward. Lasting peace will not come through instant deals. It will come only when the stakeholders – the people themselves – become the torchbearers of peace. This Roundtable is such a transparent process which ensures widest participation among all segments of opinion in the state. We are not trying to mechanically impose solutions from above. Rather, this process is throwing up possibilities which are representative in character.

Available at http://pmindia.nic.in/speech/content.asp?id=528 (accessed on 23 August 2011).

19. 'Strengthening Relations across the Line of Control', Report of the Working Group II, January 2007. Available at http://www.hinduonnet.com/nic/jk/jkreport_2.pdf (accessed on 23 September 2007).

20. 'Economic Development of Jammu and Kashmir', Report of Working Group III, March 2007. Available at http://www.hinduonnet.com/nic/jk/jkreport_3.pdf (accessed on 23 September 2007).

21. 'Ensuring Good Governance in Jammu & Kashmir', Report of Working Group IV, March 2007, Available at http://www.hinduonnet.com/nic/jk/jkreport_4.pdf (accessed on 23 September 2007).

22. 'Confidence Building Measures across Segments of Society in J&K', Report of Working Group I, January 2007. Available at http://www.hinduonnet.com/nic/jk/jkreport_1.pdf (accessed on 23 September 2007).

23. 'Ensuring Good Governance in Jammu & Kashmir'.

24. PDP was founded by her father, and former Indian Home Minister, Mufti Mohammad Sayeed in 1999. He was also the Chief Minister of J&K from 2002 to 2005.

25. The recommendation remains on paper so far. The three-member team of interlocutors for Kashmir, appointed by New Delhi in 2010, recommended 'fast-track implementation of the recommendations of the Prime Minister's Working Group on CBMs, in particular providing better relief and rehabilitation for widows and orphans of violence in the State, including widows and orphans of militants.' It needs emphasis that the comprehensive implementation of the recommendations of the working groups could have facilitated the transition process in Kashmir. Since the recommendations are not legally binding, it is the sole prerogative of the Indian government as to when and how they will be implemented. Most of the recommendations of the working groups have not been put into practice.

26. *The Tribune*, (15 January 2009).

27. *The Hindu*, (12 January 2010).

28. 'Confidence Building Measures across Segments of Society in J&K'.

29. 'Confidence Building Measures across Segments of Society in J&K'.

30. 'J&K State Human Rights Commission: The Healing Can Begin Here', 28 September 2005. Available at http://www.hrdc.net/sahrdc/hrfeatures/HRF127.htm (accessed on 23 June 2010.).

31. 'J&K State Human Rights Commission: The Healing Can Begin Here'.

32. Seema Shekhawat, 'Burden of Conscience', *Kashmir Images*, (9 August 2006).

33. B. Sorensen, 'Women and Post-Conflict Reconstruction: Issues and Sources', The War-Torn Societies Project, Occasional Paper No. 3, UNRISD, 1998. Available at http://www.unrisd.org/wsp/op3/toc.htm (accessed on 23 August 2011).

34. Kees Kingma, 'Post-war demobilization, reintegration and peace-building', Paper presented at an international conference and Expert Group Meeting on The Contribution of Disarmament and Conversion to Conflict Prevention and its Relevance for Development Cooperation, (Bonn, 30–31 August 1999). Available at http://www.bicc.de/ (accessed on 23 January 2012).

35. Seema Shekhawat, 'Addressing the Alienation', *Kashmir Times*, (28 April 2007).

36. Personal Interview, 21 May 2012.

37. As many as 4,080 militants had surrendered up to 30 November 2011. Fifteen militants surrendered in 2009 while 38 in 2008, 122 in 2007, 190 in 2006, 64 in 2005, 137 in 2004, 119 in 2003, 159 in 2002, 85 in 2001 and 104 in 2000. The highest number of 655 militants surrendered in 1996, followed by 612 in 1991, 601 in 1995, 444 in 1992, 270 in 1997, 187 in 1998, 109 in 1999, 98 in 1993 and 32 in 1994. Ravi Krishnan Khajuria, 'Ex-militants term rehab policy a mere eyewash', *The Tribune,* (23 April 2012).

38. For details of this policy see, 'Annual Report 2005–2006', Ministry of Home Affairs, Government of India, 14.

39. For an AK rifle – ₹ 15,000, for UMG, GPMG, PIKA, RPG and Sniper rifle – ₹ 25,000, for a revolver – ₹ 3,000 and for a grenade – ₹ 500. Khajuria, 'Ex-militants Term Rehab Policy a Mere Eyewash'.

40. *Greater Kashmir,* (26 December 2011).

41. Girja Shankar Kaura, 'Centre Ready for Amnesty to Kashmiri Ultras in PoK', *The Tribune,* (12 February 2010).

42. The policy document is available at http://india.gov.in/allimpfrms/alldocs/15934.pdf (accessed on 13 September 2012).

43. The clause stipulates opening of bank accounts with an initial deposit of ₹ 1,00,000 to ₹ 1,50,000. Additionally ₹ 2,500 to ₹ 3,000 will be deposited in these accounts of returnees by the government every month. There is also a provision for skill training to facilitate their reintegration into society and for employment of skilled returnees.

44. Geeta Pandey, 'Rebuilding Lives in Kashmir', BBC, (12 August 2012).

45. Personal Interview, 28 May 2012.

46. Ibid.

47. Personal Interview, 26 May 2012.

48. Personal Interview, 30 May 2012.

49. Quoted in Zulfiqar Ali, 'Kashmir Militants Give Up Fight and Head Home', *BBC Urdu,* Islamabad, (31 May 2012).

50. Personal Interview, 1 June 2012.

51. Personal Interview, 30 May 2012.

52. Personal Interview, 29 May 2012.

53. Pandey, 'Rebuilding lives in Kashmir'.

54. M. Saleem Pandit, 'Ex-militants to Help Plug Infiltration from Nepal', *The Times of India,* (23 April 2012).

55. Baba Umar, 'Return to Paradise?', *Tehelka Magazine,* 9, issue 14, (7 April 2012).

56. Personal Interview, 30 May 2012.

57. Mukeet Akmali, 'PoK Returnees Rue "Government Indifference"', *Greater Kashmir,* (28 August 2012).

58. Personal Interview, 26 May 2012.

59. Personal Interview, 23 May 2012.

60. Umar, 'Return to Paradise'.

61. 'Ex-militants in Jammu and Kashmir to Follow Anna Hazare's Path'. Available at http://post.jagran.com/Exmilitants-in-Jammu-and-Kashmir-to-follow-Anna-Hazares-path-1318843492 (accessed on 19 October 2012).

62. Personal Interview, 3 June 2011.
63. Shobna Sonpar, 'Potential Resource? Ex-militants in Jammu and Kashmir', *Intervention,* 6, no. 2, (2008): 147–53.
64. Personal Interview, 9 June 2011.
65. Rajnish Sharma, 'Hizb, LeT Trying to Rope in Ex-cadres', *Deccan Herald,* (27 August 2012).
66. *Daily News and Analysis,* 17 April 2012.
67. Manzoor-ul-Hasan, 'Cops Facilitating Ex-militants' Rehabilitation: S. M. Sahai', *Greater Kashmir,* (26 February 2012).
68. Wasim Khalid, 'Police Looking to Rehabilitate, Restore Dignity of Ex-militants', *Rising Kashmir,* (5 February 2012).
69. Khalid, 'Police Looking to Rehabilitate'.
70. Shanawaz Majid, 'CM Promises Rehabilitation of Former Militants', *Kashmir Images,* (28 June 2011).
71. Amin Masoodi, 'Rehabilitation Policy May Contribute Towards Peace Building in JK', (20 August 2012). Available at http://situationsasia.com/story/rehabilitation-policy-may-contribute-towards-peace-building-jk (accessed on 28 August 2012).

Chapter 7

Conclusion

The Kashmir case provides ample evidence of prejudiced nature of conflict and peace making, which glorified women as linchpins of the movement for secession but later did not hesitate in pushing them to the fringes of the peace process. Women as agents of change can participate in violence and can negotiate peace. They play significant roles in conflict and are equally capable of contributing to peace. The asymmetrical schema crafted under the male dominated socio-political structure has led to the negligence of gender analyses in conflict and peace. There is a need to highlight this neglect not only for the purpose of filling the void in literature, but also for ensuring women's due inclusion in peace building. The exclusion of women from the formal peace process is a reflection of the patriarchal penetration in every aspect of society and politics. Globally, gender insensitivity is considered normal as exclusion of women in the peace process is generally accepted. According women due space in peace making is not considered as urgent as negotiated peace, and this approach belies the very goal of peace building. It may not be implausible to argue that masculinized practices dehumanize the very peace making process which aims at establishing a stable and egalitarian society free from violence.

The neglect of women in formal peace finds reverberations in the writings of many scholars. 'You can't end wars simply by declaring peace. "Inclusive security" rests on the principle that fundamental social changes are necessary to prevent renewed hostilities. Women have proven time and again their unique ability to bridge seemingly insurmountable divides. So why aren't they at the negotiating table?,' argue Swanee Hunt and Cristina Posa.[1] I posit the question – where is the locus of the women in the peace building process? The answer is nowhere or, at the most, on the fringes. In its external dimensions, the Kashmir conflict is about states – India and Pakistan – and in its internal dimensions it is about masculinity – male security personnel and male militants. Urvashi Butalia is rather terse when she says, 'It is the male who is the hero, whether as an army man, or a militant….She does not count.'[2] The whole conflict and peace politics is 'confined to one domain – the domain of men while the women remain outside it.'[3] Masculinized militancy has ensured that women are neither duly acknowledged for being the much-needed cushion of the separatist struggle nor as stakeholders in peace building. The euphoria of the violent movement and the accompanied glorification of Kashmiri women as players have subsided and in its place has emerged a cold, almost negligent, recognition of their role even by members of their own group. Kavita Suri notes, 'many women have acted with courage amid the conflict, deserving praise but going unnoticed even in the eyes of their own people.'[4] It is a universal dichotomy that women are generally considered peaceful but they are denied due space in negotiating formal peace. Amidst the fierce debate on women's association with peace being rooted either in their nature or nurture, it is disturbing to note their near total absence from the formal peace processes globally.

Why Women Count?

This formulation may appear simplistic but it squarely focuses on the dilemma as to why women are not included in peace building and what the obstacles are in the process of their inclusion. There is an array of questions that needs to be addressed such as what women can contribute as peace makers, what difference can they make in the peace process as compared to male peace makers? Finally, in what capacities can they be involved in making peace sustainable? This probing is crucial since the silence has perpetuated the negligence of women; giving rise to the notion that the gender insensitive peace process is a *fait accompli*. The issue of participation of women smacks of indifference as at no time do the whys and hows of male participation become a part of the discourse in either conflict or peace. The male dominated peace process indicates the inconsiderateness towards according voice to almost half of the global population and their perspectives. Hence, fairness is the most prominent reason to put forward while talking about gender inclusive peace processes. Women account for nearly half of the world's population and therefore they should comprise half of the decision-makers in any field including peace making. In their absence lasting peace is impossible since 'half of the world's population cannot ensure a whole peace'.[5]

When women are not involved in the decision-making process their concerns remain neglected. Since their concerns do not factor in the negotiations, their representation is not deemed significant in the peace process. This exclusionary process further reinforces gender inequalities. Hence emerges a vicious circle wherein non-representation reinforces exclusion, which in turn further strengthens discriminatory practices. Women's leadership during peace negotiations can unveil a window of opportunity 'to empower women, promote gender equality, advance women's position in society, and bring wider benefits to many elements of society.'[6] Studies indicate when women consent to their issues being subdued in favour of projected larger goals set-up by male-centric processes, both women and their societies are generally at a loss.[7] A peace negotiated solely among the 'elites' excluding the participation of a majority of the people leads to instability. Hence planning and negotiations for sustainable peace cannot be solely left to the elites, most of whom are men.[8] Conflict is not gender-neutral it is in fact 'a gendered activity: women and men have different access to resources, power and decision-making before, during and after conflicts. The experience of women and men in situations of tension, war, and post-conflict reconstruction is significantly different,'[9] and hence gender-blind peace efforts cannot lead to lasting peace. Achieving sustainable peace is a complex process, hence the argument for the involvement of all sections of society including women.[10] Elisabeth Rehn and Ellen Johnson Sirleaf argue, 'post-conflict reconstruction and peace-building must support a society's transition [by]…involving women.…Indeed, investing in women may be one of the most effective means for real, sustainable development and peace-building.'[11] Women's presence can accord a humane face to the otherwise cold and complicated but crucial issues of rehabilitation and reconstruction. They can bring issues of core concern for society such as accommodation, education and childcare to the centre of the dialogue. These issues do not get prioritized if women are excluded from formal negotiations.[12] Women can develop and implement innovative ideas to make the negotiations sensitive and inclusive; the outcome of which can be practical and progressive. Azza Karam notes:

> Bringing women to the peace table is useful in so far as various individuals and groups of women put across their viewpoints in a gender-sensitive, honest, experientially defined way…women bring to the table the need to talk directly about the most difficult issues, rather than postponing them or getting entangled in bureaucratic logic. In addition, women's participation in processes of negotiated settlements is important because it transgresses the matter of 'putting rights on paper,' and enables practical actions to be taken.[13]

There are noteworthy cases wherein gender representation in the peace process has made a remarkable difference. In South Africa women made sure that their participation in the anti-apartheid movement was not undervalued in the post-apartheid era. Frene Ginwala explains the South African case:

> Conscious that the oppressed must help themselves, large numbers of women participated in the struggle for the liberation of South Africa, and as co-combatants were able to integrate into its theory the liberation of women. Continued involvement in the negotiations by women ensured that the new South Africa has a constitution that is gender-sensitive and provides a unique legal framework for genuine and effective equality.[14]

Ugandan women ensured provisions for specialized institutions and services to cater to their specific needs. In Northern Ireland, an all-women political party played an active role in the peace process and towards democratic stability in the region. In Guatemala, women's groups succeeded in including a number of critical gender specific issues such as equal access to land, medical care, education and vocational training in the peace agreement. In Cambodia, women's organizations were accorded a place in the committee set-up for drafting the new constitution. These women were able to negotiate significant constitutional guarantees including the right to vote and the right to choose a profession. In Liberia, participation of women in peace talks significantly impacted not only the transitional process but also set the stage for the exemplary political participation of women. Women of the Liberia Mass Action for Peace, led by Leymah Gbowee, who was awarded the Nobel peace prize in 2011, played a key role in the return of democracy to the war-torn country and in the election of a woman president in the post-conflict phase.[15] Women's involvement in the Bonn negotiations on Afghanistan led to the inclusion of gender-specific rights in the constitution with positive political ramifications in terms of representation in the decision-making processes.[16] These illustrations are exceptions rather than a norm. In most conflict-ridden societies, as evident in cases of Angola, Algeria, Somalia, Sierra Leone, East Timor and Zimbabwe, the gender component remains nearly absent from transition processes.

Global Invisibility

On 31 October 2000 the UNSC unanimously approved the historic Resolution 1325 on Women, Peace and Security for the advancement of gender equality. This resolution is considered a crucial international document for advancing gender equality in all processes of peace building, during and post-conflict.[17] It has been lauded as it marked the UN's full-fledged attention to gendered aspects of peace and conflict, and also brought into focus the official endorsement of the involvement of women in formal peace processes.[18]

Recognizing that women and men experience conflict and post-conflict situations differently, the resolution acknowledged the critical role that women can play in preventing and resolving conflicts and in building peace. Beginning with the recognition that women's visibility is crucial, it made a case for gender inclusive peace building. It called for full participation of women in all efforts towards conflict prevention, resolution, peace making and post-conflict reconstruction. The UN in its earlier resolutions including UNSC 1261 of 25 August 1999, UNSC 1265 of 17 September 1999, UNSC 1296 of 19 April 2000 and UNSC 1314 of 11 August 2000, in relevant statements of the UNSC President, including the one on the International Women's Day 2000, the Beijing Declaration and Platform for Action as well as in the document of the 23rd Special Session of the UN General Assembly titled 'Women 2000: Gender Equality, Development and Peace for the Twenty-First Century', emphasized gender equality in development and peace process. The October 2000 resolution reflected the core concerns of previous resolutions and documents and affirmed:

> The important role of women in the prevention and resolution of conflicts and in peace-building, and stressing the importance of their equal participation and full involvement in all efforts for the maintenance and promotion of peace and security, and the need to increase their role in decision-making with regard to conflict prevention and resolution,...[It recognized] that an understanding of the impact of armed conflict on women and girls, effective institutional arrangements to guarantee their protection and full participation in the peace process can significantly contribute to the maintenance and promotion of international peace and security,...[It urged] Member States to ensure increased representation of women at all decision-making levels in national, regional and international institutions and mechanisms for the prevention, management, and resolution of conflict.[19]

It recommended that all actors involved in conflict transformation must adopt a gender perspective when negotiating and implementing peace agreements through taking into account the specific needs of women during repatriation and for rehabilitation, reintegration and reconstruction; policymaking and implementing measures to support women's peace initiatives; involving women in the implementation of peace agreements; and ensuring the protection of and respect for human rights of women.[20] In 2008 the UNSC adopted Resolution 1820, an extension of Resolution 1325 explicitly asserting, among other things, the urgency of women's inclusion in peace efforts.

Despite being binding on all the UN member states, the resolution has not been put into practice comprehensively since there is no enforcement or accountability mechanism. Though awareness about the urgency of including women in peace building has grown internationally, the implementation of the resolution is ad hoc. Notwithstanding the fact that with the adoption of this resolution women's involvement in peace processes has been increasing, the pace is alarmingly slow at local, national as well as international levels. Women continue to remain under-represented or absent from formal peace building processes even 13 years after this UNSC resolution was passed and more than one and half decades since the adoption of the Beijing Declaration and Platform for Action. Globally, they continue to be invisible in formal peace negotiations.[21] The numerical strength of women at peace tables remains distressingly low. According to a 2011 UNSC report merely 16 per cent women participated in 585 peace agreements concluded between 1990 and 2010.[22] A study of 24 major peace processes since 1992 revealed that only 2.5 per cent of the signatories, 3.2 per cent of the mediators, 5.5 per cent of the witnesses and 7.6 per cent of the negotiators were women.[23] Another report points out that of the 11 peace agreements signed in 2011, merely two countries, Somalia and Yemen, included particular provisions for women.[24] Gender insensitivity in the peace making process in Kashmir epitomizes this dismal scenario.

Kashmir, the Prototype

The highly masculinized conflict and peace discourse determines inclusionary and exclusionary practices in Kashmir. Women's participation is not determined by their volition but by the male leadership which, by applying the analogy of a rubber band, stretches or shrinks the role of women in conflict and peace. Kashmiri women were directed by the militant leadership to broaden their traditional roles as mothers, sisters, wives and daughters to facilitate and sustain the armed resistance. Once the armed conflict subsided, the role of women shrunk to the confines of the private sphere of the four walls of a house. The scenario resembles a puppet show in which the actions of the marionettes on the stage are determined by the puppeteers. Kashmiri women were seen and heard when deemed obligatory by the leadership to project armed militancy as a mass upsurge. They indeed were successful. Initially militancy was a popular movement, wherein women participated in large numbers in demonstrations (were seen) and shouted anti-Indian and pro-freedom slogans (were heard). With the change in the course of the armed struggle, with major indigenous militant groups laying down arms and resorting to peaceful methods, it was not considered essential for women to be either seen or heard. The male separatist leadership took centre stage and pushed the women to the fringes. Was militancy a mass movement and peace building not? Are women competent to make war, not peace? Is peace making an elite, male privilege in which women can neither be actors nor beneficiaries?

The armed movement was projected by militant ideologues to be one for freedom and dignity of Kashmiri people but they failed to bestow the same to their own women. Seema Kazi argues, 'although these leaders are ostensibly committed to struggling for democracy in Kashmir, democratic rights for Kashmir women do not figure in their agenda.... [This] reflects their maintenance of the gendered status quo.'[25] Kashmiri women do not constitute a part of any formal peace talks initiated to address the conflict. They have not been provided fair representation by either the separatist leadership or by the authorities. Neither of the two sides has advocated the formal inclusion of women in peace negotiations. The impressive list of peace attempts notwithstanding, both women and their concerns are evidently absent in these attempts.[26] The political space for once highly visible women shrunk in the transitional period towards peace. Prominent women separatist leaders were either co-opted by the masculine separatist leadership or sidelined when, if at all, they raised their voice against male hegemony. Asiya Andrabi and few members of her party are sporadically visible advocating and perpetuating extremism against Kashmiri women. Farida Dar is no longer visible in the public sphere. Zamrooda Habib, leader of the Muslim Khawateen Markaz (MKM), had been relatively vocal in raising her voice against gender insensitive separatist politics,

> Women have been at the forefront during the protests and have suffered... some have been killed and crippled for life during the present agitation (and) during insurgency raped, molested and rendered destitute, widowed...but the nation isn't aware of their sacrifices and contribution. They are not given the political space in decision-making they deserve.[27]

On another occasion she has been quoted as reiterating her stance:

> Women have been suffering passively throughout the whole period of insurgency as they have been raped, molested, turned to half widows or rendered destitute as their fathers, brothers or husbands were killed by the army. They have offered numerous sacrifices by giving their beloved sons for the resistance but the nation isn't well aware of their tremendous sacrifices and contribution. They are not given the political space in decision making that they deserve.[28]

Habib has suffered the apathy of male separatist leadership. In one of her writings she recalls being disowned by Hurriyat Conference on being arrested by Indian security forces in 2003 in a smuggling case.[29] Though she is ignored by the Hurriyat Conference, her organization continues to be a part of this amalgamation. It seems there is no alternative for these women except either to subscribe to the diktats of the male leaders or perish from the public domain. 'Zamrooda argued for gender equality on many occasions but none listened to her. No one in Hurriyat Conference is bothered about MKM. Despite the apathetic attitude of the leadership, MKM is still a constituent of Hurriyat for the sake of survival in Kashmir,' contended an ex-member of MKM.[30]

The peace making process is generally considered gender neutral but a closer scrutiny reveals that the process is gender discriminatory. It is not merely an issue of neglect or ignorance but a deliberate patriarchal ploy to accord peripheral position to women in public and private spheres. The exclusion of women is by and large justified on flimsy grounds such as women are apolitical and apathetic,[31] they are busy in household chores or they are saved from several risks by maintaining a distance from peace politics. Javed Ahmed Mir, a JKLF leader has been quoted as saying, 'women aren't sure what they want. They do not have clear ideas.'[32] On being asked why women are not present in the decision-making body of the Hurriyat Conference, Syed Ali Shah Geelani, the leader of the radical faction of the organization said, 'it would expose women to unnecessary risk. They would be picked up, manhandled and arrested like other Hurriyat leaders.'[33] When I posed this question to an ex-militant leader the response was, 'women have to perform many routine activities. They are busy in families and hence are not free like men to travel and spend time outside their homes.'[34] What do these statements imply? That only men are political and interested in political issues, they are not busy in family affairs and hence have free time to engage in public affairs or they are brave enough to confront the risks involved in peace making for the sake of their community, including women. How does this justify involving women in conflict as fighters and supporters and denying them any role in peace building? Is it not an irony that men are prepared to shoulder the 'risk' of peace making all alone but are not hesitant to share the risks of armed conflict with women? When it comes to peace, risk is cited as a factor for excluding women but when it comes to violent movements the risk factor does not appear on the horizon. There is intrinsic patriarchal resistance on the part of Kashmiri men even to acknowledge the significant position of women in conflict, as a result of which, women's exclusion from the peace process has not resulted in the needed introspection and action. One of my respondent's observations reflected this asymmetry, 'when we are not considered equal by men at home how can we even dream of being equal in public life in terms of recognition of our role in the *azadi* movement and demanding our due place in the peace building process?'[35]

Patriarchy Prevails

The space for redefining gender relations in violent struggles including that in Kashmir remains a contested one. The issue becomes more complicated in conflict situations such as in Nepal, where the leaders of the Maoist movement envisioned an egalitarian society devoid of patriarchy. The initial pledge of gender equality was abandoned once arms are laid down and negotiations began. The male dominated power politics in this later phase gave rise to a genuine inkling that the pledge of parity was a ploy to garner mass support. Nevertheless, in conflict situations there are instances when armed women enjoyed semblance of parity and power with their male counterparts. It is contended by many scholars that not all the experiences of women are subjugating; some of them are also empowering since war 'destroys the patriarchal structures of society that confine and degrade women. In the very breakdown of morals, traditions, customs, and community, war also opens up new beginnings.'[36] A number of studies indicate that empowerment, if any, is at the most ambivalent.[37] At times women actors suffer in gender-specific ways including sexual abuse at the hands of their male counterparts.[38] Even if it is established that empowerment takes place during the conflict, the puzzling question that follows is why does not the newly gained agency persist in post-conflict period? Why is the agency provisional? Isn't it a case of premeditated utilization of women, by luring them to join violence, to achieve a 'sacrosanct' goal? The persistence of patriarchy before, during and in post-conflict situation shapes the involvement of women in conflict and peace. The patriarchal ideology does not cease to operate in conflict situations; at the most, if at all, it gets partially subverted to re-erupt as soon as the transition process starts. This partial collapse of the chauvinistic order in times of conflict is incidental. Even if it is intentional, the aim is certainly not reshaping gender equations but sustaining the rebel movement.

Even if gender relations are challenged momentarily for the duration of the conflict it can be a significant respite from the patriarchal tangle that carries on unchallenged during times of relative peace. Is conflict empowering from a gender perspective? Scores of my respondents from Nepal and Sri Lanka responded affirmatively. For them life as a combatant was better than the pre and post-conflict one. A Nepalese ex-combatant asserted that, 'if given a choice I will prefer to go back to the period of conflict. It was a much better life.'[39] Restoration of peace in terms of return to a pre-conflict scenario is rather discomforting for armed women. The post-conflict scenario brings forth in its trail a number of gender-specific problems ranging from economic to societal. Since the concerns of female ex-combatants are not genuinely addressed in peace and reintegration programmes, they suffer more, in both the short and long term, than their male counterparts. Generally, there is no support for these women to rejoin mainstream society. Many female ex-combatants deal with the experience of inclusion in war and exclusion in peace. In Nepal, out of the 3,558 identified female combatants, more than 3,000 opted for voluntary retirement and only 218 women demanded reintegration in the Nepal Army.[40] The ex-combatants have to negotiate their space in a highly patriarchal society, which is a long and arduous process. Sharada Khadka gives details of the situation of female ex-combatants in Nepal:

> Female ex-combatants are at the forefront of some of the most conflict-ridden and painful slow social transformations within post-war Nepal. They have experienced war-time empowerment and currently a sense of disillusionment, indeed a difficult experience. Firstly, they went through incredible difficulties and formative experiences during the war, which taught them new warrior skills, a sense of empowerment. Secondly, after the discharge, they are found to have to cope with the feudal, gender differentiated society that they had abandoned long ago and hoped to radically transform by the barrel of their guns.[41]

In the aftermath of the negotiated settlement of the Maoist conflict in Nepal, the involvement of women in peace and politics remains visibly low. To quote a 2012 report:

> The post-conflict transition period has not put an end to inequality. Despite the 33 percent representation of women in the CA (Constituent Assembly), their decision making powers remained indistinct. With political parties being deeply entrenched in patriarchal norms and values, women were given little say. Women politicians continue to be side-lined in positions of power within the political parties. Despite party manifestos underscoring women's rights issues, violence faced by women politicians themselves are unaddressed. Women's participation in the peace negotiations has remained insignificant, and they are under-represented in most government and non-government bodies, especially at decision making levels.[42]

The marginalization of women is pervasive in several South Asian countries even if the conflict is settled through negotiations, as in Nepal or through confrontation, as in Sri Lanka. In Sri Lanka the civil war came to an end with the victory of government forces over the LTTE. There are programmes that the Sri Lankan government has initiated ostensibly to facilitate reintegration and rehabilitation of the Tamil community but women continue to be at the receiving end. 'Anecdotal evidence suggests that violence against women and structural discrimination has increased in former conflict areas due to lack of participation of women,' claims the 2012 Civil Society Monitoring Report.[43] The problems of female ex-combatants are further compounded by lack of support from within the community, forcing many to relocate to India. Several of them do not receive any financial assistance and are forced to do menial jobs for survival. Many of my Sri Lankan respondents have learnt new languages and acquired new identities to assimilate with the Indian population. In the Indian state of Punjab, as in the case of Sri Lanka, Indian security personnel gained a military victory over the militants. In the post-Khalistan movement scenario no formal process was initiated by New Delhi to address the concerns of the Sikh community. Ex-militants, their supporters and the community at large were left to their own means. Many women supporters of Khalistan returned to a 'normal' life with stipulations by their families to forget their past as a 'bad dream'. Some others were forced to leave their native places, and many others had to lead a 'compromised' life. One respondent said:

> The choice was between leaving the village or to marry an elderly sick man who actually needed a nurse to attend to him. I chose the second option. My husband was critical and died after one and half year of the marriage. His death made me the owner of his house and of fertile land. I now have social acceptance, economic sustenance and a son as a family. What else can a woman, particularly an ex-militant, aspire for? In our society, it is better to lead the life of a widow than remaining unmarried or leaving the *pind* (village) and resettling in an unknown place.[44]

While in case of Nepal and Sri Lanka gender equality was a proclaimed goal of the rebel groups, in Kashmir it was not an issue during the armed struggle. Women's issues were completely sidelined to ensure that the focus was on the goal of *azadi*. Men and women equally shared this patriarchal ideology. For a majority of my respondents, gender was never a matter of discussion. Sabeena reasoned:

> Gender equality will be achieved once we are independent from India. Rather it will be realized automatically after *azadi*. Since *azadi* has not become a reality so far, women are suffering from discrimination. I am sure once we achieve our goal, women will enjoy equality. Asking for equality while fighting for independence would have been imprudent. It could have diluted the struggle and divided Kashmiris.[45]

Most Kashmiri women do not even assert for a place in both conflict and peace narratives. During an interview, a mainstream female political leader of Kashmir, Mehbooba Mufti, was posed the question, 'where are the women in peace process?' and her response was 'conditions were not conducive to talk about women's experience of the conflict at the moment, that would be possible only when things were better.'[46] There is a deafening silence on the part of a majority of the women who are reluctant to stake their claim in peace making. *Ham kya kar sakte hain?* (what can we do?) is the oft-repeated response. Many consider their involvement in militancy 'not worth mentioning'. The marginalization is accepted as given.[47] Rita Manchanda argues:

> Part of the difficulty of making women's activism in peace building visible and therefore mainstreaming gender in the political activity of peace agreements and the actual planning for a society's reconstruction, is that women themselves see their activity as non political and an extension of their domestic concerns – 'stretched roles.' Moreover, women's visibility is further obscured by the fact that their language of support and resistance flows from their cultural experience, especially of being disempowered.[48]

Few women are vocal in asserting their appropriate place in both the conflict and peace discourse but their numerical strength is abysmally low.[49] I have contended in an earlier writing.[50]

> Women's participation in militancy added to the tagging of the whole struggle for a just cause but, it added nothing to the discourse of women's empowerment, rather it accentuated their victimization in many ways, thus giving rise to the problematique: are women supporters of militancy actually perpetrators or are they victims?

The conflict in Kashmir, in many ways, provided an occasion for women to accomplish agency by challenging patriarchal norms. The traditional social structure and gendered hierarchies could have been challenged with the opening of, even though in a limited manner and for a limited time, the public space for women. But such a prospect wilted in the embryo.

In Kashmir, patriarchy did not cease to exist even momentarily during the conflict period. Women were assigned selective tasks, which were deemed as a mere extension of their traditional roles. They were simply followers. There was not even token representation of women in the formal militant leadership or in the higher ranks. Even in women's victimization, patriarchal values played a crucial role. Women confronted discrimination from 'all men surrounding them, whether militants, or security forces, or their own families.'[51] Particularly in the context of rape, prejudicial practices factored starkly. The security forces and militants raped and abused women. Militant ideologues persuaded the victims of rape, committed by Indian security personnel, to publicly testify in order to draw the attention of the international community. With a decline in armed militancy the same leaders turned an ostrich eye to their plight. Public testimonies, at the behest of militant leaders, in a conservative society later led to the ostracism of many Kashmiri women. To draw on a popular analogy once the euphoria of *azadi* ebbed, these rape victims found themselves between the hard rock of the insensitive separatist leadership which used and abused them and the deep sea of society which commended their 'bravery' during the conflict but did not hesitate to abandon them after the conflict. Raped women were exploited as a tool to evoke mass sentiments and seek international attention by the male leadership but no genuine attempts were made to seek justice for the victims or to challenge associated social stigmas. The most vocally narrated case is of Kunan Poshpura village where scores of women were raped by Indian security personnel in February 1991. According to Amnesty International:

> Reports suggest that hundreds of soldiers, many of whom were drunk, arrived at the village around 11 p.m. The men were taken from their houses and tortured during the night and interrogated about Kashmiri militant activity while large numbers of women, reportedly aged between 13 and 80 years old, were raped at gunpoint. The incident came to light through a letter dated 7 March 1991 (No. conf/1956-61) from the local magistrate, S. M. Yasin, to the State Commissioner of Kashmir, Wajahat Habibullah. The local magistrate confirmed the allegations after he visited the village on 5 March. He stated that, 'The armed forces had turned violent and behaved like beasts.[52]

The security forces and state authorities discredited the reports confirming the abuses.[53] At the insistence of separatist leaders, victimized women of the village testified only to be dumped by one and all.[54] Kazi notes, 'Kashmir's militant leaders have cashed in on public anger against rape by the military, yet their own patriarchal rhetoric does not in any way alter the social realities of rape survivors.'[55] Similarly Manchanda argues, 'women raped by security forces are exploited in the propaganda war to expose the human rights violations of the state. But as in Kashmir, the pro-separatist political ideologues fail to take on the challenge of locating rape in gender politics, reinforcing the notion of feminisation of honour, thus condemning the raped women to social ostracism in a patriarchal society.'[56] Zenab, raped by two security personnel during a cordon search, narrated:

> We have been used and abused by everyone. I was raped by two security personnel during a cordon and search operation. I was one of the three women who testified the rape in public. Our narratives were recorded and later the

cassettes were sent to the media and some international organizations. Later I was asked by my in-laws to leave the house. I requested a local militant for help. He came to our house with his group and convinced my family to allow me to stay. After a week I was thrown out of the house by my husband. This time militants did not help. They expressed their helplessness. I was advised by a militant to take divorce and remarry. Was it feasible, remarriage of a raped woman? Twelve years have passed since the rape and the public testimony. I am single and live alone in this place where no one is aware of my past. The Indians raped me physically and then I was raped mentally by my own people – my leaders, my society and my family.[57]

Notably, in 1995 MKM had proposed that ex-militants should be 'persuaded' to marry the raped women to set an example for the Kashmiri youth but the idea was rejected by Hurriyat leaders.[58] It is an irony that during a Hurriyat's hunger strike in New Delhi in 1998, to highlight the issue of rape in Kashmir, no woman was present. This women-specific issue was talked about in an all-man show for the reason that 'Hurriyat leaders did not believe that the presence of their women members was necessary.'[59]

Patriarchy did not subside even momentarily in Kashmir, it, in fact, strengthened. Hence, instead of bringing temporary agency, as was claimed by some of my respondents from other South Asian conflicts, it accentuated their subjugation. The reinforcement of patriarchy was evident in women-specific militant diktats such as veiling, prohibition of sterilization and abortion and closure of beauty salons. Being caught between the guns of militants and security forces societal control over women's public and private lives increased as is evident from the narration of a respondent:

> Before militancy we did not have such a restrictive lifestyle. But now you can notice a visible increase in control over women. For instance, most women now wear the veil or at least wear a headscarf. This is because on the one hand the extremist militant groups force us to do so and on the other hand we have to save ourselves from Indian security personnel. There is also the issue of social acceptability. Our society has become more conservative. Even our women political leaders, for example Mehbooba Mufti, have to wear the headscarf for acceptability. I keep a close watch on every move of my teenage daughter. She wants to lead a different life but I cannot allow that. She at times insists on buying a trouser, a shirt and also a mobile. Though we can afford these items but I cannot take the risk. I do not even permit her to watch television. If she does anything prohibited by militants the whole family will suffer.[60]

Though militancy is receding, its patriarchal outlook persists as reflected in recent calls by extremist elements for veiling and prohibiting the use of mobile phones by young women. To reproduce a warning by the militants:

> People should ensure that girls observe purdah (veil) in public places. If we spot any woman without purdah we will sprinkle acid on her face,' handwritten posters of Lashkar Al Qaeda and Alqaeda Mujahideen warned. The posters, appearing at many mosques in militancy-hit Shopian district a few days ago, threatened, 'If we spot any girl using mobile phone, she will be shot dead.[61]

Guns Matter

In most global conflicts men usually take up arms. Arguably no conflict has witnessed a higher numerical strength of female active combatants as compared to male combatants. Women are primarily visible in support roles and their numerical strength may be, at times, higher than men as performers of auxiliary tasks. The discourse on conflict and peace usually revolves around those who wield guns and not around those who support their operations from the margins. Women in support roles are not considered combatants, hence their involvement is undervalued. Vivi Stavrou and Josefa Dombolo argue,

> 'Not labeling the work of non-combatant women soldiers as soldiering, continues the gender discrimination of the division of labour whereby critical work that is essential for survival, is simply considered a natural extension of women's domestic obligations and hence neither worthy of remuneration nor significant enough for women to qualify for training and livelihoods programs.'[62]

Gender invisibility in the peace discourse is a direct outcome of the presumption that 'women are external, far removed from the scene of actual combat' and for this purpose 'false dichotomies of home vs. Warfront' are constructed.[63] The presumption that is quite widespread in Kashmir is that since women did not take up arms the value of their contribution is of less significance than that of armed men. 'Women did not risk their lives as we did by taking up arms, hence our (men's) contribution to the struggle cannot be equated with that of women who merely helped us,' said one male ex-militant in Kashmir.[64] Kazi aptly sums up this generalization, 'while the attempt to retain combat as a fundamental and decisive marker of the public-private dichotomy is not unique to Kashmir, its significance relates to the unstated, albeit manifest, reluctance of Kashmiri men to accept women as political equals.'[65] The commonly held assumption is that men who took up arms did something extraordinary and women's role as caretakers and nurturers is perceived as mundane. It is assumed that men carrying weapons need to be dealt with either through force or pacifism and women supporters will automatically fall in the line; and armed men need specific attention and not unarmed female supporters. Ani Colekessian contends:

> Peace process has often assumed a realist approach to security, in which the function of efforts has focused namely on disarming perceived violent [male] combatants...at the expense of a holistic, gender-sensitive, approach to security. Such an approach ignores the unarmed roles of members involved in armed groups, particularly those of women who may not be perceived as an immediate security threat.[66]

What if women are armed? Are they then accorded the same status as their male counterparts in peace making? As discussed earlier with reference to female combatants in Nepal and Sri Lanka, the prospects are actually dim.

Female participants in violence can be categorized in three broad, at times overlapping, categories – combatants, supporters and dependents.[67] Female combatants take up arms, while female supporters are associated with armed forces and groups, either by 'coercion' or 'volition', to perform auxiliary tasks such as porters, cooks, nurses, spies, translators and radio operators. The dependents are those women who constitute a part of households of combatants such as wives, daughters, mothers, sisters and other female members of the extended family. All these categories of women should be accorded due attention in the peace and rebuilding processes. Post-conflict peace attempts have implications for women, whether they participated in combat, have family members who did, or are members of a community endeavouring to integrate former combatants.[68] Peace building efforts should include all those who took up arms, those who supported violence, the families of the instigators of violence and those who suffered the violence. A UN report on gender in disarmament, demobilization and reintegration (DDR) notes:

> Although there may often be pressures to get the guns out of the hands of combatants, it is important to understand more than just the needs, interests and situation of combatants. There are at least two important pieces in a reintegration initiative: the combatant and the family/society into which they are to be reintegrated. Just as the combatant's life has changed during the conflict, so have the lives of non-combatants. Family members not directly participating in the fighting may have still been victims of violence: they may have fled their homes, had to take on new responsibilities and learn new skills, overcome harsh obstacles and be carrying their own war horrors. These families also need support if they are to successfully receive and reintegrate ex-combatants. Specific issues relating to gender roles and responsibilities can arise in this process.[69]

The argument for inclusion of all women in peace building may be a logical one and termed desirable, but in the current dismal scenario it seems to be untenable as even armed women are not accorded due space in the peace process. These women may have fought as cadres or even commanded a battalion of fighters but when it comes to peace making they are visible nowhere, neither in decision-making nor in availing the major or even equal dividends of the transition process. The needs and concerns of female ex-combatants do not constitute a crucial part of either peace negotiations or policies. The generally accepted notion of combatants as being only men fighters has to be primarily held responsible for this omission. Excluding armed women from the category of combatants prohibit them from being the primary target of peace initiatives, including DDR.[70] Unarmed female supporters are excluded from DDR programmes since they do not have weapons to meet the first condition of the programme – disarmament. The DDR process for men is generally emphasized as vital to the transition process while for women it has been deemed, at the most, a 'social concern' that does not need specific attention. Megan MacKenzie elaborates:

> Men and masculinity are securitized post-conflict while women – even when they act in highly securitized roles such as soldiers – are desecuritized and, in effect, de-emphasized in post-conflict policy making. The impact of this categorization has been that the reintegration process for men has been securitized, or emphasized as an essential element of the transition from war to peace. In contrast, the reintegration process for females has been deemed a social concern and has been moralized as a return to normal.[71]

The predominance of male ex-militants is not the only reason for gender insensitivity in peace and reconstruction efforts; the projected preponderance of women as victims aids the lopsided processes towards return to normalcy.

Asymmetrical Victimization Discourse

Despite burgeoning research on women as participants in war the general assumption that men are perpetrators and women are victims dominates the theory and practice of the conflict discourse. The traditional security paradigm is based on the gender stereotype of men being the soldiers and women the victims. Women continue to be perceived as marginal to situations of war, and victims at best, and hence their multiple experiences of conflict receive scant attention from various quarters including policymakers and the media. If one scans media reports of the ongoing war in Syria one can easily come across images of women and children herded in refugee camps as victims and images of men-rebels carrying guns.

Undoubtedly women are affected in terms of human rights violations in conflict situations. It is indubitable that women experience conflict-related violence perhaps in a more wretched way than other groups. The irony is that women who are considered the worst sufferers of the conflict remain at the periphery of the peace process. Where do all these 'worst sufferers' go when the formal peace process is negotiated? Once formal peace is attempted women are ignored not only by both the parties but also by the international community. Their victimization receives attention but not their post-conflict concerns. Rehn and Sirleaf elaborate on this issue by quoting a woman from Kosovo:

> It is really amazing...that the international community cared only about Kosovar women when they were being raped – and then only as some sort of exciting story. We see now that they really don't give a damn about us. What we see here are men, men, men from Europe and America and even Asia, listening to men, men, men from Kosovo. Sometimes they have to be politically correct so they include a woman on a committee or they add a paragraph to a report. But when it comes to real involvement in the planning for the future of this country, our men tell the foreign men to ignore our ideas. And they are happy to do so – under the notion of 'cultural sensitivity.'[72]

Kashmir is no exception to this trend. The mainstream discourse on militancy has not accorded a place to women except as victims. In the initial years of militancy women were the face of the militancy, they continue to be the face of victimization but are nowhere in the peace process. Neither the government nor the militant leadership acknowledges that beyond victimization, women have an existence. Talk to anyone about women in Kashmir and they promptly cite instances of abuse of women by Indian security forces. Not many seem to be interested in discussing inclusion of women in conflict and exclusion in peace. The fallout of this scenario is that women are neither recognized as active agents of conflict nor stakeholders in peace. Challenging the victimization discourse in Kashmir Aaliya Anjum says:

> As Kashmiri masses were riding high on the wave for 'azadi'...women did not remain impervious to the charged political landscape. They were pushed by circumstance or sentiment of nationalism to engage either as victim-activists, protesters or as separatist politicians. However, a Kashmiri woman's identity and place in historical accounts describing her position in the ongoing struggle – more often than not – is seen to rest at being a 'victim.' Relegating women's engagement in conflict situations to the passive space of victimhood is an anticipated outcome of the unequal distribution of power in gender relations. However, this narrative obfuscates their role as active participants, which is of equal, if not greater, significance – and which has increasingly become an accentuating facet of their participation during the recent years of the conflict.[73]

The simplistic portrayal of women as hapless victims needs to be critically challenged in an exercise not only to bring into the forefront their multi-faceted experiences but also to accord them due space in peace building. The UNSC Resolution 1325 explicitly reorients the victim discourse by acknowledging that women's experiences of conflict go beyond victimhood; they can be agents of violence as well. The resolution hence 'encourages all those involved in the planning for disarmament, demobilization and reintegration to consider the different needs of female and male ex-combatants and to take into account the needs of their dependants.'[74]

Reshaping Peace Building

In short, the story is that women are at the margins of peace processes globally. Does this scenario imply women do not make peace? Yes, they do. But, their peace activism is largely unorganized and gets undervalued when formal negotiations start. Women are quite active in negotiating peace in informal spaces and even facilitating the formal process towards peace. Once the stage is set for formal negotiations women are pushed back as it is appropriated by the male leadership. It is an irony that women can be involved in informal peace making as healers and reconcilers but not in the formal decision-making process. Rashmi Goswami sums up this situation:

> When the state initiates to involve them, it is really to be go-betweens, to play the role of the 'healer' or the 'pacifier.' There has been no effort on the side of the state or non-state agencies to involve women in actual negotiations. This merely goes to re-emphasise the lack of understanding of peace in terms of mutuality and equality, and of viewing the peace process as a kind of 'settlement.'[75]

Increasingly women are asserting their rights, recognizing the significance of migrating from the informal space of crafting peace to the formal sphere of peace making.[76] This migration from the informal to the formal is gradually gaining ground in Kashmir. I cite two instances. Athwaas, a women's group has actively advocated a gender inclusive peace process. Following is an excerpt of an open letter written by the coordinator of the group to the Prime Minister of India:

> The Prime Minister of India Dr. Manmohan Singh has invited all the political parties and groups, including the separatist leaders, to begin exploring a joint solution for peace in Jammu and Kashmir. However, the Prime Minister has

once again excluded the voices of 50 per cent of the population in the process. We, the Athwaas members – an alliance of women from Jammu, Kashmir and Ladakh – welcome and support the initiative, but we strongly urge the Honourable Prime Minister to include women's perspectives, insights and understanding in the dialogue process to ensure a long lasting, creative and sustainable solution. In the last 20 years of political unrest and continued violence, it has been the women who have held the fabric of the society, their families and communities together. They have rejected violence as a means to achieve political goals and reached out to adversaries for rebuilding human relationships.[77]

In 2010 a Kashmiri women's delegation, invoking applicability of UN Resolution 1325 to Kashmir, submitted a memorandum to the Home Secretary of India to involve women in the peace process. It was contended by some analysts that this memorandum led to the appointment of a woman to the three member team of interlocutors on Kashmir by New Delhi in 2010 to assess the ground situation and recommend measures towards normalcy.[78] The presence of a woman in the panel ensured inclusion of the word women scores of times in the final report.[79] Should the inclusion of this five letter word a number of times in the report be applauded? Probably yes, keeping in view though there is plethora of reports on Kashmir submitted by interlocutors, working groups, committees etc. in the past; in none of them women figured significantly and whenever they did, it was as victims, that too as widows. In the report submitted by the most recent team of interlocutors to the Government of India, I did not find any specific suggestion or recommendation to ensure gender parity in peace and reintegration initiatives although at a few places it has been indicated that women need to be part of the overall process. The report reads,

> At a broader level, the role of women in peacemaking – and especially in peace-building – is now recognized as contributing significantly to a meaningful peace process. Though women are active in various supportive ways in Jammu and Kashmir, they have not been sufficiently involved by government in "the healing touch".[80]

Token representation or inclusion of a single woman in one committee cannot bring desired results. More so, representation alone will not ensure gender equality. The presence of a large number of women on the peace table 'is not necessarily the automatic formula for gender parity'.[81] Also, gender parity in terms of both representation and consideration of their concerns should not be limited to the victimization discourse. The peace building process has to include women beyond victimization and customary charting out of policies to 'help the vulnerable'. Gender should be mainstreamed as early as negotiations and throughout policymaking, implementation and evaluation. It must be a core component of agenda setting, deliberations, policymaking and implementation of those policies. It has to become an essential tool for all steps of peace building and for this to happen the voices of women have to be more organized, sharp, precise and vocal.

I do not intend to prescribe an exhaustive list of dos and dont's to be adopted in making the peace process gender sensitive. Impressive recommendations are accessible in various reports of the UN and other organizations to achieve the objective. The UNSC Resolution 1325 and Convention on Elimination of All Forms of Discrimination Against Women provide ample guidance in this regard. The need is to localize the recommendations for maximum benefits. The recipe of gender sensitive peace making is available and it needs to be improvised to cater to specific contexts. What I consider significant in the context of Kashmir is due emphasis on the gendered contribution of women in the armed conflict. Their involvement must be acknowledged, which may goad leaders at both ends of the spectrum to work towards inclusive peace. As discussed earlier, gender exclusion from the peace and reintegration process not only leads to persistence of inequality in society and in polity but also jeopardizes prospects of sustainable peace. If peace initiatives have to positively impact the situation in the region it is imperative to espouse a comprehensive approach to include women and their concerns in peace attempts. The separatist groups involved in talks must ensure that women are accorded due representation. Indian and state governments must also ensure that female officials are part of negotiating teams. There is a need to discuss women-specific concerns in peace efforts. For instance, there should be a provision for proper rehabilitation of women supporters of militancy. They did not handle weapons but helped those who took up arms and hence stood up against the state. If the male militants have been provided an opportunity to surrender and seek assistance to start life afresh why cannot the same provision be made available for women who shun violence and intend to return to the mainstream? If the Government of India aims to reintegrate ex-militants who wielded guns, how can such a policy exclude women who were active supporters of armed militants? Why is a high premium put by the state on male militants who carried guns and no notice is taken of those who hid the guns under their veils? These women, like their male counterparts, had grievances against the Indian state and hence supported the violent movement. Why are no specific steps taken to address the grievances of this support group? Gender sensitive budgeting for reconstruction programmes is crucial to ensure that women benefit. To ensure greater effectiveness in addressing women specific issues, a gender sensitive work ethic and culture must be imparted to public servants including security personnel through various training programmes.

Policies for real empowerment should be integral to the peace making process to 'facilitate the struggle for social justice and women's equality through a transformation of economic, social, and political structures.'[82] Capacity building through socio-economic and political empowerment will ensure gender equality in all programmes of reconstruction and resource distribution. Rehn and Sirleaf argue:

> Reconstruction provides a rare opportunity for women not only to help shape emerging political, economic and social structures, but to benefit from the large amount of funds....Although women may benefit broadly from the positive forces of reconstruction, there is no doubt...that the vast majority of aid...is not being directed to women. They certainly will not receive their fair share without deliberate planning....For women to benefit equitably from transitional aid, specific policy and programme strategies are needed.[83]

Women's active participation in reconstruction programmes needs special attention because, as a UN report suggests:

> Women and men have unequal access to resources following conflict. Given existing gender biases and inequalities in most societies, men are often better positioned to take advantage of reconstruction initiatives....Special attention is generally required to ensure that women... are not excluded from programmes and...benefit from reconstruction efforts. Without these efforts,...[peace] activities run the risk of widening gender inequalities.[84]

Omission of gender in conflict and peace needs to be interrogated squarely and addressed effectively for ensuring conflict transformation. The aim of sustainable peace cannot be realized when the process is exclusive and discriminatory. It is imperative to ensure gender parity in peace building not as a favour or a privilege but as a matter of right. Women must be rightfully acknowledged as stakeholders in peace.

Endnotes

1. Swanee Hunt and Cristina Posa, 'Women Waging Peace', *Foreign Policy*, no. 124, (May–June 2001): 1.
2. Urvashi Butalia, 'Speaking Peace: An Introduction', in *Speaking Peace: Women's Voices from Kashmir*, ed., Urvashi Butalia, (New Delhi: Kali for Women, 2002), xvi.

3. Uma Chakravarti, 'A Kashmir Diary: Seven Days in an Armed "Paradise,"' in Butalia, *Speaking Peace*, 116.

4. Kavita Suri, 'Women in the Valley: From Victims to Agents of Change', in *Kashmir: New Voices, New Approaches*, eds, W. P. S. Sidhu, B. Asif and C. Samii, (Boulder: Lynne Rienner, 2006), 82.

5. Valerie Norville, 'The Role of Women in Global Security', Special Report No. 264, United Nations Institute of Peace, (January 2011). Available at http://www. usip.org/files/resources/SR264-The_role_of_Women_in_Global_Security.pdf (accessed on 23 January 2012).

6. Camille Pampell Conaway, 'The Role of Women in Stabilization and Reconstruction, Stabilization and Reconstruction', Series No. 3, United Nations Institute of Peace, (August 2006), 3. Also see Paula Banerjee, ed., *Women in Peace Politics*, (New Delhi: Sage Publications, 2008) and Sanam Naraghi Anderlini, *Women Building Peace: What They Do, Why It Matters*, (Boulder: Lynne Rienner Publishers, 2007).

7. Kumari Jayawardena, *Feminism and Nationalism in the Third World*, (London: Zed Books, 1986).

8. Jayawardena, *Feminism and Nationalism*.

9. 'Conflict Prevention and Resolution: The Role of Women', Council of Europe, 2004. Available at http://assembly.coe.int/Documents/AdoptedText/ta04/ ERES1385.htm (accessed on 23 March 2012).

10. Kees Kingma, 'Post-war demobilization, reintegration and peace-building'. Paper presented at an international conference and Expert Group Meeting on The Contribution of Disarmament and Conversion to Conflict Prevention and its Relevance for Development Cooperation, (Bonn, 30–31 August 1999). Available at http://www.bicc.de/ (accessed on 23 January 2012).

11. Elisabeth Rehn and Ellen Johnson Sirleaf, *Women, War and Peace: The Independent Experts' Assessment on the Impact of Armed Conflict on Women and Women's Role in Peace-building*, (New York: UNIFEM, 2002), 134.

12. Azza Karam, 'Women in War and Peace-building: The Roads Traversed, The Challenges Ahead', *International Feminist Journal of Politics*, 3, no. 1, (2000): 12.

13. Karam, 'Women in War and Peace-building', 11.

14. Frene Ginwala, 'Foreword', in *The International IDEA Handbook on Women in Parliament: Beyond Numbers*, ed., Azza Karam, (Stockholm: International IDEA, 1998), 15.

15. 2011 was a crucial year for women in conflict and transition societies. A major reason is that the Nobel peace prize was awarded to three women: President Ellen Johnson Sirleaf and Leymah Gbowee of Liberia, and Tawakkul Karman of Yemen. Further, for the first time the Nobel Committee's citation included a direct reference to UN resolution 1325. Emanuela C. Del Re, 'The Role of Women in Transition Societies', *Shared Space: A research journal on peace, conflict and community relations in Northern Ireland*, issue 13, (March 2012): 31.

16. 'Bonn and Beyond: Negotiating the Future of Women's Rights in Afghanistan', ActionAid, November 2011. Available at http://www.actionaid.org.uk/doc_lib/bonn_and_beyond.pdf (accessed on 29 January 2012).

17. Earlier, the Beijing Platform for Action had dealt with this issue in a comprehensive manner. It advocated, among other things, increasing participation of women at conflict resolution and decision-making levels and promoting women's contribution to foster a culture of peace. Beijing Platform for Action. Available at http://www.un.org/womenwatch/daw/beijing/platform (accessed on 15 June 2011).

18. Caroline Cohn, 'Feminist Peacemaking: In Resolution 1325, the United Nations Requires the Inclusion of Women in All Peace Planning and Negotiation', *The Women's Review of Books*, 21, no. 5, (February 2004): 8–9.

19. United Nations Security Council, 2000. Available at http://www.un.org/events/res_1325e.pdf (accessed on 2 January 2011).

20. United Nations Security Council, 2000.

21. Li Fung, 'Engendering the Peace Process: Women's Role in Peace Building and Conflict Resolution', in *Listening to the Silences: Women and War*, eds, Helen Durham and Tracy Gurd, (Netherlands: Koninklijke Brill BV, 2005), 213–15.

22. Quoted in Bishnu Pathak, 'Women and DDR-Disarmament, Demobilization, Reintegration'. Available at http://www.transcend.org/tms/2011/09/women-and-ddr-disarmament-demobilization-reintegration/ (accessed on 23 August 2012).

23. 'Women's Participation in Peace Negotiations: Connections between Presence and Influence', UNIFEM, (August 2010), 3. Available at http://www.unifem.org/attachments/products/0302_WomensParticipationInPeaceNegotiations_en.pdf (accessed on 23 August 2012).

24. 'Women and Peace and Security: Guidelines for National Implementation', UN Women, 4. Available at http://www.unwomen.org/wp-content/uploads/2012/10/02B-Plan-on-Women-and-Peace-and-Security.pdf (accessed on 22 August 2012).

25. Seema Kazi, *Between Democracy & Nation: Gender and Militarisation in Kashmir*, (New Delhi: Women Unlimited, 2009), 176.

26. See Seema Shekhawat, 'Gender-sensitive Peace Process in Jammu and Kashmir', in *Sustainable Development in Conflict Environments*, eds, Hari Dhungana and Marty Logan, (Nepal: CISC, 2007), 156–66.

27. Rita Manchanda, 'Kashmiri Women Demand Participation in Peace Process', (4 February 2011). Available at http://peacetalks.hdcentre.org/2011/02/kashmiri-women-demand-participation-in-peace-process/ (accessed on 14 August 2011).

28. Mushtaq Ul Haq, 'Kashmir Burns Again', (3 October 2010). Available at http://koshurpinta.blogspot.in/search?updated-min=2010-01-01T00:00:00%2B05:30&updated-max=2011-01-01T00:00:00%2B05:30&max-results=36 (accessed on 30 August 2011).

29. Quoted in Manchanda, 'Kashmiri Women Demand Participation in Peace Process'.

30. Personal Interview, 24 June 2011.

31. In the domain of security in International Relations women are on the fringes and 'hard' issues such as conflict and peace are considered extraneous and even uninteresting to women. More often than not I have heard men arguing that politics is not an area of interest for women, be it for peace or anything else.

Women are happier in their homes and families. Neither do women have an understanding of issues such as war and peace and nor are they interested in participating in these political processes. They contribute to the movement of their community when they are asked to do so and go back to their homes when their job is over.

opined a male ex-combatant. Personal Interview, 20 June 2011.

32. Sudha Ramachandran and Sonia Jabbar, *The Shades of Violence: Women and Kashmir*, (New Delhi: WISCOMP, 2003), 36.

33. Quoted in Rita Manchanda, 'Guns and Burqa: Women in the Kashmiri Conflict', in *Women, War and Peace in South Asia: Beyond Victimhood to Agency*, ed., Rita Manchanda, ed., (New Delhi: Sage Publications, 2001), 94.

34. Personal Interview, 15 June 2011.

35. Personal Interview, 18 June 2011.

36. M. Turshen, 'Women's War Stories', in *What Women Do in Wartime: Gender and Conflict in Africa*, eds, M. Turshen and C. Twagiramariya, (London and New York: Zed Books, 1998), 20.

37. See, for instance, Neloufer De Mel, *Women & the Nation's Narrative: Gender and Nationalism in Twentieth Century Sri Lanka*, (Lanham, Md.: Rowman & Littlefield, 2001) and Darini Rajasingham-Senanayake, 'Between Reality and Representation: Women's Agency in War and Post-Conflict Sri Lanka', *Cultural Dynamics*, 16, nos. 2 & 3, (2004): 141–68.

38. Kamla Swaroop, 'Women in Conflict exploited sexually', (19 May 2005). Available at http://www.worldsecuritynetwork.com/Other/Sarup-Kamala/Women-In-Conflict-exploited-sexually (accessed on 2 December 2011). A 2012 report on Nepal contends, 'anecdotal evidence indicates female combatants were asked by superiors to agree to sexual favours for male combatants to "boost their morale."' 'Women Count: Security Council Resolution 1325, Nepal', Civil Society Monitoring Report 2012, 5. Available at http://www.gnwp.org/wp-content/uploads/2010/02/Nepal_Report.pdf (accessed on 10 December 2012). The Maoist movement in India has been afflicted by numerous reported cases of abuses of female cadres. My interactions with ex-Maoist female combatants from Nepal and India also highlighted this issue.

39. Personal Interview, 23 January 2012.

40. 'Women Count: Security Council Resolution 1325, Nepal', 4.

41. Sharada Khadka, 'Female Combatants and Ex-combatants in Maoist Revolution and Their Struggle for Reintegration in Post-war', Unpublished Master's Thesis, University of Tromsø, (2012), 59–60.

42. 'Women Count: Security Council Resolution 1325, Nepal', 5.

43. For details see, 'Women Count: Security Council Resolution 1325, Sri Lanka', Civil Society Monitoring Report 2012, 5. Available at http://www.gnwp.org/wp-content/uploads/2010/02/SriLanka_Report.pdf (accessed on 10 December 2012).

44. Personal Interview, 10 June 2012.

45. Personal Interview, 22 May 2012.

46. Chakravarti, 'A Kashmir Diary: Seven Days in an Armed "Paradise,"' 133.

47. Personal Interview, 26 May 2011.

48. Rita Manchanda, 'Women, Conflict & Peace', South Asia Forum for Human Rights (SAFHR). Available at http://www.safhr.org/index.php?option=com_content&view=article&id=204: women-conflict-a-peace&catid=46:women-and-peace&Itemid=90 (accessed on 14 August 2011).

49. 'We women were the backbone of the mass movement. Now, look, how we have been acknowledged for that crucial role – by exclusion of us and our issues from peace politics,' Sabeena said. Personal Interview, 20 May 2012.

50. Seema Shekhawat, 'Engendering Armed Militancy in Kashmir: Women as Perpetrators of Violence', in *Understanding Collective Political Violence*, ed., Yvan Guichaoua, (Basingstoke: Palgrave Macmillan, 2012), 142.

51. Butalia, 'Speaking Peace: An Introduction', xxi. An instance may be cited of a woman tortured by Indian security personnel in Handwara in 2004. Sajjad Lone, a separatist leader, promised to fight for justice for her. Justice remained a mere assurance. Later, the victim was socially ostracized and was forced to leave her native place. Anuradha Bhasin Jamwal, 'Women in Kashmir Conflict: Victimhood and Beyond', in *Women Building Peace between India and Pakistan*, eds, Shree Mulay and Jackie Kirk, (New Delhi: Anthem Press, 2007), 94.

52. Amnesty International Press Release UA 108/91, 1991.

53. This was neither the first nor the last time that authorities discredited allegations of rape. There are a number of cases including the one of Mehtaba and her two daughters who were gang raped by Indian security personnel in 1998. Their complaint was discredited and all the three victims were branded as 'known keeps of militants,' *Kashmir Times*, (3 July 1998).

54. Following the incident of rape, the village witnessed the abandonment of some married women by their husbands, while unmarried ones remained single. Gauri Chaudhury et al., *Women's Testimonies from Kashmir: 'The Green of the Valley is Khaki*, (Bombay: Women's Initiative, 1994), 10–11.

55. Kazi, *Between Democracy & Nation: Gender and Militarisation in Kashmir*, 163.

56. Rita Manchanda, 'Where Are The Women in South Asian Conflicts?', in *Women, War and Peace in South Asia: Beyond Victimhood to Agency*, ed., Rita Manchanda, (New Delhi: Sage Publications, 2001), 23.

57. Personal Interview, 12 June 2011.

58. Manchanda, 'Guns and Burqa: Women in the Kashmiri Conflict', 91.

59. Manchanda, 'Guns and Burqa: Women in the Kashmiri Conflict'.

60. Personal Interview, 27 May 2011.

61. *Indian Express*, (12 August 2012).

62. Vivi Stavrou and Josefa Dombolo, 'Breaking the Silence: Girls Abducted During Armed Conflict in Angola', A Christian Children's Fund Angola research project funded by the CIDA Children Protection Research Fund, 2006. Available at: http://www.uottawa.ca/childprotection/present_angola.pdf (accessed on 19 August 2011).

63. Seema Kazi, 'Key Components for an Equitable and Long Lasting Peace, Armed Conflicts and Women in Kashmir.' Available at http://www.lolapress.org/elec1/edit_e.htm (accessed on 21 June 2012).

64. Personal Interview, 31 May 2012.

65. Kazi, *Between Democracy & Nation: Gender and Militarisation in Kashmir*, 143.

66. Ani Colekessian, 'Reintegrating Gender: A Gendered Analysis of the Nepali Rehabilitation Process', Working paper, United Nations International Research and Training Institute for the Advancement of Women, 2009, 5.

67. 'Operational Guide to the Integrated Disarmament, Demobilization and Reintegration Standards', United Nations, 2010, 194. Available at http://www.operationspaix.net/DATA/DOCUMENT/444~v~The_New_Operational_Guide_to_the_Integrated_Disarmament_Demobilization_and_Reintegration_Standards.pdf (accessed on 22 August 2011).

68. Rehn and Sirleaf, *Women, War and Peace*, 114.

69. 'Gender Perspectives on Disarmament, Demobilization and Reintegration (DDR)', Briefing Note 4, The Department for Disarmament Affairs in collaboration with the Office of the Special Adviser on Gender Issues and the Advancement of Women United Nations (March 2001), 2. Available at http://www.un.org/disarmament/HomePage/gender/docs/note4.pdf (accessed on 22 August 2011).

70. DDR, considered essential for a successful transition from war to peace, is briefly defined by the UN as: Disarmament as the collection, documentation and control and disposal of weapons; demobilization as the formal and controlled discharge of active combatants from armed forces or other armed groups; and reintegration as a process by which ex-combatants acquire civilian status and gain sustainable employment and income.

71. Megan MacKenzie, 'Securitization and Desecuritization: Female Soldiers and the Reconstruction of Women in Post-Conflict Sierra Leone', *Security Studies*, 18, no. 2, (2009): 241–61.

72. Rehn and Sirleaf, *Women, War and Peace*, 125.

73. Aaliya Anjum, 'Kashmir: The forgotten conflict, The militant in her: Women and resistance', (2 August 2011). Available at http://www.aljazeera.com/indepth/spotlight/kashmirtheforgottenconflict/2011/07/2011731995821770.html (accessed on 14 August 2011).

74. UNSC 1325 Resolution 2000.

75. Roshmi Goswami, 'Reinforcing Subordination: An analysis of Women in Armed Conflict Situations', in *Women in Action*, no. 3, (1999): 19.

76. Manchanda, 'Women, Conflict & Peace'.

77. Ashima Kaul, Co-ordinator Athwaas, Srinagar. Available at http://www. peacedirectusa.org/women-in-the-peace-process-in-kashmir/ (accessed on 23 April 2012).

78. Manchanda, 'Kashmiri Women Demand Participation in Peace Process'.

79. The team of interlocutors comprised Radha Kumar, M. M. Ansari and Dileep Padgaonkar (Chairperson). The report of the interlocutors titled *A New Compact with the People of Jammu and Kashmir* is available at http://mha.nic.in/pdfs/J&K-InterlocatorsRpt-0512.pdf (accessed on 4 September 2012).

80. Report of the interlocutors, 145–46.

81. Karam, 'Women in War and Peace-building: The Roads Traversed, The Challenges Ahead', 13.

82. S. Bisnath and D. Elson, 'Women's Empowerment Revisited', UNIFEM. Available at http://www.undp.org/unifem/progressww/empower.html (accessed 30 October 2003).

83. Rehn and Sirleaf, *Women, War and Peace*, 27.

84. 'Gender Perspectives on Disarmament, Demobilization and Reintegration (DDR)', 1.

Select Bibliography

Abdullah, Farooq, *My Dismissal*, New Delhi: Vikas Publications, 1985.

Addis, Elisabetta Russo, E., Valeria and Lorenza, Sebesta, eds, *Women Soldiers: Images and Reality*, New York: St. Martin's Press, 1994.

Akbar, M. J. *India: The Siege Within: Challenges to a Nation's Unity*, Harmondsworth: Penguin, 1985.

———. *Kashmir Behind the Vale*, New Delhi: Viking, 1991.

Alison, Miranda, *Women and Political Violence: Female Combatants in Ethno-National Conflict*, London: Routledge, 2009.

Anand, A. S. *The Constitution of Jammu and Kashmir*, New Delhi: Universal Law Company, 1998.

Anderlini, Sanam Naraghi, *Women Building Peace: What They Do, Why It Matters*, Boulder: Lynne Rienner Publishers, 2007.

Ann, Adele, *Women Fighters of Liberation Tigers*, LTTE: Jaffna, 1993.

Azhar, Edward E. and Chung-in Moon, eds, *National Security in the Third World: The Management of Internal and External Threats*, Aldershot: Edward Elgar, 1988.

Aziz, M. A. *Struggle for Liberation of Kashmir*, Karachi: Ferozsons, 1965.

Bamzai, P. N. K., *Kashmir and Power Politics: From Lake Success to Tashkent*, New Delhi: Metropolitan, 1966.

———. *A History of Kashmir*, New Delhi: Metropolitan, 1973.

Banerjee, Paula, ed., *Women in Peace Politics*, New Delhi: Sage Publications, 2008.

Barker, Gary, *Dying to be Men: Youth, Masculinity and Social Exclusion*, London: Routledge, 2005.

Bazaz, Prem Nath, *Daughters of Vitasta: A History of Kashmiri Women from Early Times to the Present Day*, Srinagar: Gulshan Publishers, 2003.

Beauvoir, Simone de, *The Second Sex*, translated by H. M. Parshley, London: Vintage, 1997.

Behera, Navnita Chadha, *Demystifying Kashmir*, Washington: Brookings Institute, 2006.

———. *State, Identity and Violence: Jammu, Kashmir & Ladakh*, New Delhi: Manohar Publishers, 2000.

Bennett, Olivia, Jo, Bexely and Kitty Warnock, eds, *Arms to Fight, Arms to Protect: Women Speak out About Conflict*, London: Panos, 1995.

Berger, Thomas U., *Cultures of Antimilitarism: National Security in Germany and Japan*, Baltimore: John Hopkins University Press, 1998.

Bhasin, Kamla, Ritu Menon and Nigat Said Khan, eds, *Against All Odds: Essays on Women, Religion and Development from India and Pakistan*, New Delhi: Kali for Women, 1994.

Bhatia, K. L., *Jammu and Kashmir: Article 370 of Constitution of India*, New Delhi: Deep and Deep Publishers, 1997.

Bloeria, Sudhir S. *The Battles of Zojila, 1948*, New Delhi: Har-Anand Publications, 1997.

Bloom, Mia, *Dying to Kill: The Allure of Suicide Terror*, New York: Columbia University Press, 2005.

Bose, Sumantra, *States, Nations, Sovereignty: Sri Lanka, India and the Tamil Eelam Movement*, New Delhi: Sage Publications, 1994.

———. *The Challenge in Kashmir: Democracy, Self-Determination and a Just Peace*, New Delhi: Sage Publications, 1997.

———. *Kashmir: Roots of Conflict, Paths to Peace*, New Delhi: Vistaar Publications, 2003.

Bourgois, Peter and Nancy Scheper-Hughes, *Violence in War and Peace*, Oxford: Blackwell Publishing, 2004.

Brittan, Arthur, *Masculinity and Power*, Oxford: Blackwell, 1989.

Brod, Harry, *The Making of Masculinities*, London: Allen & Unwin, 1987.

Brod, Harry and Michael Kaufman, eds, *Theorizing Masculinities*, London: Sage Publications, 1994.

Buchbinder, David, *Masculinities and Identities*, Melbourne: Melbourne University Press, 1994.

Bunch, Charlotte, *Passionate Politics: Feminist Theory in Action*, New York: St. Martin's Press, 1987.

Burr, Vivien, *An Introduction to Social Constructionism*, London: Routledge, 1995.

Butalia, Urvashi, ed., *Speaking Peace: Women's Voices from Kashmir*, New Delhi: Kali for Women, 2002.

Butler, Judith, *Gender Trouble*, New York: Routledge, 1990.

Buzan, Barry and Hansen, Lene, *The Evolution of International Security Studies*, Cambridge: Cambridge University Press, 2009.

Cady, Linell E. and Simon Sheldon, eds, *Religion and conflict in South and Southeast Asia: Disrupting Violence*, New York: Routledge, 2007.

Cheldelin, Sandra I. and Maneshka Eliatamby, eds, *Women Waging War and Peace, International Perspectives on Women's Roles in Conflict and Post-Conflict Reconstruction*, New York: Continuum, 2011.

Chenoy, Anuradha M., *Militarism and Women in South Asia*, New Delhi: Kali for Women, 2002.

Chodorow, Nancy, *The Reproduction of Mothering: Psychoanalysis and the Sociology of Gender*, Berkeley: University of California Press, 1978.

Chopra, Pran, *India, Pakistan and the Kashmir Tangle*, Delhi: HarperCollins India, 1994.

Chopra, Radhika, ed., *Reframing Masculinities: Narrating the Supportive Practices of Men*, New Delhi: Orient Longman, 2006.

Chopra, Surendra, *UN Mediation in Kashmir*, Kurukshetra: Vishal Publications, 1971.

Chopra, V. D. *Genesis of Indo-Pakistan Conflict on Kashmir*, New Delhi: Patriot Publications, 1990.

Cohen, Stephen P., *India: Emerging Power*, Washington DC: Brookings Institution Press, 2001.

Cohn, Carol, *Women and Wars*, London: Polity Press, 2013.

Connell, Robert, *Gender and Power: Society, the Person and Sexual Politics*, Cambridge: Polity, 1987.

———. *Masculinities*, Cambridge: Polity, 1995.

Cooke, Miriam and Angela Woollacott, eds, *Gendering War Talk*, Princeton: Princeton University Press, 1993.

Coser, Lewis A., *The Functions of Social Conflict*, New York: Free Press, 1956.

D'Amico, Francine and Peter R. Beckman, eds, *Women in World Politics: An Introduction*, Westport, CT: Bergin & Garvey, 1995.

Dabla, Bashir Ahmad, *Multi-Dimensional Problems of Women in Kashmir*, New Delhi: Gyan Publishing House, 2007.

Dabla, Bashir Ahmad, Sandeep K. Nayak and Khurshid ul Islam, *Gender Discrimination in the Kashmir Valley: A Survey of Budgam and Baramulla District*, New Delhi: Gyan Publishing House, 2000.

Daly, Mary, *Gyn/Ecology: The Metaethics of Radical Feminism*, Boston: Beacon Press, 1978.

Dang, Satyapal, *Genesis of Terrorism: An Analytical Study of Punjab Terrorists*, New Delhi: Patriot Publishers, 1988.

Dasgupta, C., *War and Diplomacy in Kashmir 1947–48*, New Delhi: Sage Publications, 2002.

DasGupta, Sumona, *Breaking the Silence: Women and Kashmir*, New Delhi: Women in Security, Conflict Management and Peace, 2002.

Davis, Nira Yuval, *Gender and Nation*, London: Sage Publications, 1997.

De Pauw, Linda Grant, *Battle Cries and Lullabies: Women in War from Prehistory to the Present*, Norman: University of Oklahoma Press, 1998.

Detraz, Nicole, *International Security and Gender*, Cambridge: Polity Press, 2012.

Dhungana, Hari and Marty Logan, eds, *Sustainable Development in Conflict Environments: Challenges and Opportunities*, Kathmandu: Centre for International Studies and Cooperation, 2007.

Dixit, J. N., *India-Pakistan in War and Peace*, New Delhi: India Today Group, 2002.

Drew, Fredric, *The Jummoo and Kashmir Territories*, New Delhi: Oriental Publishers, 1971.

Elshtain, Jean Bethke, *Women and War*, New York: Basic Books, 1987.

Elshtain, J. B. and S. Tobias, *Women, Militarism, and War*, Savage, MD: Rowman & Littlefield, 1990.

Embree, Ainslie T. and Stephen N. Hay, *Sources of Indian Tradition: Modern India and Pakistan*, Volume 2, New York: Columbia University Press, 1988.

Enloe, Cynthia, *Does Khaki Become You?*, London: Pluto Press, 1983.

———. *Bananas, Beaches and Bases: Making Feminist Sense of International Politics*, Berkeley: University of California Press, 1990.

————. *The Morning After: Sexual Politics at the End of the Cold War,* Berkeley: University of California Press, 1993.

————. *Maneuvers: The International Politics of Militarizing Women's Lives,* Berkeley: University of California Press, 2000.

Ferguson, J. P., *Kashmir: A Historical Introduction,* London: Centaur Press, 1961.

Ferguson, Kathy, *The Man Question: Visions of Subjectivity in Feminist Theory,* Berkeley: University of California Press, 1993.

Francke, Linda Bird, *Ground Zero: The Gender Wars in the Military,* New York: Simon & Schuster, 1997.

Fraser, Antonia, *The Warrior Queens,* New York: Knopf, 1989.

Fuss, Diana, *Essentially Speaking: Feminism, Nature and Difference,* New York: Routledge, 1989.

Ganai, Abdul Jabbar, *Kashmir: National Conference and Politics,* Srinagar: Gulshan Publishers, 1984.

Ganguly, Rajat, *Kin State Intervention in Ethnic Conflicts: Lessons from South Asia,* New Delhi: Sage Publications, 1998.

Ganguly, Sumit, *The Origins of War in South Asia: The Indo-Pakistani Conflicts Since 1947,* Boulder: Westview Press, 1994.

————. *The Crisis in Kashmir: Portents of War, Hopes of Peace,* New Delhi: Foundation Books, 1997.

————. *Conflict Unending: India-Pakistan Tensions Since 1947,* New Delhi: Oxford University Press, 2002.

Ganjoo, S. K., *Kashmir: History and Politics,* New Delhi: Commonwealth Publishers, 1998.

Genovese, Michael A., ed., *Women as National Leaders: The Political Performance of Women as Heads of Government,* Thousands Oaks: Sage Publications, 1993.

Gilligan, Carol, *In a Different Voice: Psychological Theory and Women's Development,* Cambridge: Harvard University Press, 1982.

Giyas-ud-Din, Peer, *Understanding the Kashmiri Insurgency,* New Delhi: Anmol Publishers, 1992.

Goldstein, Joshua S. *International Relations,* Delhi: Pearson Education, 2003.

————. *War and Gender: How Gender Shapes the War System and Vice Versa,* Cambridge: Cambridge University Press, 2003.

Griffiths, Martin, ed., *International Relations for the 21st Century,* London: Routledge, 2007.

Grover, Verinder, ed., *The Story of Kashmir: Yesterday and Today,* New Delhi: Deep and Deep Publications, 1995.

Guichaoua, Yvan, ed., *Understanding Collective Political Violence,* Basingstoke: Palgrave Macmillan, 2012.

Gupta, Sisir, *Kashmir: A Study of India Pakistan Relations,* Bombay: Asia Publishing House, 1966.

Hari Om, *Beyond the Kashmir Valley,* New Delhi: Har-Anand Publications, 1998.

Hirsch, Marianne and Evelyn Fox Keller, eds, *Conflicts in Feminism,* New York: Routledge, 1990.

Hooper, Charlotte, *Manly States: Masculinities, International Relations, and Gender Politics,* New York: Columbia University Press, 2001.

Horowitz, Donald L. *Ethnic Groups in Conflict*, Berkeley: University of California Press, 1985.

Hussain, Syed T. *Reflections on Kashmir Politics*, Delhi: Rima Publishing House, 1987.

Hutt, Michael, ed., *Himalayan 'People's War': Nepal's Maoist Rebellion*, London: Hurst & Company, 2004.

Isaksson, Eva, ed., *Women and the Military System*, New York: St. Martin's, 1988.

Jackson, Robert and Georg Sørensen, *Introduction to International Relations: Theories and Approaches*, Oxford: Oxford University Press, 2010.

Jaffrelot, Christophe, ed., *Pakistan: Nationalism Without a Nation*, New Delhi: Manohar Publishers, 2002.

Jagger, Alison M. and Paula S. Rothenberg, eds, *Feminist Frameworks: Alternative Theoretical Accounts of the Relations Between Women and Men*, New York: McGraw-Hill, 1984.

Jagmohan, *My Frozen Turbulence in Kashmir*, New Delhi: Allied Publishers, 2000.

Jayawardena, Kumari, *Feminism and Nationalism in the Third World*, London: Zed Books, 1986.

Jones, David E., *Women Warriors: A History*, Washington: Brassey's, 1997.

Kaldor, Mary, *New & Old Wars, Organized Violence in a Global Era*, Cambridge: Polity Press, 1999.

Karim, Afsir, *Counter Terrorism: The Pakistan Factor*, New Delhi: Lancer International, 1991.

Katzenstein, Peter J., ed., *The Culture of National Security: Norms and Identity in World Politics*, New York: Columbia University Press, 1996.

Kazi, Seema, *Between Democracy & Nation: Gender and Militarisation in Kashmir*, New Delhi: Women Unlimited, 2009.

Khan, M. Akbar, *Raiders in Kashmir*, Islamabad: National Book Foundation, 1975.

Khan, M. Ishaq, *Kashmir's Transition to Islam: The Role of Muslim Rishis*, Delhi: Manohar Publishers, 2002.

Khan, Nighat Saeed, Rubina Saigol and Afiya Shahbano Zia, eds, *Locating the Self: Perspectives of Women and Multiple Identities*, Lahore: ASR Publications, 1994.

Khan, Nyla Ali, *Islam, Women, and Violence in Kashmir: Between India and Pakistan*, London: Palgrave Macmillan, 2010.

Klare, Michael and Peter Kornbluh, eds, *Low-Intensity Warfare: Counterinsurgency, Proinsurgency, and Antiterrorism in the Eighties*, New York: Random, 1991.

Korbel, Josef, *Danger in Kashmir*, Princeton: Princeton University Press, 1954.

Koul, Mohan Lal, *Kashmir: Wail of a Valley*, New Delhi: Gyan Sagar Publications, 1999.

Kronsell, Annika and Erika Svedberg, eds, *Making Gender, Making War*, London: Routledge, 2011.

Kuehnast, Kathleen, Chantal de Jonge Oudraat and Helga Hernes, eds, *Women and War: Power and Protection in the 21st Century*, Washington DC: United States Institute of Peace Press, 2011.

Kumar, Dev P., *Kashmir Return to Democracy*, New Delhi: Cosmo Publications, 1996.

Kurshid, Salman, *Beyond Terrorism: New Hope for Kashmir*, New Delhi: UBS Publishers Distributors Ltd., 1994.

Lamb, Alastair, *Crisis in Kashmir: 1947 to 1966*, London: Routledge and Kegan Paul, 1966.

————. *Kashmir: A Disputed Legacy 1846–1990*, Hertfordshire: Roxord Books, 1991.

Lawrence, Walter R., *The Valley of Kashmir*, Jammu: Kashmir Kitab Ghar, 1996.

Lodge, David, ed., *Modern Criticism and Theory*, London: Longman, 1988.

Lorber, Judith and Susan A. Farrell, eds, *The Social Construction of Gender*, Newbury Park: Sage Publications, 1991.

Lorber, Judith, *Paradoxes of Gender*, New Haven: Yale University Press, 1994.

Lorentzen, Lois Ann and Jennifer Turpin, eds, *The Women and War Reader*, New York: New York University Press, 1998.

Madhok, Balraj, *A Story of Bungling in Kashmir*, New Delhi: Asia Publishing House, 1973.

Mahajan, M. C., *Accession of Kashmir to India*, Sholapur: Institute of Public Administration, 1962.

Mahapatra, Debidatta Aurobinda, *World Order, Multipolarism and Terrorism: The Indian Approach*, New Delhi: New Century Publications, 2011.

————. ed., *Conflict and Peace in Eurasia*, New York: Routledge, 2013.

————. *Making Kashmir Borderless*, New Delhi and Colombo: Manohar Publishers and Regional Centre for Strategic Studies, 2013.

Mahapatra, Debidatta Aurobinda and Seema Shekhawat, *Conflict in Kashmir and Chechnya: Political and Humanitarian Dimensions*, New Delhi: Lancers Publications, 2007.

————. *Kashmir Across LOC*, New Delhi: Gyan Publishing House, 2008.

Maheshwari, Anil, *Crescent over Kashmir: Politics of Mullaism*, New Delhi: Rupa and Co., 1993.

Manchanda, Rita, ed., *Women, War and Peace in South Asia: Beyond Victimhood to Agency*, New Delhi: Sage Publications, 2001.

McGlen, Nancy E. and Meredith Reid Sarkees, *Women in Foreign Policy: The Insiders*, New York: Routledge, 1993.

Mearsheimer, John J., *The Tragedy of Great Power Politics*, New York: W. W. Norton & Company, 2001.

Mir, Amir, *The True Face of Jihadis: Inside Pakistan's Network of Terror*, New Delhi: Roli Books, 2006.

Mohanty, Chandra Talpade, Ann Russo and Lourdes Torres, eds, *Third World Women and the Politics of Feminism*, Bloomington: Indiana University Press, 1991.

Moore, C. W., *The Mediation Process: Practical Strategies for Resolving Conflict*, San Francisco: Jossey Bass, 1986.

Moser, Caroline O. N. and Fiona C. Clark, eds, *Victims, Perpetrators or Actors?: Gender, Armed Conflict and Political Violence*, New Delhi: Kali for Women, 2001.

Mulay, Shree and Jackie Kirk, eds, *Women Building Peace between India and Pakistan*, New Delhi: Anthem Press, 2007.

Nayar, Kuldip, *Wall at Wagah: India-Pakistan Relations*, New Delhi: Gyan Publishing House, 2003.

Nelson, Barbara J. and Najma Chowdhury, eds, *Women and Politics Worldwide*, New Haven and London: Yale University Press, 1994.

Newberg, Paula R., *Double Betrayal: Repression and Insurgency in Kashmir*, Washington: Carnegie Endowment for International Peace, 1995.

Okin, Susan M., 'Is Multiculturalism Bad for Women?', in *Is Multiculturalism Bad for Women*, eds, Joshua Cohen, Matthew Howard and Martha C. Nussbaum, Princeton: Princeton University Press, 1999.

Peterson, V. Spike, ed., *Gendered States: Feminist (Re)Visions of International Relations Theory*, Boulder and London: Lynn Reinner Publishers, 1992.

Pierson, Ruth Roach, *Women and Peace: Theoretical, Historical and Practical Perspectives*, London: Croom Helm, 1987.

Pirages, Dennis and Sylvester, Christine, eds, *Transformations in the Global Political Economy*, London: Macmillan, 1990.

Prakhar, Gulab Mishra, *Indo-Pakistan Relations: From Tashkent to Shimla*, New Delhi: Ashish Publications, 1987.

Prashar, Avineet and Vivek, Paawan, eds, *Conflict and Politics of Jammu & Kashmir: Internal Dynamics*, Jammu: Saksham Books International, 2007.

Pruitt, D. G. and J. Z. Rubin, *Social Conflict: Escalation, Stalemate, and Settlement*, New York: Random House, 1986.

Puri, Balraj, *Jammu and Kashmir: Triumph and Tragedy of Indian Federalism*, Delhi: Sterling Publishers, 1981.

———. *Kashmir: Towards Insurgency*, New Delhi: Orient Longman, 1993.

———. *Kashmir: Insurgency and After*, New Delhi: Orient Blackswan, 2008.

Qureshi, Hashim, *Kashmir: The unveiling of Truth*, Delhi: Renaissance Publishing House, 1999.

Ramachandran, Sudha and Sonia Jabbar, *The Shades of Violence: Women and Kashmir*, New Delhi: WISCOMP, 2003.

Ramazanoglu, Caroline, *Feminism and the Contradictions of Oppression*, London and New York: Routledge, 1989.

Rashid, Afsana, *Widows and Half Widows: Saga of Extra-Judicial Arrests and Killings in Kashmir*, Delhi: Pharos Media & Publishing, 2011.

Reardon, Betty, *Sexism and the War System*, Syracuse: Syracuse University Press, 1996.

Rehn, Elisabeth and Ellen Johnson Sirleaf, *Women, War and Peace: The Independent Experts' Assessment on the Impact of Armed Conflict on Women and Women's Role in Peace-building*, New York: UNIFEM, 2002.

Sahni, Sati, *Kashmir Underground*, New Delhi: Har-Anand Publications, 1999.

Salmonson, Jessica Amanda, *The Encyclopedia of Amazons: Women Warriors from Antiquity to the Modern Era*, New York: Paragon House, 1991.

Samaddar, Ranbir and Helmut Reifeld, eds, *Peace as Process: Reconciliation and Conflict-Resolution in South Asia*, New Delhi: Manohar Publishers, 2001.

Sapiro, Virginia, *Women in American Society*, Palo Alto, CA: Mayfield, 1986.

Schofield, Victoria, *Kashmir in Conflict: India, Pakistan and the Unending War*, London: IB Tauris, 2003.

Schor, Naomi and Elizabeth Weed, eds, *The Essential Difference: Another Look at Essentialism*, Bloomington: Indiana University Press, 1994.

Scott, Joan Wallach, *Gender and the Politics of History*, New York: Columbia University Press, 1988.

Seifert, R., *War and Rape-Analytical Approaches*, Geneva: Women's International League for Peace and Freedom, 1993.

Sexena, H. L., *The Tragedy of Kashmir*, New Delhi: Nationalist, 1975.

Sharoni, S., *Gender and the Israeli-Palestinian Conflict: The Politics of Women's Resistance*, New York: Syracuse University Press, 1995.

Shekhawat, Seema, *Conflict and Displacement in Kashmir: The Gender Dimension*, Jammu: Saksham Books International, 2006.

Shekhawat, Seema and Debidatta Aurobinda Mahapatra, *Contested Border and Division of Families in Kashmir: Contextualizing the Ordeal of the Kargil Women*, New Delhi: Women in Security, Conflict Management and Peace, 2009.

Shepherd, Laura, *Gender, Violence and Security*, London: Zed Books, 2008.

Shrestha, Ava Darshan and Rita Thapa, eds, *The Impact of Armed Conflicts on Women in South Asia*, New Delhi: Manohar Publishers, 2007.

Sidhu, W. P. S., B. Asif and C. Samii, eds, *Kashmir: New Voices, New Approaches*, Boulder: Lynne Rienner, 2006.

Sikand, Yoginder, *Religion, Peace and Dialogue in Jammu and Kashmir*, New Delhi: Women in Security, Conflict Management and Peace, 2006.

Singh, Bhim, *Murder of Democracy in Jammu & Kashmir*, New Delhi: Har-Anand Publications, 2002.

Singh, L. P., *India's Foreign Policy: The Shastri Period*, New Delhi: Uppal Publications, 1980.

Singh, Tavleen, *Kashmir: A Tragedy of Errors*, New Delhi: Viking, 1995.

Sjoberg, Laura, *Gender and International Security: Feminist Perspectives*, London and New York: Routledge, 2010.

Sjoberg, Laura and Caron E. Gentry, *Mothers, Monsters, Whores: Women's Violence in Global Politics*, London: Zed Books, 2007.

———, eds, *Women, Gender, and Terrorism*, Athens, GA: University of Georgia Press, 2011.

Skjelsbaek, Inger and Dan Smith, eds, *Gender, Peace and Conflict*, New Delhi: Sage Publications, 2001.

Spelman, Elizabeth, *Inessential Woman: Problems of Exclusion in Feminist Thought*, Boston: Beacon Press, 1988.

Stiehm, Judith Hicks, *Bring Me Men and Women: Mandated Change at the US Air Force Academy*, Berkeley: University of California Press, 1981.

———. ed., *It's Our Military, Too!*, Philadelphia: Temple University Press, 1996.

Sylvester, Christine, *Feminist International Relations: An Unfinished Journey*, Cambridge: Cambridge University Press, 2002.

———. *War as Experience: Contributions from International Relations and Feminist Analysis*, London: Routledge, 2013.

Teng, M. K. and C. L. Gadoo, *White Paper on Kashmir*, New Delhi: Geoffrey Bell and Publishers, 1991.

Tetreault, Mary-Ann, ed., *Women and Revolution in Africa, Asia and the New World,* Columbia: University of South Carolina Press, 1994.

Thomas, Raju G. C., *Indian Defense Policy,* Princeton: Princeton University Press, 1986.

———. ed., *Perspectives on Kashmir: The Roots of Conflict in South Asia,* Boulder: Westview Press, 1992.

Tickner, J. Ann, *Gender in International Relations: Feminist Perspectives on Achieving Global Security,* New York: Columbia University Press, 1992.

———. *Gendering World Politics, Issues and Approaches in the Post–Cold War Era,* New York: Columbia University Press, 2001.

Tong, Rosemarie, *Feminist Thought: A Comprehensive Introduction,* Boulder: Westview, 1989.

Turshen, M. and C. Twagiramariya, eds, *What Women Do in Wartime: Gender and Conflict in Africa,* London and New York: Zed Books, 1998.

Weinstein, Laurie and Christie White, *Wives and Warriors: Women and the Military in the United States and Canada,* Westport: Bergin & Garvey, 1997.

Wendt, Alexander, *Social Theory of International Politics,* Cambridge: Cambridge University Press, 1999.

West, Lois A., ed., *Feminist Nationalism,* London: Routledge, 1997.

Wilby, Adele Ann, *Women Fighters of Liberation Tigers,* Jaffna: LTTE Publication Section, 1993.

Wirsing, Robert G., *Kashmir in the Shadow of War: Regional Rivalries in a Nuclear Age,* New York: M. E. Sharpe, 2003.

Wolf, Virginia, *Three Guineas,* London: Hogarth Press, 1977.

Yami, Hisila, *People's War and Women's Liberation in Nepal,* Raipur: Purvaiya Prakashan, 2006.

Yasin, Mohammad and A. Qaiyum Rafiqi, eds, *History of the Freedom Struggle in Jammu and Kashmir,* New Delhi: Light and Life Publishers, 1980.

Zalewski, Marysia and Parpart, Jane, eds, *The 'Man' Question in International Relations,* Boulder, CO: Westview Press, 1998.

Index